THE LEARNING FRAMEWORK IN NUMBER

Sara Miller McCune founded SAGE Publishing in 1965 to support the dissemination of usable knowledge and educate a global community. SAGE publishes more than 1000 journals and over 800 new books each year, spanning a wide range of subject areas. Our growing selection of library products includes archives, data, case studies and video. SAGE remains majority owned by our founder and after her lifetime will become owned by a charitable trust that secures the company's continued independence.

Los Angeles | London | New Delhi | Singapore | Washington DC | Melbourne

THE LEARNING FRAMEWORK IN NUMBER

PEDAGOGICAL TOOLS FOR ASSESSMENT AND INSTRUCTION

ROBERT J. WRIGHT

DAVID ELLEMOR-COLLINS

Los Angeles | London | New Delhi
Singapore | Washington DC | Melbourne

Los Angeles | London | New Delhi
Singapore | Washington DC | Melbourne

SAGE Publications Ltd
1 Oliver's Yard
55 City Road
London EC1Y 1SP

SAGE Publications Inc.
2455 Teller Road
Thousand Oaks, California 91320

SAGE Publications India Pvt Ltd
B 1/I 1 Mohan Cooperative Industrial Area
Mathura Road
New Delhi 110 044

SAGE Publications Asia-Pacific Pte Ltd
3 Church Street
#10-04 Samsung Hub
Singapore 049483

Editor: James Clark
Assistant editor: Robert Patterson
Production editor: Victoria Nicholas
Copyeditor: Jane Fricker
Proofreader: Bryan Campbell
Marketing manager: Dilhara Attygalle
Cover design: Sheila Tong
Typeset by: C&M Digitals (P) Ltd, Chennai, India
Printed in the UK by Bell and Bain Ltd, Glasgow

Library of Congress Control Number: 2017952667

British Library Cataloguing in Publication data

A catalogue record for this book is available from
the British Library

ISBN 978-1-5264-0275-2
ISBN 978-1-5264-0276-9 (pbk)

Brief Table of Contents

Detailed Table of Contents

The Learning Framework in Number

Glossary   135

Appendix 1: Instructional Settings   141

Bibliography   145

Index   153

List of Charts

List of Boxes

List of Figures

List of Tables

About the Authors
and the Contributor

Dr Robert J. (Bob) Wright holds Bachelor's and Master's degrees in mathematics from the University of Queensland (Australia) and a doctoral degree in mathematics education from the University of Georgia. He is an adjunct professor in mathematics education at Southern Cross University in New South Wales. Bob is an internationally recognized leader in assessment and instruction relating to children's early arithmetical knowledge and strategies, publishing six books, and many articles and papers in this field. His work over the last 25 years has included the development of the **Mathematics Recovery** Programme, which focuses on providing specialist training for teachers to advance the numeracy levels of young children assessed as low-attainers. In Australia and New Zealand, Ireland, the UK, the USA, Canada, Mexico, South Africa and elsewhere, this programme has been implemented widely, and applied extensively to classroom teaching and to average and able learners as well as low-attainers. Bob has conducted several research projects funded by the Australian Research Council including the most recent project focusing on assessment and intervention in the early arithmetical learning of low-attaining 8- to 10-year-olds.

David Ellemor-Collins holds a Bachelor's degree with honours in mathematics and philosophy from Harvard University, and a Graduate Diploma in Education from the University of Melbourne. David works as a mathematics teacher, as he has done for 20 years across primary schools, high schools and universities. As a specialist in arithmetic instruction, he publishes articles for both researchers and practitioners, designs curriculum materials, and provides professional development to teachers. He has co-authored a book with Bob, and collaborated on Bob's recent research project on intervention with low-attaining 8- to 10-year-olds. David is completing a doctoral degree in mathematics education at Southern Cross University, focusing on instruction in multiplication and division.

Dr Tran Le Thi holds a Bachelor's degree in mathematics from Quy Nhon University, Vietnam, a Master's degree in Science and Technology Education (Mathematics) from La Trobe University in Melbourne, and a Doctor of Philosophy degree in mathematics education from Southern Cross University in New South Wales. Her PhD thesis identified and illuminated the key elements in intensive, one-to-one instruction in whole number arithmetic. Thi worked as a mathematics lecturer at Binh Dinh College in Vietnam for seven years before commencing a PhD programme. She is a contracted academic at Southern Cross University where her work includes teaching and research in the School of Education.

Foreword

In this book, Robert J. Wright and David Ellemor-Collins do not view children's minds as *tabula rasa* upon entering school, nor do they regard children's mathematical learning as simply imprinting conventional school mathematics on children's minds. Rather, they fully acknowledge children's mathematics, which are the mathematical ways of operating that children construct as a result of interacting in their social-cultural milieu in all of its aspects and of maturation of the central nervous system. Acknowledging children's mathematics is a basic principle for any adult who is involved in children's mathematics education simply because children are human beings not unlike adults. With nothing else being said, adults do not need to interact with children in order to impute some kind of mathematics to them; that is, children's mathematics. But adults do need to interact with children in order to construct what children's mathematics might consist of. Throughout this book, the authors celebrate children as mathematical thinkers and learners and fully subscribe to the position that teachers construct what children's mathematics might consist of in the context of teaching children. However, children's mathematics is not simply lodged in teachers' minds through their senses in a way analogous to how a postage stamp is stuck on an envelope. Rather, in the context of teaching children, teachers must interpret children's mathematical language and actions and continually test their interpretations in order to construct experiential models of children's mathematics. Because such experiential models are constructed by teachers it might seem that the models would be isomorphic to teachers' ways and means of operating mathematically. But teachers must become the children and put their own mathematical ways and means of operating 'on the side', as it were, and construct a 'mathematics' – some experiential model of children's mathematics – that, were children to have it, the children would produce the observed mathematical behavior. That is, teachers must learn to think mathematically as if they were the children. In doing so, the goal is for teachers to construct a 'mathematics' that fits within the constraints of children's mathematical language and actions.

Through their own work teaching children, through their research with children and teachers, as well as through their interpretation of the research of others, Wright and Ellemor-Collins have developed a comprehensive *Learning Framework in Number* (LFIN) across the first six grades in school that represents their generalized models of the mathematics of children across those six grades. Their LFIN represents a major step forward toward the inclusion of children's mathematics in mathematics curricula for children. Correlated with age ranges, three broad bands of numeracy are laid out and, within each band, domains of number knowledge are specified and developed. But to regard LFIN simply as a blueprint for mathematics curricula for children would be to drastically short-change it. Also included is a vision of how assessment within the domains of number knowledge can be used to inform mathematics teaching and children's learning. Based on assessment, the authors advocate that teachers pitch instruction just beyond the cutting edge of students' learning. In this way, the tasks that teachers present to children are at a level that makes sense to them in terms of their current knowledge. But to solve the tasks, children would need to reorganize their approach, develop new strategies, or gain new insights.

The LFIN is a model that is finely tuned to children's mathematics in its levels of complexity and sophistication. In the model, children's mathematical behavior constitutes raw material for teachers' interpretative and constructive activity concerning pedagogical decisions. The teaching approach is inquiry-based and children are routinely engaged in 'thinking hard to solve numerical problems'. In this context, it is important to note that the authors leave open the possibility that teachers may well encounter children operating numerically in ways that are not accounted for in their LFIN model. Furthermore, the model does not prescribe what teachers are to do given current assessment results. The authors' understanding of teachers as rational and creative is essential, especially in those cases where children meet situations subsequent to an assessment that their current mathematics is not sufficient to solve. These cases can be particularly challenging because it is children's actions that determine the effectiveness of a planned intervention rather than the intentions of the teacher. If children do not engage in effective action regardless of a teacher's interventions, the creative teacher must 'step back' and work to establish learning trajectories that may not be pre-specified and that occasion children's effective action. The authors' view of teachers as rational and creative especially recommends the LFIN and Mathematics Recovery Program. When coupled with their emphasis on children's mathematics, the program is revolutionary.

Leslie P. Steffe

Acknowledgements

This book is a culmination of several interrelated research projects conducted over the last 25 years, many of which come under the collective label of Mathematics Recovery. All of these projects involved undertaking research, development and implementation in collaboration with teachers, schools and school systems. These projects have received significant support from the participating schools, school systems and jurisdictions.

The authors wish to express their sincere gratitude and appreciation to all of the teachers, students and project colleagues who have participated in, and contributed to, these projects. We also wish to thank the following organizations for funding and supporting one or more projects which have provided a basis for writing this book: the Australian Research Council under Grant No. AM9180064 and Grant No. LP0348932; Southern Cross University; the government and Catholic school systems of the north coast region of New South Wales, Australia; the New South Wales Department of Education and Training; the School District of Oconee County and the South Carolina Department of Education; many other school districts across the United States; the University of Liverpool, and Wigan, Sefton, Salford, Stockport, Knowsley and Cumbria Education Authorities in England; Flintshire County Council in Wales; the Ministry of Education in the Bahamas; Catholic Education Melbourne (Australia); The First Peoples Center for Education (USA); the Department of Education and Science, Ireland; The Kentucky Center for Mathematics; the Frontier School Division, Manitoba, Canada; the University of Strathclyde, and Glasgow, Edinburgh, and Stirling Education Authorities in Scotland; Fundación Educación, Voces y Vuelos, IAP in Mexico; and Trinity College, South Australia.

Finally, we wish to thank the following people for their contributions to the development and refinement of important ideas in this book: Andrea Dineen, Peter Gould, Lucy Kett, Kurt Kinsey, Thi Tran Le, Jim Martland, Petey MacCarty, Joanne Mulligan, Vicki Nally, Rumiati, Ann Stafford, Garry Stanger and Pam Tabor.

Catholic Education Melbourne

A special acknowledgement

The material in this book is drawn from two major initiatives focusing on intervention in the number learning of low-attaining students in the range from the Foundation Year (Kindergarten/Prep) to 4th Grade. The first of these focused mainly on the Foundation Year to 1st Grade, and the second extended this range to 4th Grade. The second of these two initiatives involved an extended collaboration between the authors of this book and *Catholic Education Melbourne (CEM)*. This collaboration began with a three-year Linkage Research Project (2004–6) funded jointly by the Australian Research Council (under Grant #LP0348932) and CEM. Commencing in 2009, this collaboration has continued each year via CEM's Number Intervention F-4 Project. Each year, throughout this period, the first author has provided an extended programme of professional learning with one or more cohorts of CEM teachers, and the second author has contributed significantly to the development and refinement of the pedagogical tools which are the focus of this book. This intensive and extensive collaboration between the teachers and the authors has enabled ongoing development and review related to the Number Intervention F-4 Project. The authors wish to acknowledge the very significant contribution CEM teachers have made to the focus and content of this book. We also wish to acknowledge the following leaders and learning consultants from CEM for their significant roles in the Number Intervention F-4 Project: Judy Connell, Valerie Everist, David Huggins, Lucy Kett, Gerald Lewis, Simon Lindsay, Leanne Murray, Vicky Nally and Paul Sedunary.

Series Preface

This book – *The Learning Framework in Number: Pedagogical Tools for Assessment and Instruction* is a significant and important addition to the current Mathematics Recovery Series. The six books in this series address the teaching of **early number**, whole number arithmetic and fractions in primary, elementary and secondary education. These books provide practical help to enable schools and teachers to give equal status to numeracy intervention and classroom instruction. The authors are internationally recognized as leaders in this field and draw on considerable practical experience of delivering professional learning programmes, training courses and materials.

The books are:

Early Numeracy: Assessment for Teaching and Intervention, 2nd edition, Robert J. Wright, Jim Martland and Ann K. Stafford, 2006.

Early Numeracy demonstrates how to assess students' mathematical knowledge, skills and strategies in addition, subtraction, multiplication and division.

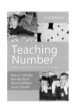

Teaching Number: Advancing Children's Skills and Strategies, 2nd edition, Robert J. Wright, Jim Martland, Ann K. Stafford and Garry Stanger, 2006.

Teaching Number sets out in detail nine principles which guide the teaching, together with 180 practical, exemplar teaching procedures to advance children to more sophisticated strategies for solving arithmetic problems.

Developing Number Knowledge: Assessment, Teaching and Intervention with 7–11 Year-Olds, Robert J. Wright, David Ellemor-Collins and Pamela Tabor, 2012.

Developing Number Knowledge provides more advanced knowledge and resources for teachers working with older students.

Teaching Number in the Classroom with 4–8 Year-Olds, 2nd edition, Robert J. Wright, Garry Stanger, Ann K. Stafford and Jim Martland, 2014.

Teaching Number in the Classroom shows how to extend the work of assessment and intervention with individual and small groups to working with whole classes.

Developing Fractions Knowledge, Amy J. Hackenberg, Anderson Norton and Robert J. Wright, 2016.

Developing Fractions Knowledge provides a detailed progressive approach to assessment and instruction related to students' learning of fractions.

The Learning Framework in Number: Pedagogical Tools for Assessment and Instruction, Robert J. Wright and David Ellemor-Collins, 2018.

This book presents a learning framework across the whole K to 5 range, and provides three sets of pedagogical tools for the framework – assessment schedules, models of learning progressions and teaching charts. These tools enable detailed assessment and profiling of children's whole number **arithmetic knowledge**, and the development of specific instructional programmes.

The series provides a comprehensive package on:

1. How to identify, analyse and report students' arithmetic knowledge, skills and strategies.
2. How to design, implement and evaluate a course of intervention.
3. How to include both assessment and teaching in the daily numeracy programme in differing class organizations and contexts.

The series draws on a substantial body of recent theoretical research supported by international practical application. Because all the assessment and teaching activities have been empirically tested the books are able to show the teacher the possible ranges of students' responses and patterns of their behaviour.

The books are a package for professional development and a comprehensive resource for experienced teachers concerned with intervention and instruction from Kindergarten to primary, elementary and secondary levels.

Online Resources

The Learning Framework in Number is supported by a range of downloadable resources available at: **https://study.sagepub.com/wrightLFIN**

These include:

- The downloadable **LFIN Assessment Kit** including printable resources necessary for carrying out the assessments detailed in the book
- The downloadable **LFIN Teaching Kit** including printable resources for use in classroom teaching

Introduction

This book presents a complete Learning Framework in Number (LFIN) across the primary grades K to 5. The LFIN provides a coherent overview of instruction in whole number arithmetic. It is organized into key **domains** of number from emergent numeracy through to strong additive and multiplicative arithmetic, which teachers can use to organize their assessment, planning and instruction.

Central to the LFIN are what we call *pedagogical tools*, that is, carefully designed materials that teachers can apply in their pedagogy. The LFIN incorporates a comprehensive suite of three main types of pedagogical tools: assessment schedules, models of learning progressions and teaching charts.

- An *assessment schedule* is a sequence of groups of **tasks** that teachers can use to assess students' levels of knowledge in a domain of number.
- A *learning progression* is presented as a table of levels that enables charting of students' current knowledge of a key aspect of number. We refer to each table of levels as a *model* of a learning progression.
- A *teaching chart* sets out interrelated progressions of instructional procedures to serve as a map for targeted, responsive instruction in a domain of number.
- Each of these tools is content-specific, and has developed from our ongoing work in teachers' professional learning.

Along with a broad consensus of mathematics educators, we do not regard learning number to be simply a task of memorizing facts or procedures. Rather, for each student, learning number demands a progression of increasing conceptual sophistication, along with the development of a rich network of number relationships. Supporting most students with this learning requires a responsive, targeted, **enquiry-based instruction** over several years of schooling. The LFIN and the suite of pedagogical tools are designed to enable such responsive instruction.

The purpose of the book

The purpose of this book is to provide the LFIN and pedagogical tools for teachers to use in their work with K to 5 students. Each tool is presented in a ready-to-use format, with sufficient instructions for teachers to use them, and with commentaries to highlight the details of students' number learning associated with each tool.

Using the book

The LFIN and pedagogical tools have been designed for intensive intervention. To this end, they are detailed. They can support subtle individual assessment and tailored, finely-graded individual instruction. Nevertheless, our experience is that teachers who learn to use these tools in intervention also bring the tools to their classroom teaching, and with great success. The core of the materials serves excellently for regular teaching. Teachers can skim the detail, and use the core tasks of the assessment schedules, the core levels of the models, and the core instructional progressions of the teaching charts. Meanwhile, the richer detail can still be of benefit at times in regular classroom teaching. So, all teachers of number and arithmetic can use the LFIN and tools in this book.

The tools are fully explained here, and the earlier books in the series furnish further compatible information on assessment and instruction. Nevertheless, to teach number well there is much to learn. We heartily recommend dedicated programmes of professional learning to make the most of these materials. For more on professional learning, see Purple Book Chapter 11 and Red Book Chapter 1. Note that these books are described in the latter part of this chapter.

We are convinced that these tools can contribute enormously to teachers' pedagogical knowledge and work, and so in turn, lead to much improved learning of arithmetic in our students and to a strong foundation for all their mathematics learning.

The background to the book

The tools and methods presented in this book are a culmination of an extensive and ongoing programme of research and development related to the teaching of number and arithmetic in the primary and elementary grades. In the case of the first author, this work spans at least 25 years, and includes several multi-year projects funded by the Australian Research Council (ARC) and a range of education departments and jurisdictions. One outcome of this work is Mathematics Recovery, a programme focusing on intensive intervention for low-attaining students in the early years of school. This programme was developed by the first author in New South Wales (Australia) and has been widely implemented internationally. As well, the programme has been extensively adapted to classroom teaching for average and able learners, and it provided a basis for earlier books in the series.

Since 2004, the authors have collaborated on a project focusing on intervention in the number learning of low-attaining 8- to 10-year-olds. The project is funded by the Australian Research Council (under Grant No. LP0348932) and Catholic Education Melbourne (CEM), and extends our earlier work on intensive intervention for younger students. Since 2012, we have also pursued a project on intervention in multiplication and division. The collaborative work of the authors of this book over the last 12 years, along with the first author's earlier work, provides a basis for the writing of this book.

With all of our research and development work, we have drawn extensively on a range of international research and development related to students' learning of arithmetic. Equally, our work depends on intensive, long-term collaborations with teachers, schools and school systems. We have drawn extensively on their insights into students' learning and purposeful instruction, as well as their trialling of the range of pedagogical tools that we have developed. This book in particular, is the outcome of these long-term collaborations with teachers.

The book should be of interest to all who are concerned with finding new ways to teach number and with advancing the levels of learning in schools. Teachers, advisers, numeracy consultants, mathematics supervisors, curriculum leaders and learning support personnel, as well as teacher educators and researchers whose work relates to this field, will find much of interest from both theoretical and practical perspectives.

The structure of the book

The book is structured using the basic order in which the pedagogical tools are learned and used by teachers. We begin with the organizing framework (LFIN). Then follows the approach to assessment and tools for assessment, and finally the approach to instruction and tools for instruction.

In Chapter 1 we provide an overview of the Learning Framework in Number (LFIN) and introduce the three types of pedagogical tools that are the focus of this book: assessment schedules, models of learning progressions and teaching charts.

In Chapter 2 we describe our approach to assessment. This includes an account of Video-recorded Interview-based Assessment (VIBA) and its particular usefulness in teacher professional learning; guidelines for conducting assessment interviews; guidelines for videotaping assessment interviews; and guidelines for coding and analysing assessment interviews.

In Chapter 3 we present the assessment schedules. We explain the format of the schedules, and how they are used to guide assessment interviews. We give an overview of the set of schedules. We then present the nine schedules, along with detailed commentaries for each schedule on students' responses to the assessment tasks.

In Chapter 4 we present the models of learning progressions. We explain the format of the models, and how they are used both to summarize assessment and to give direction to teaching. We give an overview of the set of models. We then present the nine models and, for each model, a detailed commentary on the significance of the levels and the sense of progression through the model.

In Chapter 5 we describe our enquiry-based approach to instruction. This includes guiding principles of instruction; key elements of instructional interaction in intervention; and characteristics of students' problem solving. Chapter 5 also includes a description of the broad trajectory of instruction in number across grades K to 5, and an overview of instruction in each domain.

Finally, in Chapter 6 we present the teaching charts. We explain the format of the charts, and how they are used to guide both moment-to-moment teaching and lesson planning. We give an overview of the set of teaching charts. We then present the 10 charts, along with commentaries for each chart on the main teaching procedures and progressions.

Useful reference sources are gathered at the end of the book, including:

- an extensive glossary of technical terms used in the book;
- an appendix which contains descriptions of key **instructional settings** used in the book;
- copies of two key charts from the book, the LFIN Chart and the Models Chart; and
- a comprehensive bibliography of relevant works.

The book's website has master documents for printing the materials in the LFIN Assessment Kit, and the LFIN Teaching Kit.

Using the earlier books in the series

This book is the sixth entry in the Math Recovery series which addresses assessment, instruction and intervention in early number and whole number arithmetic in the range from Kindergarten to 5th grade. Four earlier books are listed below. For ease of use, we refer to each book according to the cover colour: the Blue Book, the Green Book, the Purple Book and the Red Book.

Blue Book   *Early Numeracy: Assessment for Teaching and Intervention*

Green Book   *Teaching Number: Advancing Children's Skills and Strategies*

Red Book   *Developing Number Knowledge: Assessment, Teaching and Intervention with 7–11 Year-Olds*

Purple Book   *Teaching Number in the Classroom with 4–8 Year-Olds*

This book is an important addition to the series because for the first time it presents a learning framework across the whole K to 5 range, and provides a complete suite of pedagogical tools for that framework: assessment schedules, models of learning progressions and teaching charts. The new LFIN has been developed from earlier frameworks and organizers, to offer a coherent framework extending from preschoolers' emergent number knowledge through to the relatively sophisticated arithmetical knowledge typical of successful learners at 4th- and 5th-grade levels. The assessment schedules and models from our earlier books have been radically revised, reorganized, extended and furnished with new commentaries. The teaching charts are all new.

While an extensive amount of the material in this book is new to the series, the book relates closely to the four earlier books. Our strong recommendation to readers is that they use this book in conjunction with the earlier books. The earlier books provide detailed information related to many aspects of the pedagogical tools in this book. The earlier books also offer more extensive descriptions of our general approach to assessment and instruction. Thus, in the earlier books, the reader will find additional information that can be applied in coming to understand the content and significance of all of the pedagogical tools. To this end, a table in Chapter 1 lays out the links from this book to the chapters of the earlier books. Cross-references to the earlier books are provided throughout this book.

Developing fractions knowledge

Finally, please note that, as well as this new book and the four books listed above, a sixth book in the Mathematics Recovery Series, entitled *Developing Fractions Knowledge*, is also available.

1

The Learning Framework in Number: An Overview

We organize our approaches to assessment and teaching using what we call a learning framework. We name it the Learning Framework in Number: the LFIN. There are several major features in the LFIN: bands, domains, schedules, models, teaching charts, ranges, dimensions, and so on. The LFIN is a rich system which connects all these features into a coherent approach to instruction in children's number knowledge. This chapter explains the main features in the LFIN, how the pedagogical tools are organized in the LFIN, how the LFIN is used to support instruction, and further information related to the LFIN.

An introduction to using the LFIN

The LFIN is organized into nine key domains of number knowledge, and incorporates three main types of pedagogical tools. Here is a brief example of how the domains and tools are used to organize assessment and teaching.

A teacher, Vicki, selects three domains to address with her student, Sam, broadly appropriate for Sam's number knowledge. Vicki uses a distinctive approach to initial assessment: Video-recorded Interview-based Assessment (VIBA). The VIBA approach is explained in Chapter 2. The assessment involves Vicki conducting an assessment interview with Sam, using the three *assessment schedules* – the first main type of tool – for the three selected domains. The schedules are presented in Chapter 3. Each assessment schedule provides refined groups of assessment tasks, which Vicki works through strategically, to assess Sam's knowledge in that domain.

After the assessment interview, Vicki reviews the video-recording of the interview, annotating Sam's responses on each assessment schedule. Each of the three domains she has assessed has associated *models* of the learning progressions in the domain – the second main type of tool – which give sequences of levels or stages of knowledge. The models are presented in Chapter 4. Vicki analyses Sam's responses to determine levels and stages which give a profile of his current knowledge across the three domains.

Next, Vicki consults a *teaching chart* for each domain – the third main type of tool – to develop an instructional plan targeting Sam's level of knowledge in each domain. The teaching charts are presented in Chapter 6. As Vicki's teaching gets underway, the teaching charts guide the subsequent progressions in the instruction. In the next school term, Vicki can assess Sam again, using the same three schedules, and analyse the levels on the same models, to track his progress.

In summary, the teacher uses assessment schedules to assess a student's knowledge, she uses models to summarize those assessments, and she uses teaching charts to guide instruction that responds to those assessments. The assessment schedules, models and teaching charts are the three main types of pedagogical tools of the teacher's trade. The LFIN enables coordination of the tools across the domains.

The first three sections of this chapter explain these domains and tools, and how they are coordinated. The latter two sections provide further information related to the LFIN.

Bands and domains in the LFIN

The LFIN spans three broad bands of number learning. Table 1.1 sets out the three bands and indicative age ranges for each. Our main focus is on Band 2, Early Number (EN), and Band 3, Middle Number (MN).

Table 1.1   Bands and domains

Broad bands	Ages	Domains
1. Very Early Number (VEN)	2 to 5	1. Very Early Number
2. Early Number (EN)	4 to 8	2A. Early Number Words & Numerals
		2B. Early Structuring
		2C. Early Arithmetical Strategies
3. Middle Number (MN)	6 to 10	3A. Number Words & Numerals
		3B. Structuring Numbers 1 to 20
		3C. Conceptual Place Value
		3D. Addition & Subtraction to 100
		3E. Early Multiplication & Division
		3F. Multiplicative Basic Facts

Within Band 2 and Band 3, the LFIN identifies key domains of number learning. The table sets out these domains – three in Early Number and six in Middle Number. The domains have letter codes, 2A to 2C and 3A to 3F, and colour codes, which we use throughout the materials.

Domains

Our sense of these domains has developed over years of our research and teaching. Each domain is regarded as a substantial area of number learning. From the perspective of the teacher, each domain can be somewhat distinct from the other domains, involving distinctive assessment tasks and instructional procedures. Each is worth sustained instructional attention over many months, probably two to three years in the case of the larger domains (e.g. 3B, 3D and 3F). Acquiring sound knowledge of a domain is a significant accomplishment in mathematics learning.

There are, of course, important connections and overlaps between the domains. Instruction within each domain includes developing these connections to other domains.

Overview of each domain

Below is a brief description of each domain. More detailed accounts of each domain are developed in later chapters, through the descriptions of the assessment schedules, models and teaching charts in each domain.

1. Very Early Number

Our purpose in including Very Early Number as Band 1 is to highlight that typically, children acquire significant number knowledge prior to starting school. As well, there is significant very early number knowledge that is not included in the curriculum for students in the first year of school. Insights into this knowledge are provided by the work of developmental psychologists who have observed and documented the number knowledge typical of, for example, 2-, 3- and 4-year-olds.

2A. Early Number Words and Numerals

This domain involves knowledge of basic spoken **number word sequences** by ones, both forward and backward, such as 'one, two, three, … twenty' and 'thirty-two, thirty-one, thirty, twenty-nine, twenty-eight'. The domain also involves reading and writing **numerals**. For both number words and numerals, the domain focuses on the range up to 100.

2B. Early Structuring

This domain involves knowledge of **finger patterns** for numbers up to 10, and standard spatial configurations, such as dice and domino patterns. The domain also involves knowledge of small combinations and **partitions**, such as small **doubles** (1&1, 2&2, 3&3, 4&4, 5&5), and five-pluses (5&1, 5&2, 5&3, 5&4, 5&5), and additional emerging knowledge of addition and subtraction in the range 1 to 10.

2C. Early Arithmetic Strategies

Early arithmetic strategies refers to a progression of counting-based strategies that children use to solve counting, **additive** and **subtractive tasks**, such as counting the items in a collection, determining the number of items in two collections, or the number of items remaining after some items are removed. These strategies arise in situations where the items to be counted are in the child's visual field or are screened and thus unavailable to count perceptually. These strategies include the advanced **counting-by-ones** strategies, that is, **counting-on** and counting-back.

3A. Number Words and Numerals

This domain extends from Domain 2A, into the range to 1000 and beyond. The domain involves knowledge of number word sequences and **numeral sequences**, including sequences by 1s, 10s and 100s. This domain also involves reading and writing numerals, up to 5-digit numerals and further.

3B. Structuring Numbers 1 to 20

This domain involves number combinations and partitions in the range 1 to 20, and facility with mental strategies for addition and subtraction that do not involve counting-by-ones. The domain progresses from the finger patterns of Domain 2B, to the use of five-frames, **ten-frames** and the **arithmetic rack**, and increasingly to reasoning about **bare numbers** with independence from any such **settings**. The domain includes the significant sub-domain of Structuring Numbers 1 to 10.

3C. Conceptual Place Value

This domain involves flexibly **incrementing** and **decrementing** numbers by 1s, 10s and 100s. This informal knowledge of 1s, 10s and 100s is foundational in mental strategies for **multi-digit** computation, and can be distinguished from conventional place value knowledge.

3D. Addition and Subtraction to 100

This domain involves facility with **mental computation** for addition and subtraction in the range to 100, and beyond, using relatively sophisticated mental strategies. The domain includes the sub-domain of **Higher Decade Addition and Subtraction**.

3E. Early Multiplication and Division

This domain involves the early development from **perceptual**, counting-based strategies toward abstract multiplicative reasoning. The domain is focused in the range 1 to 30, and involves facility with basic multiplicative contexts such as equal groups and **arrays**. Also included is skip-counting, that is, sequences by 2s, 3s, 4s and 5s.

3F. Multiplicative Basic Facts

This domain involves facility with mental computation for multiplication and division in the range to 100, and beyond. This includes using strong multiplicative mental strategies, and increasing automaticity with **basic facts** of multiplication and division.

The LFIN Chart

The domains are used to organize our intervention work. Assessment materials, teaching materials, lesson plans, student profiles, and so on, are all organized in terms of the domains. In particular, the three sets of pedagogical tools presented in this book – the assessment schedules, the models and the teaching charts – are organized in terms of the domains.

The organization of the domains and pedagogical tools is shown in the *Learning Framework in Number* Chart, or LFIN Chart (see below). This is the main organizing chart for the LFIN. A copy of the LFIN Chart is included in Appendix 2. Here we explain the organization of the domains in the chart, and in the next section we explain the organization of the tools.

Learning Framework in Number

Domains, Models, Assessment Schedules and Teaching Charts

BAND 2
Early Number (EN)

2A	2B	2C
Early Number Words & Numerals	Early Structuring	Early Arithmetical Strategies

NID: ⓪①②③④...
BNWS: ⓪①②③④⑤...
FNWS: ⓪①②③④⑤...

SN20: ⓪①②③...

SEAL: ⓪①②③④⑤

BAND 3
Middle Number (MN)

3A	3B	3C	3D	3E	3F
Number Words & Numerals	Structuring Numbers 1 to 20	Conceptual Place Value	Addition & Subtraction to 100	Early Multiplication & Division	Multiplicative Basic Facts

...③④⑤⑥
...④⑤⑥⑦
...④⑤⑥⑦

...②③④⑤⑥⑦

10
20

CPV: ⓪①②③④

A&S: ⓪①②③④⑤⑥

EM&D: ⓪①②③④⑤⑥

MBF: ①abcd...⑤abcd

Model names

FNWS:	Forward Number Word Sequences
BNWS:	Backward Number Word Sequences
NID:	Numeral Identification
SN20:	Structuring Numbers 1 to 20
SEAL:	Stages of Early Arithmetical Learning
CPV:	Conceptual Place Value
A&S:	Addition & Subtraction to 100
EM&D:	Early Multiplication & Division
MBF:	Multiplicative Basic Facts

Assessment schedule   Teaching chart   Model of a learning progression

⓪①②... level or stage numbers on model

Bands

The main progression in the chart is from the Early Number Band in the upper row, to the Middle Number Band in the lower row. The three EN domains address basic knowledge of number words and numerals up to 100, finger patterns to 10, and solving arithmetic tasks using strategies based on counting-by-ones. The six MN domains progress to number words and numerals beyond 1000, using relatively sophisticated **non-counting strategies** for mental addition and subtraction, and using relatively sophisticated multiplicative strategies for mental multiplication and division.

Horizontal progressions

Within each band, there is a suggestion of progression from left to right across the row. To align with this progression, the colour codes start with green on the left, and progress in a colour wheel sequence left to right.

- In Early Number: Green/Yellow/Pink
- In Middle Number: Green/Yellow/Orange/Red/Blue

So, in Early Number, we typically address Domain 2A (Early Number Words and Numerals) first in assessments and lessons, though we will also work concurrently on Domains 2B (Early Structuring) and 2C (Early Arithmetic Strategies). Further, we regard Domain 2A as, in part, developing foundational knowledge needed for Domain 2C, such as knowing a **backward number word sequence** (2A) that is used in a counting-down-from **strategy** for a subtraction task (2C).

In Middle Number, we often address Domains 3A, 3B and 3C for some time before introducing instruction on Domains 3D or 3E. Domains 3B and 3C are each regarded as, in part, developing important foundations for Domain 3D; and some facility in 3D and 3E is important, in turn, for Domain 3F.

Vertical progressions

There are also vertical progressions down the first two columns of domains. As noted in the overview of the domains above, Domain 2A (Early Number Words and Numerals) extends into Domain 3A (Number Words and Numerals). Likewise, Domain 2B (Early Structuring) extends into Domain 3B (Structuring Numbers 1 to 20). These vertical pairings are indicated by the matched colour codes.

Each of these pairs could be considered as one long domain extending across both bands. However, it is not simply a case of the numbers getting bigger in Middle Number. In each pair, the MN Domain involves significant changes in instruction from the EN Domain, and we find it useful to regard them as distinct domains. For example, in progressing from Domain 2A to Domain 3A, the instruction integrates numeral sequences more with number word sequences, and brings new attention to place value for reading and writing multi-digit numerals.

In contrast to the pairings of 2A–3A and 2B–3B, Domain 2C (Early Arithmetical Strategies) does not descend directly to Domain 3C (Conceptual Place Value). Domain 3C has its own colour code. Nevertheless, there are affinities down this column. For example, Domain 2C tasks typically involve covered collections of counters, while Domain 3C tasks typically involve covered collections of **base-ten materials**; also, Domain 2C focuses on students' strategies based on counting-by-ones, while Domain 3C focuses on students' strategies based on counting by 1s, 10s and 100s. More generally, Domain 2C can be regarded as descending to all of Domains 3B, 3C and 3D, since Domain 2C addresses early strategies for additive tasks, while Domains 3B, 3C and 3D involve more sophisticated strategies for different types of additive tasks.

Three main pedagogical tools in the LFIN

Below, we explain how each of the three main pedagogical tools is coordinated with the domains, and how they are represented in the LFIN Chart.

Assessment schedules

There is one assessment schedule for each domain. The schedules are represented in the LFIN Chart by an icon of a single page, one in each domain.

The schedules are presented in Chapter 3. Have a look at some schedule pages to see what they are like. A printed schedule is typically two pages long. There is room on a copy of the printed schedule to annotate the student's responses when reviewing a videotaped assessment interview, and to record the model level or stage assessed. Each schedule is organized into task groups, which are graduated sequences of similar tasks, used for assessing particular levels of knowledge and strategies on specific topics in the domain. There is much to learn about how to present each task, and the range of possible responses from students: this is the subject of Chapter 3.

Models of learning progressions

In the LFIN chart, the models associated with each domain are written in narrow paler strips down the right-hand edge of the domain, marked with an icon of a square boxed list. The sequence of level or stage numbers is listed in each strip, using circled numbers such as:

SEAL: ⓪①②③④⑤

These circled numbers are used for levels and stages throughout the materials.

Each model is described in Chapter 4. As well, Chapter 4 includes a one-page summary of all the models, which we refer to as the Models Chart. There is much to learn about the levels in each model, and how to analyse students' responses to determine their levels. This is the subject of Chapter 4.

FNWS, BNWS and Numeral Identification models

Domain 2A, Early Number Words and Numerals, and Domain 3A, Number Words and Numerals, share three models that extend across both Band 2 and Band 3:

Forward Number Word Sequences (**FNWS**)

Backward Number Word Sequences (**BNWS**)

Numeral Identification (NID)

Domain 2A addresses the lower levels of the three models, while Domain 3A addresses the higher levels. This is indicated in the chart by the incomplete lists of level numbers in the strips beside each domain. The level numbers shown are the levels assessed by each assessment schedule. That is, Schedule 2A includes tasks that assess Levels ⓪ to ⑤ on FNWS and BNWS, and ⓪ to ④ on NID; while Schedule 3A can assess levels ④ to ⑦ on FNWS and BNWS, and ③ to ⑥ on NID. There is an overlap. Thus the levels used for Domain 2A overlap with the levels used for Domain 3A.

These three models are relatively straightforward models to assess. They are also closely connected: the BNWS model levels correspond with the FNWS model levels, and the NID levels are similar to the number word sequence levels. Charting a student's levels across these three models provides a good summary of their knowledge of number words and numerals.

Structuring Numbers 1 to 20 model

The pair of Structuring Numbers domains 2B–3B share a single model that extends across both bands, called the Structuring Numbers 1 to 20 model. Again, 2B addresses the lower levels, and 3B the higher levels, of this shared model. The exact ranges of levels assessed by Schedules 2B and 3B are shown on the LFIN Chart.

SEAL model

Domain 2C, Early Arithmetical Strategies, has the model called the Stages of Early Arithmetical Learning, or SEAL – a model of early conceptual development in number and the only model in the LFIN comprised of stages rather than levels. This is explained further in Chapter 4.

Conceptual Place Value, Addition and Subtraction, and Multiplication and Division models

Each of the last four domains has a model:

3C. Conceptual Place Value (CPV)

3D. Addition and Subtraction to 100 (A&S)

3E. Early Multiplication and Division (EM&D)

3F. Multiplicative Basic Facts (MBF)

The names of the models for 3C, 3D, 3E and 3F are synonymous with the domains.

Teaching charts

The teaching charts are represented in the LFIN Chart by an icon of a wide page with a heading banner. Each domain has one teaching chart except Domain 3B, Structuring Numbers 1 to 20, which has two charts. The teaching laid out for 3B is extensive, and we find it helpful to separate it into two charts: Chart $3B_{10}$ for Structuring Numbers 1 to 10, and Chart $3B_{20}$ for Structuring Numbers 1 to 20.

Each teaching chart is described in Chapter 6. Have a look at some charts to see what they are like. A printed teaching chart is one or two pages long, in landscape orientation. Each regular cell in a chart lists a teaching procedure, that is, a particular kind of instructional task in a particular topic. The teaching procedures are organized into topics, ranges and phases. The layout of the cells in the chart suggests potential progressions in the instruction: progressions across the rows, down the columns, and so on. The chart may address a broader range of topics than what is assessed in the schedule. There is much to learn about how to do the teaching procedures, the range of possible responses from students, and how to pursue progressions in the instruction. This is the subject of Chapter 6.

Summary of the LFIN Chart

So, in summary, the LFIN Chart shows the following:

- Two main bands: Band 2 Early Number and Band 3 Middle Number
- Nine domains:
    - three in EN: 2A, 2B, 2C
    - six in MN: 3A, 3B, 3C, 3D, 3E, 3F
- Domains 2A–3A and 2B–3B spanning both bands
- Nine assessment schedules: one for each domain
- Ten teaching charts: one for each domain, plus an extra for 3B
- Nine models:
    - three models associated with Domains 2A–3A spanning both bands
    - one model associated with Domains 2B and 3B spanning both bands
    - one model associated with each of Domains 2C, 3C, 3D, 3E, and 3F
- The model level numbers or stage numbers assessed by each schedule.

These are the basic elements of the LFIN.

Progression of the LFIN across grades K to 5

The LFIN Progressions across K to 5 Chart

A second important chart is the LFIN Progressions across K to 5 Chart (see below). The Progressions K to 5 Chart shows the progression of instruction in the LFIN, across the school grades K to 5. The chart is organized in the two bands of number learning – Early Number and Middle Number – with the domains listed in order.

For the purposes of intervention, a domain is typically addressed after it has been addressed in regular classroom teaching. The chart shows, across the row of each domain, indicative grade levels for intervention instruction in that domain. The letter codes indicate the phases of Starting (S), Working-on (W) and Consolidating (C) instruction, and the corresponding brightening-and-fading colour across the row indicates the building-and-tapering of instructional attention to that domain.

For a student at a given grade, the chart suggests the domains that are likely to be assessed, and to become the focus of teaching. A teacher will typically address three to five domains at any one time, including consolidating one or two earlier domains, working on two current domains, and perhaps starting one new domain. Following are two examples.

For a typical grade 1 intervention student

Initial assessment:

- assess Schedules 2A, 2B, 2C;
- determine profile of levels on the associated models: FNWS, BNWS, NID, SN20 and SEAL;
- possibly assess Schedule 3C, determining a level on model CPV.

Teaching:

- consolidating Charts 2A and 2C;
- working on Chart 2B;
- later, starting Charts 3A, 3B and 3C.

LFIN: Progressions across K to 5

BAND		Domains and Models		K	1	2	3	4	5
2 Early Number (EN)	**2A**	Early Number Words & Numerals		W	C				
		FNWS: 0①②③④⑤ ...							
		BNWS: 0①②③④⑤ ...							
		NID: 0①②③④ ...							
	2B	Early Structuring		S	W	C			
		SN20: 0①②③ ...							
	2C	Early Arithmetical Strategies		W	C				
		SEAL: 0①②③④⑤							
3 Middle Number (MN)	**3A**	Number Words & Numerals			S	W	C		
		FNWS: ...④⑤⑥⑦							
		BNWS: ...④⑤⑥⑦							
		NID: ...③④⑤⑥							
	3B	Structuring Numbers 1 to 20			S	W	W	C	C
		SN20: ...②③④⑤⑥⑦							
	3C	Conceptual Place Value			S	W	W	C	C
		CPV: 0①②③④							
	3D	Addition & Subtraction to 100				S	W	W	C
		A&S: 0①②③④⑤⑥							
	3E	Early Multiplication & Division					S	W	C
		EM&D: 0①②③④⑤⑥							
	3F	Multiplicative Basic Facts					S	W	W
		MBF: ①abcd–⑤abcd							

S = Starting   W = Working-on   C = Consolidating

⊞ Model   ☐ Assessment schedule   ☐ Teaching chart

For a typical grade 3 intervention student

Initial assessment:

- assess Schedules 3A, 3B and 3C;
- determine profile of levels on the associated models: FNWS, BNWS, NID, SN20 and CPV;
- possibly assess Schedule 3D, determining a level on model A&S.

Teaching:

- consolidating Chart 3A;
- working on Charts 3B, 3C and 3D;
- later, starting Chart 3E or 3F, as time becomes available.

A layered progression

The Progressions across K to 5 Chart show an important characteristic of the LFIN approach overall: work in the domains is not a lock-step progression, rather, it is a layered and interwoven progression.

- At any one time, teaching addresses several domains concurrently.
- Within each domain, instructional attention builds and tapers.
- New domains are introduced while earlier domains continue.
- New domains are connected to earlier domains.

Assessing a student on a single topic, determining she or he is at Level ②, and then delivering instruction pitched at Level ②, is relatively straightforward. Important in the use of the LFIN is that we do not assess and teach on one topic alone, and do not regard the student as being at a single level. Instead, we try to understand how the student is advancing on several interconnected fronts, and develop instruction to address those several fronts concurrently. The LFIN serves as a map, to keep track of where we are and where we are trying to go, on what is an idiosyncratic and multi-layered trajectory.

Further layers in the LFIN

Progressions of ranges

Within each domain, assessment and instruction are often organized by a progression in the range of numbers involved, progressing from lower numbers to higher numbers. There are three standard schemes of ranges which are used in several LFIN tools. We present them here, and refer to them as needed throughout the book.

Place value ranges

One scheme is the *place value ranges*, making a progression through 1-, 2-, 3- and 4-digit numbers.

Range 1	1 to 10
Range 2	1 to 20
Range 3	1 to 100
Range 4	1 to 1000
Range 5	Beyond 1000

Variants of this scheme are involved in the assessment schedules, models and teaching charts in four different domains:

2A. Early Number Words and Numerals

3A. Number Words and Numerals

3C. Conceptual Place Value

3D. Addition and Subtraction to 100

For example, the Numeral Identification model associated with Domains 2A and 3A follows this scheme closely:

Level ⓪: Emergent numeral identification

Level ①: Numerals to 10 – Identify

Level ②: Numerals to 20 – Identify

Level ③: Numerals to 100 – Identify

Level ④: Numerals to 1000 – Identify & write

Level ⑤: Numerals to 10,000 – Identify & write

Level ⑥: Numerals to 100,000 – Identify & write

Addition ranges

For addition and subtraction in the range 1 to 20, we have a scheme of four ranges of additive tasks. This Addition Ranges scheme is involved in organizing Domains 2B Early Structuring and 3B Structuring Numbers 1 to 20.

To describe the ranges, we regard any basic addition or subtraction task as involving three numbers: two *parts* and one *whole* (the largest number).

Task	Parts		Whole
3 + 6 = 9	3	6	9
16 – 8 = 8	8	8	16
19 – □ = 13	6	13	19

We then describe the ranges in terms of the size of the parts and wholes. The four ranges are presented in the Addition Ranges Grid. Example tasks are given in the table below.

	Range	Examples			
Range 1	Parts ≤ 5	2 + 2	8 – 3	1 + □ = 5	10 – □ = 5
Range 2	Whole ≤ 10	3 + 6	9 – 7	2 + □ = 8	10 – □ = 4
Range 3	Parts ≤ 10	7 + 8	16 – 8	10 + □ = 16	11 – □ = 4
Range 4	Whole ≤ 20	13 + 3	19 – 11	15 + □ = 17	19 – □ = 13

The progression of these four ranges has a numerical pattern which makes it easy to work with in practice. At the same time, importantly, the progression has a pedagogical rationale. Range 1 consists of tasks where each part can be counted on the fingers of a single hand. These are typically the earliest additive tasks that students solve. Range 2 tasks can be solved using the fingers of both hands, and include the key partitions of 10 (1&9, 2&8, 3&7, 4&6, 5&5). Range 3 consists of tasks which 'cross over 10', requiring the development of non-counting strategies, a significant advance in sophistication. Range 3 also completes the traditional 'Basic Facts of Addition': all sums up to 10 + 10. Range 4 completes the mastery of all additive combinations in the range 1 to 20.

Multiplication ranges

For multiplication and division, we have a scheme of five ranges of multiplicative tasks. This multiplicative scheme appears in Domains 3E Early Multiplication and Division and 3F Multiplicative Basic Facts. In 3F, instruction progresses systematically through each of these five ranges, developing distinctive multiplicative strategies for the facts in each range, and then working toward automaticity with those facts. This progression is explained further in Chapter 6.

To describe the ranges, we regard any basic multiplication or division task as involving three numbers: two **factors** and one **product** (the largest number).

Addition Ranges Grid

	Range	Notes
Range 1	Parts ≤ 5	Earliest tasks. Each part can be counted on one hand. Key combinations: small doubles, partitions of 5, five-pluses.
Range 2	Whole ≤ 10	Completes range 1 to 10. Key combinations: partitions of 10.
Range 3	Parts ≤ 10	Tasks cross over 10. Develop non-counting strategies. Key combinations: large doubles, ten-pluses.
Range 4	Whole ≤ 20	Completes range 1 to 20. Key combinations: partitions of 20.

+	1	2	3	4	5	6	7	8	9	10	11	12	...
1	1+1	1+2	1+3	1+4	1+5	1+6	1+7	1+8	1+9	1+10	1+11	1+12	
2	2+1	2+2	2+3	2+4	2+5	2+6	2+7	2+8	2+9	2+10	2+11	2+12	...
3	3+1	3+2	3+3	3+4	3+5	3+6	3+7	3+8	3+9	3+10	3+11	3+12	
4	4+1	4+2	4+3	4+4	4+5	4+6	4+7	4+8	4+9	4+10	4+11	4+12	...
5	5+1	5+2	5+3	5+4	5+5	5+6	5+7	5+8	5+9	5+10	5+11	5+12	
6	6+1	6+2	6+3	6+4	6+5	6+6	6+7	6+8	6+9	6+10	6+11	6+12	...
7	7+1	7+2	7+3	7+4	7+5	7+6	7+7	7+8	7+9	7+10	7+11	7+12	
8	8+1	8+2	8+3	8+4	8+5	8+6	8+7	8+8	8+9	8+10	8+11	8+12	
9	9+1	9+2	9+3	9+4	9+5	9+6	9+7	9+8	9+9	9+10	9+11		
10	10+1	10+2	10+3	10+4	10+5	10+6	10+7	10+8	10+9	10+10			

+	1	2	3	4	5	6	7	8	9
11	11+1	11+2	11+3	11+4	11+5	11+6	11+7	11+8	11+9
12	12+1	12+2	12+3	12+4	12+5	12+6	12+7	12+8	
13	13+1	13+2	13+3	13+4	13+5	13+6	13+7		
14	14+1	14+2	14+3	14+4	14+5	14+6			
15	15+1	15+2	15+3	15+4	15+5				
16	16+1	16+2	16+3	16+4					
17	17+1	17+2	17+3						
18	18+1	18+2							
19	19+1								

For example:

Task	Factors		Product
2 × 6 = 12	2	6	12
25 ÷ 5 = 5	5	5	25
36 ÷ □ = 9	9	4	36

We consider factors of basic facts as either *low factors* (2, 3, 4, 5) or *high factors* (6, 7, 8, 9). We then describe the ranges of tasks in terms of the size of the two factors involved. The five ranges are presented in the Multiplication Ranges Grid. Example tasks are given in the table below.

	Range	Examples			
Range 1	2s and 10s	2 × 6	10 × 4	10 × □ = 70	18 ÷ 9
Range 2	Low × low	3 × 4	5 × 5	3 × □ = 15	20 ÷ 4
Range 3	Low × high	4 × 7	8 × 3	5 × □ = 45	24 ÷ 4
Range 4	High × high	6 × 8	7 × 7	9 × □ = 54	42 ÷ 7
Range 5	Factor > 10	12 × 4	5 × 36	8 × □ = 176	256 ÷ 4

As with the addition ranges, this progression of multiplication ranges is sufficiently simple to work with in practice. At the same time, the progression has a pedagogical rationale. Range 1, involving doubles and **multiples** of 10, are among the earliest multiples learned, as they are already key combinations of addition. Range 2 tasks, with factors of only 3, 4 and 5, can be visualized as small arrays, and calculated using additive strategies. Range 3 tasks, the higher multiples of 3, 4 and 5, are not so readily learned. These are typically the first tasks requiring the development of relatively sophisticated multiplicative computation strategies. Range 4 tasks, all with high factors, include the most demanding basic facts to calculate and learn. Range 5 tasks involve a 2-digit factor. These products are generally not **habituated**; rather, they require well-organized multiplicative computation strategies, which build on knowledge of all the previous ranges. The significance of these ranges is elaborated on in the commentaries on the 3F Schedule, Model and Teaching Chart, in Chapters 3, 4 and 6 respectively.

Dimensions of mathematization

Consider an example. To learn Domain 3C, Conceptual Place Value, students need to progress through coordinating increasingly complex combinations of base-ten **units**: from just incrementing by 10s, to switching between 10s and 1s, through to incrementing and decrementing by mixtures of 100s, 10s and 1s. Students also need to extend the range of numbers they can work in as described in the previous section: the range to 100, then the range to 1000, and then beyond 1000. Furthermore, students usually begin CPV tasks in a setting of visible materials, and need to then progress from dependence on the visible setting, to fluency with bare number tasks. Thus, the student is really progressing on several related fronts within the one domain. We call these different progressions *dimensions of mathematization*.

We have developed a framework of ten key dimensions in number and arithmetic learning:

- Extending the range
- Varying the orientation
- Increasing the complexity
- Distancing the setting
- Notating and formalizing
- Refining strategies
- Structuring numbers
- Unitizing
- Decimalizing
- Organizing and generalizing.

They are each described briefly below, and summarized in the Dimensions of Mathematization chart. (See also Red Book, Chapter 2, pp. 14–19.)

Multiplication Ranges Grid

	Range	Notes
Range 1	2s and 10s	Doubles and decuples. The most familiar multiples. These are already key addition facts.
Range 2	Low × low	Low 3s, 4s and 5s. Small arrays, learned via addition. These small products are used to derive larger products.
Range 3	Low × high	High 3s, 4s and 5s. First earnest engagement with developing multiplicative strategies.
Range 4	High × high	High 6s, 7s, 8s, 9s. Requires multiplicative strategies. Includes the most demanding basic facts.
Range 5	Factor > 10	Tasks beyond the traditional basic facts. Strategies derive from knowledge of the earlier ranges.

×	2	3	4	5	6	7	8	9	10
2	2×2	2×3	2×4	2×5	2×6	2×7	2×8	2×9	2×10
3	3×2	3×3	3×4	3×5	3×6	3×7	3×8	3×9	3×10
4	4×2	4×3	4×4	4×5	4×6	4×7	4×8	4×9	4×10
5	5×2	5×3	5×4	5×5	5×6	5×7	5×8	5×9	5×10
6	6×2	6×3	6×4	6×5	6×6	6×7	6×8	6×9	6×10
7	7×2	7×3	7×4	7×5	7×6	7×7	7×8	7×9	7×10
8	8×2	8×3	8×4	8×5	8×6	8×7	8×8	8×9	8×10
9	9×2	9×3	9×4	9×5	9×6	9×7	9×8	9×9	9×10
10	10×2	10×3	10×4	10×5	10×6	10×7	10×8	10×9	10×10

>10				
11×2	11×3	11×4...		
	....25×3	25×4	25×5...	
		...5×34	5×35	5×36...
			...8×65	8×66	8×67...

Range 5

Learning Framework in Number © Wright & Ellemor-Collins, 2018 (Sage)

Dimensions of Mathematization

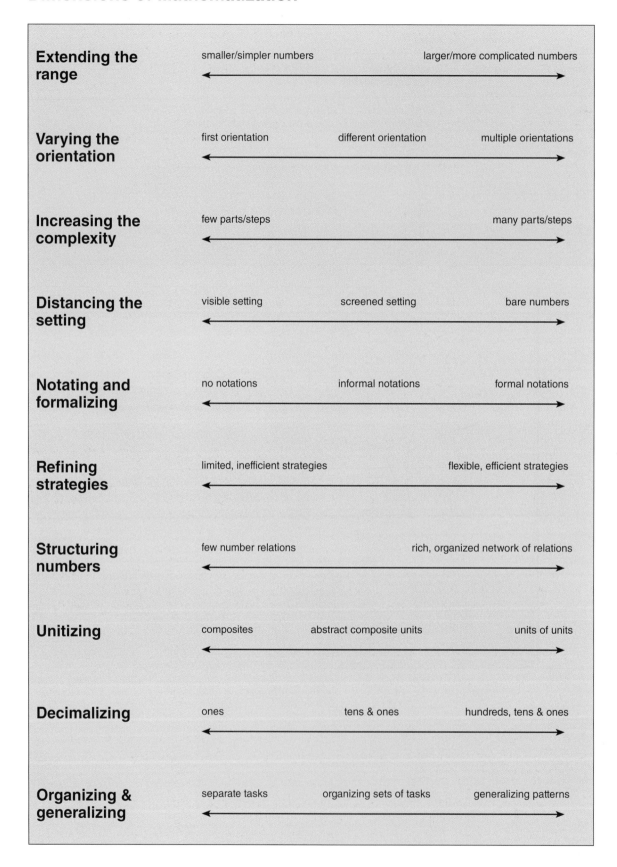

Extending the range	smaller/simpler numbers		larger/more complicated numbers
Varying the orientation	first orientation	different orientation	multiple orientations
Increasing the complexity	few parts/steps		many parts/steps
Distancing the setting	visible setting	screened setting	bare numbers
Notating and formalizing	no notations	informal notations	formal notations
Refining strategies	limited, inefficient strategies		flexible, efficient strategies
Structuring numbers	few number relations		rich, organized network of relations
Unitizing	composites	abstract composite units	units of units
Decimalizing	ones	tens & ones	hundreds, tens & ones
Organizing & generalizing	separate tasks	organizing sets of tasks	generalizing patterns

Extending the range

Extending the range involves a progression from handling smaller or simpler numbers to larger or more complicated numbers. This dimension arises on a broad-scale through the whole development of arithmetic, from adding in the range 1 to 5 through to adding numbers in the thousands. The dimension also arises on finer scales, as in the scheme of four ranges for structuring numbers 1 to 20, described in the previous section.

Varying the orientation

Orientation refers to the choice of which values are given, and which are to be determined, in an arithmetic task. For example, tasks about the relation $8 \times 5 = 40$ could be presented in several different orientations, including:

> What is 8 5s?
>
> How many 5s in 40?
>
> What is 40 divided into 8 shares?

Often, learning arithmetic involves varying the orientation. In particular, students need to develop the **inverse relationships** of addition with subtraction, and multiplication with division.

Increasing the complexity

By increasing the arithmetic complexity we mean developing more arithmetic parts in the tasks. Common ways to increase complexity include progressing:

- from adding two numbers, to adding three numbers;
- from tasks that do not involve **regrouping**, to tasks that do;
- from division without a remainder to division with a remainder.

Distancing the setting

Instruction in a topic often begins in an instructional setting such as counters or ten-frames. The student can progress through different degrees of distance from the setting, such as: (1) manipulating the materials; (2) seeing the materials but not manipulating them; (3) leaving the materials behind a screen; and (4) solving tasks posed in verbal or written form without materials, which we refer to as *bare number* tasks. Instruction frequently works back and forth along this dimension, **screening**, then revealing, then re-screening materials.

Notating and formalizing

Instruction in a topic often involves developing some notation. Arithmetic tasks can be notated: for example, the task '16 and how many more to make 20?' presented on the arithmetic rack can be notated as $16 + \square \rightarrow 20$. Also, computation strategies can be notated: a counting-on strategy for solving this task can be notated as jumps on a number line. Progressions in the dimension of **notating** can include:

- shifting from not using notation to using notation;
- shifting from informal notation toward formal notation; and
- shifting from teacher writing to student writing.

Refining strategies

Students' first attempts in a topic typically involve inefficient, unsophisticated computation strategies. Learning in the topic then involves refining those strategies, by curtailing steps, and using more number relations. Examples of refinements include progressing:

- from counting-on, to using a non-counting strategy such as adding-through-ten;
- from adding 30 in three jumps of 10, to adding 30 as one jump;
- from always adding with a **jump strategy**, to flexibly using jump, **split-jump**, or compensation for suitable tasks.

Structuring numbers

By structuring numbers we mean noticing number relations, and organizing numbers into an increasingly dense network of number relations. With additive structuring, for example, students can progress from thinking of 8 only as the number after 7, to recognizing 8 as double 4, as 5 and 3, as 2 less than 10, as related to 18 and 28, and so on. Students can also come to see relations between these relations: from 5 + 3 to 4 + 4, and to 10 − 2. Multiplicative structuring can involve relating 8 × 5 to double 4 × 5, and also to 4 × 10; while relating 9 × 5 to 5 more than 8 × 5, or 5 less than 10 × 5, or half of 9 × 10. Thus, for students, numbers increasingly become nodes in networks of relations.

Unitizing

By **unitizing** we mean students coming to regard numbers as units, that is, as single whole objects that can be counted. For example, when a student counts how many 3s in 12 as 'one 3, two 3s, three 3s, four 3s', the 3s are regarded as units. Unitizing can involve, for example, reasoning that if there are four 3s in 12, then there are eight 3s in 24, which involves counting units of units. Unitizing compounds in layers: addition can involve constructing units, multiplication involves constructing units of units. Unitizing is fundamental to conceptual development in arithmetic. It can be regarded as a special form of structuring numbers.

Decimalizing

By **decimalizing** we mean developing the practice of organizing numbers into 1s, 10s, 100s, 1000s, and so on; developing *base-ten thinking*. For example:

- Building 16 with materials as one 10 and six 1s.
- Organizing mental computation for adding 25 to 47 by adding 10, then another 10, then 5.
- Recognizing that, in the numeral 145, the 4 stands for four 10s.

Decimalizing is a special form of unitizing, learning to use the most important units in our number system.

Organizing and generalizing

Organizing can involve making categories. For example, a student separates a set of ten-frame cards into the **five-wise** and **pair-wise** configurations. As well, organizing can involve making an ordered list. For example, a student lists the partitions of 6 in order: 0 + 6, 1 + 5, 2 + 4, 3 + 3.

Organizing is closely aligned with **generalizing** about number relations. For example, considering the ordered list of partitions of 6, how many partitions of 7 would there be, or of 8? How many partitions of *n*? Generalizing is perhaps the most generic form of mathematizing. All the dimensions could be regarded as forms of generalizing.

Using dimensions to understand domains

The framework of 10 dimensions of mathematization provides another layer in the LFIN. We can describe any single domain in the LFIN, in terms of the subset of dimensions that are prominent in that domain. For example, learning in Domain 3C, Conceptual Place Value, involves an interweaving of three key dimensions: increasing the complexity, extending the range and **distancing** the setting. So, the model of the learning progression for CPV is described in terms of those three dimensions. Likewise, the teaching chart for CPV is explained in terms of those three dimensions. The rows and columns of the teaching chart lay out how the instruction progresses on several dimensions in that domain.

In general, we use the dimensions to help understand the learning and instruction in each domain. Dimensions are invoked in commentaries on learning progressions in Chapter 4, and in commentaries on teaching charts, in Chapter 6. On a finer scale, we also use the dimensions to describe potential **micro-adjustments** in moment-to-moment instruction. These uses of the dimensions in instruction are discussed further in Chapter 5.

Broader view of the LFIN

We have introduced many layers in the LFIN:

- bands
- domains
- assessment schedules
- models
- stages and levels
- teaching charts
- grades
- ranges
- dimensions.

The LFIN can be understood first as a higher level organizer, holding all these layers, as laid out in the main LFIN Chart. However, for each layer of the LFIN, there are rich descriptions of details: details about each assessment task in a schedule, about each level in a model, about each teaching procedure in a teaching chart, and so on. The remaining chapters of this book outline some of these rich descriptions. And we think of all this rich description as part of the LFIN. Thus, with a broader view, the LFIN can be understood as referring to all the rich pedagogical knowledge we can lay out about instruction in number and arithmetic.

Over time, the LFIN in this broad sense can become a teacher's working map, which can zoom in from the high level organizer down through the layers to these rich details, at any given moment of working with a student. For example, a teacher is beginning a lesson with a grade 1 student. At the zoomed out level, she orients herself to Band 2, and within Band 2 to Domain 2A, Early Number Words and Numerals. Within 2A, she zooms in first on FNWS, Forward Number Word Sequences. Within FNWS, she has zoomed in further on Level ② in the FNWS model, where she is aware of an important but subtle distinction, in whether her student can say the number word after a given number, without dropping back to one. She selects a particular teaching procedure on number word after tasks from the 2A Teaching Chart, working with a numeral track, with attention to subtle calibrations in the dimension of distancing the setting. When she has given these tasks some time, she can zoom back out to link to other aspects of Domain 2A, such as BNWS and numerals; and later she zooms out again to attend to other Domains 2B, and 2C. Her whole lesson, carefully targeted and responsive to her student, is organized within the LFIN.

The LFIN and teachers' professional learning

An important part of learning our approach is just by getting your hands dirty with the pedagogical tools: doing VIBA assessments using the assessment schedules, trying to analyse your students' levels on the models, choosing which key topics to focus on in the teaching charts, and teaching students. Through this experience, you will learn about the schedules and models and charts.

At the same time, another important part of learning our approach is to become acquainted with the LFIN, and to reflect on your experience in the context of the LFIN. In this way, as you use the schedules, models and charts, you will be able to make increasing sense of how to fit them all together.

The LFIN as an organizer for professional learning

The LFIN is designed as an organizer for instruction. It is also an organizer for teachers' professional learning about instruction. As you learn more, the LFIN becomes a place to hang new knowledge, an organizer for developing increasing expertise in the assessment and instruction of whole number arithmetic. Your sense of each domain, and each tool within the domains, will develop and become personalized over time.

In the end, you will develop your own rich knowledge of the LFIN. You will create for yourself a detailed pedagogical map for instruction in number. With any student at any moment, you will know a great deal about what you might look for and what tasks you might pose. Developing such expertise can be immensely rewarding.

Teachers learning the LFIN charts

We give overviews of the LFIN in the form of charts and tables. Two main charts were introduced in this chapter:

- The LFIN Chart
- The Progressions across K to 5 Chart

Two further charts will be important:

The Assessment Schedules Overview Chart, presented in Chapter 3

The Models Chart, presented in Chapter 4

The LFIN Chart and the Models Chart are also reproduced in Appendix 2, for ease of reference.

These charts bring together considerable detail about the pedagogical tools, and the links between them. At first encounter, they can be daunting, but keep returning to them. As you work with the materials, you will become familiar with them. They become important references for assessment, planning and teaching.

Teachers learning domains

The domains make good units of study for professional learning. For each domain, we can:

- characterize what constitutes facility in the domain;
- appreciate the significance of that knowledge for students' arithmetic learning;
- learn how to assess students' knowledge and misconceptions in the domain, using the assessment schedules;
- describe progressions of learning in the domain, using the models; and
- describe key topics and progressions in instruction toward facility in the domain, using the teaching charts.

Thus, teachers can learn a great deal about any one domain.

As you learn a new domain, you can make connections to domains you know well. This is how strong knowledge of the whole LFIN develops.

The LFIN is for teachers, not for students

Keep in mind that the LFIN is a tool for teachers. Teachers can learn the LFIN, but students do not need to learn the LFIN; they need to learn the mathematics. For example, students do not need to learn what 'Conceptual Place Value' means. They need to learn to increment by 1s, 10s and 100s. Furthermore, when they are doing some Conceptual Place Value tasks, they do not need to know they are working in a different domain from when they were doing some Number Words and Numerals tasks. From the perspective of the student, a task in any one domain can simply be a challenge about numbers. The domains are not compartments for the students' knowledge, they are organizers for the teacher's work. Our goal for the student is an increasingly interconnected, coherent, sophisticated knowledge of arithmetic. We can look back over all the instructional work and knowledge teachers use to reach that goal. The LFIN is like a map laid out over all of that.

The LFIN is for guidance, not doctrine

When first learning the LFIN, it may feel overly compartmentalized, complicated, or rigid. As you make it your own, let it instead become a rich, insightful guide. The purpose of the LFIN is to provide good tools and a good map, so you as a teacher have the resources and knowledge to develop your own responsive teaching with your students.

Links to the earlier books in the series

The LFIN and pedagogical tools described in this book have developed from earlier frameworks and tools from the four earlier books in the series. While the material in this book is new or extensively revised, the book relates closely to the four earlier books. These earlier books can provide detailed information related to many aspects of the LFIN, and to our general approach to instruction.

  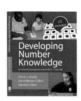

Blue Book   *Early Numeracy: Assessment for Teaching and Intervention*

Green Book   *Teaching Number: Advancing Children's Skills and Strategies*

Red Book   *Developing Number Knowledge: Assessment, Teaching and Intervention with 7–11 Year-Olds*

Purple Book   *Teaching Number in the Classroom with 4–8 Year-Olds*

The Blue Book focuses on assessment, and includes descriptions of six assessment schedules. The Green Book focuses on teaching, and includes descriptions of 30 key topics. The Purple Book and Red Book address both assessment and teaching, for early and middle primary respectively. Both include whole chapters devoted to each domain.

Table 1.2 sets out, for each domain in the LFIN, relevant assessment schedules, key topics and chapters in the four earlier books. All of these sections provide detailed information relevant to the domains.

Table 1.2 Links to earlier books in the series

LFIN Domains	Blue Book Schedules	Green Book Key Topics	Purple Book Chapters	Red Book Chapters
Early Number				
2A. Early Number Words & Numerals	1.1	5.1, 5.2, 6.1, 6.2, 7.1, 7.2	3	
2B. Early Structuring	2.1	5.4, 5.5, 6.4, 6.5, 7.4, 7.5	5	
2C. Early Arithmetical Strategies	1.1	5.3, 5.6, 6.3, 7.3	4, 6	
Middle Number				
3A. Number Words & Numerals	1.1	8.1, 8.2		3
3B. Structuring Numbers 1 to 20	2.1, 2.2	8.5	7	4
3C. Conceptual Place Value	1.2	8.3, 9.1		5
3D. Addition & Subtraction to 100	1.2	8.4, 9.2, 9.3, 9.4, 9.5	8, 9	6
3E. Early Multiplication & Division	3.1, 3.2	6.6, 7.6, 8.1, 8.6, 9.6	10	7
3F. Multiplicative Basic Facts				7

Three other sections of particular note are:

Blue Book, Chapters 2–5:   Provide detailed overviews relevant to the three Early Number domains 2A, 2B, 2C, especially to 2C and the SEAL model.

Green Book, Chapter 2:   Provides a detailed overview of the general approach to one-to-one intervention teaching.

Red Book, Chapter 2:   Describes the organization of Middle Number instruction using domains, and the progression of learning and teaching across the domains.

2

Approach to Assessment

We advocate attentive, assiduous assessment as fundamental to good instruction. We use a distinctive approach of Video-recorded Interview-based Assessment (VIBA). Teachers use individual assessment interviews to develop detailed profiles of each student's knowledge. An initial assessment interview is used to inform what instruction is needed with each student. Since instruction begins with assessment, we describe the approach to assessment early in this book.

This chapter has four parts:

Video-recorded Interview-based Assessment (VIBA)

Conducting Assessment Interviews

Video-recording Assessment Interviews

Coding and Analysing Assessment Interviews

Assessment involves two main pedagogical tools: the assessment schedules are used in assessment interviews, and the models of learning progressions are used in analysing assessments. The schedules and the models are presented in the next two chapters.

Video-recorded Interview-based Assessment (VIBA)

A typical VIBA assessment proceeds as follows. A teacher selects two to four schedules addressing several domains of number knowledge. Using the schedule, she conducts an assessment interview with a single student for 10–20 minutes, in which she poses tasks from the schedule. She observes closely the responses of the student, trying to understand how the student is thinking about each task, and occasionally asking the student to explain his strategies. Her main aim is to identify the student's most advanced thinking on each type of task on the schedule, and she may select less advanced or more advanced tasks in her attempts to ascertain the student's limits. She takes no notes during the assessment interview; instead, she records the interview on video. Afterwards, she watches the video, noting the student's response to each task on a copy of the schedule used, in a process we refer to as *coding*. Along with coding the responses, she analyses the responses, to determine what stage or level the student has demonstrated on the relevant learning progression model. The stage or level forms part of the profile of the student's current number knowledge.

Objective of VIBA

The key objective of VIBA is to learn as much as possible about the student's current number knowledge and strategies. The more we know about these, the more targeted is our instruction, and the more targeted the instruction, the more likely learning is to occur.

Distinctiveness of VIBA

VIBA is different from approaches that simply record a student's success on a series of tasks. Instead, the purpose is to understand the student's knowledge and strategies. The teacher brings her increasingly expert knowledge of the tasks and learning progressions, and her attentive observation of the student, to assess many aspects of the student's numerical thinking, such as: how the student appears to construe additive tasks, how the student uses number words, number relationships taken for granted, particular computation strategies, particular procedures using fingers, self-talk and level of certitude. Other, non-mathematical aspects can also be observed, such as the student's body language, verbal fluency and motor coordination. Teachers find it valuable to take the time to notice such aspects of students' thinking, and to reflect on how to approach them in teaching.

VIBA is also different from approaches where the teacher does not record the interview but instead writes notes as the interview proceeds. With video-recording the teacher can give all of her attention to posing tasks, observing, reflecting, and when appropriate making comments and asking follow-up questions. This can create a distinctive atmosphere of respectful attention on the student's thinking. Furthermore, reviewing the video enables assessment of aspects that otherwise might be overlooked, as students' numerical reasoning can involve subtle clues which are very difficult to interpret in real time. It is common to replay key moments of the video several times, in order to understand what the student was doing. Appreciating the value of video-recording might be difficult without experiencing it. When teachers commence professional learning based on the VIBA approach most are very surprised by the usefulness of video to provide insight into students' thinking.

Using the assessment schedules and models for VIBA

Learning VIBA involves three areas of professional learning: the general assessment interview technique; the assessment schedules; and the models of learning progressions. These are addressed respectively in Chapters 2, 3 and 4.

Conducting an interview also requires knowledge of the assessment schedules. The teacher needs to learn the words and actions associated with presenting each kind of assessment task. She also needs to use her judgement during the course of the interview to pose additional tasks that take account of the student's responses to the assessment tasks. Thus it is important to learn how to select the task groups to be presented and which tasks to present within each task group, according to the student's responses. Developing expertise in the use of a schedule involves coming to know how to present each task, the range of potential responses to the tasks, and how different tasks might elicit different levels of sophistication in the student's thinking. Chapter 3 presents the schedules, including commentaries on each task group of each schedule.

Finally, analysing an interview requires knowledge of the models of learning progressions. Each model is associated with certain task groups from a schedule. Developing expertise in the use of the model involves coming to know the meaning of the levels or stages, and how responses on different tasks can be characterized in terms of a level or stage. Also, the LFIN can be regarded as including a rich body of knowledge about students' number learning beyond the basic models, which can be brought to the analysis of an assessment. Chapter 4 presents the models.

Teachers learning from VIBA videos

Watching assessment interviews on video is a powerful experience for teachers. They learn about children's thinking, and they also reflect on their own modes of interacting with students. Using VIBA, teachers develop knowledge that strengthens their use of interview assessment with and without video. Their increased knowledge of students' mathematical thinking also helps teachers develop instructional strategies. When teachers watch assessment videos together, they see other teachers' efforts, think hard about students' strategies, become inspired by students' thinking, and share instructional strategies. Using VIBA as an assessment tool contributes to ongoing professional learning that has much relevance to both intensive intervention and classroom teaching.

The benefits of VIBA

The use of video-recording has considerable advantages for the interviewer. These can be described under the following five headings: (a) data gathering; (b) analysis; (c) reflection; (d) communication; and (e) accreditation.

Data gathering

Video-recording allows a very rich documentation of the student's responses to the tasks. During the interview, total attention is given to the student's responses to tasks. The interviewer can then decide to re-pose tasks, revisit items, and seek confirmation of conjectures relating to the student's strategy or probe to ascertain more information about the student's reasoning.

Analysis

The recording can be reviewed several times if necessary in order to determine whether or not the student satisfies the criteria for a particular level or stage. Having colleagues review video records can lead to rich discussion about students' behaviours, actions and utterances.

Reflection

Viewing tapes in a group is a most valuable activity during professional learning sessions. Colleagues can reflect on what has occurred during the interview and offer interpretations of the student's reasoning and explanations.

Communication

Video-recording can provide a powerful tool for communication with colleagues, parents and other professionals. Digital recordings can be readily edited, annotated, and reproduced in a variety of formats. Libraries of clips can be built up, and can be used to further professional learning and dissemination.

Accreditation

Video-recorded assessment interviews and teaching sessions can be compiled, with relative ease, into case studies that serve to document not only the student's progress but also the progress of the teacher in her professional learning.

When to use VIBA

Administering assessment interviews using the VIBA approach can be a significant undertaking that can be quite time consuming. Worth keeping in mind is that undertaking assessments using VIBA can make a significant contribution to teachers' professional learning, particularly when using an approach involving an instructional leader working with a team of trainee intervention specialists. As well, VIBA will generate very detailed assessment information which can be a basis for planning intervention instruction or a means of documenting students' current levels of knowledge. Further, the VIBA approach can be used to document students' progress over the course of a term or a school year. Documenting students' progress in that way can serve to highlight the effectiveness of a programme of intervention instruction. As well, we have seen many instances where the VIBA approach has been adapted for use by classroom teachers at the start of the school year, as a basis for planning classroom instruction that is very well targeted to the range of students' needs.

Conducting assessment interviews

Adapted from the Blue Book:

> Wright et al. (2006a). *Early Numeracy: Assessment for Teaching and Intervention* (2nd edn). London: Sage, Chapter 3 (pp. 32–4).

In order to administer the assessment interviews correctly the interviewer needs to learn the words and actions associated with presenting each kind of assessment task. It is also necessary to learn the general interview technique, which involves observation and questioning in order to elicit information about the student's knowledge and strategies.

Practice, review and reflection

Becoming competent in administering the assessment requires extensive practice, review and reflection. Learning how to conduct the assessment should involve interviews with several students, the review of videotapes and then repeating this whole process several times. Experience has taught us that trainee assessors benefit greatly from working in pairs or trios. They can take turns to present aspects of the assessment schedule and to observe and give feedback to one another on the correct administration of the tasks and how to maintain the climate of the interview. We have found that students do not seem to be perturbed by the presence of others. Following presentation of the tasks, much can be learned by the trainees working together to observe and interpret the videos of students' responses. Through practice, review and reflection, the interviewer becomes attuned to the nature and range of students' responses to the tasks and the techniques involved in posing additional questions when necessary.

Assessing more able students

It is recommended that the first assessment interviews with students be undertaken with more able students. These students tend to more readily understand the tasks and are more likely to be successful, and thus it is usually easier to conduct the interview with such students. As well, knowing how more able students respond to the tasks is equally as important as knowing how low-attaining students respond. Assessing able students can help the teacher to develop detailed pedagogical knowledge of the range of student responses to the tasks.

Re-posing and rephrasing tasks

Administering the assessment involves the interviewer following a prescribed schedule. It is important that the tasks are presented as described in the schedule. The interviewer should avoid presenting the task a second time, unless it is deemed necessary, because this can be counterproductive if the student has already started to solve the task. By continuing to speak the interviewer can interrupt the student's thought processes. In cases where additional clarification for the student seems necessary, the interviewer may re-pose a task and repeat statements in the script. For example, this becomes particularly apparent when students are asked to state the number word just before a number word in the backward number word sequence aspect. Some students will state the number word after rather than the one before, reflecting their unfamiliarity with this task item. The interviewer may also rephrase or make variations to the verbal instructions, but the nature and conditions of the task should not be varied. In the initial stages of learning to administer the assessment, it is advisable to follow the scripts closely. With experience the interviewer will become more fluent and flexible in presenting the tasks, and more skilful at probing the student's initial response.

Revisiting tasks

The interviewer must refrain from providing any verbal or non-verbal clues to the student. The tasks have the purpose of providing insight into the student's numerical thinking, and this information is equally as important as whether the student answers the task correctly. In cases where the interviewer thinks that the student may have made a random error, tasks may be re-posed at a later time during the course of the interview. The re-posing of tasks at the end of a section of items is called revisiting. It allows us to see whether the student made a slip or miscalculation or whether the original response resulted from a lack of knowledge. An example is if a student identifies '32' as 'thirty-eight', and there does not appear to be an explanation for the answer. In a case such as this, it is of interest to see if the student gives the same answer when the task is presented again, later in the interview. Revisiting tasks is useful if this is considered likely to provide additional information about the student's knowledge and strategies.

Eliciting the most advanced strategy

The importance of closely observing the student's response to a task was emphasized above. This is particularly important for tasks involving the generation and use of a strategy. In order to elicit the student's most advanced strategy it is necessary first to understand the student's current strategy. Eliciting the student's most advanced strategy typically involves asking, 'Can you do that another way?' 'Do you have another way to check that?' If the student describes a strategy involving counting-by-ones, it is often useful to ask 'how did you know when to stop?'

While it can be useful to ask the student to explain their solution, doing so is not always the best response. In particular, asking the student to explain how they obtained their answer should not become a routine directive. Related to this, directing the student, in advance of presenting a task or immediately after a task is presented, to work aloud or to be ready to describe how they obtained their answer should generally be avoided. This can confound the task for the student. They are required to simultaneously solve the task and generate an explanation. Rather, one should observe, very closely, the student's words and actions, and use one's observations as a basis for subsequent questions and tasks. Keep in mind the important goal of finding the cutting edge of the student's knowledge. Typically this will involve finding out what the student both can and cannot do.

Monitoring the student's ease and comfort

At the beginning of the interview, the interviewer should take steps to make the student feel as comfortable as possible. As well as asking the student their name and other particulars, the interviewer should explain the purpose of the interview and tell the student what is expected of them during the interview. The interviewer should monitor and be sensitive to the student's state of ease and comfort during the course of the interview.

Using motivation sparingly

In most cases it is not necessary to provide ongoing encouragement and motivation to the student because, typically, students seem to gain intrinsic satisfaction from solving the tasks. Thus, as a general rule, the interviewer should not routinely comment on the correctness of the student's responses. It may be appropriate to do so when, for example, the student expresses particular interest in whether they have answered correctly. Confirming that a student has correctly answered all or most of a group of tasks often seems to have a positive motivational effect on the student. In similar vein, affirming sound effort on the part of the student in attempting to solve tasks usually proves to be motivational when it is genuine and not overdone. Thus, it is appropriate to use motivation and encouragement sparingly.

'Talking to the camera'

This technique involves making a statement during the course of the interview that refers to an observation or realization concerning the student's strategy. The interviewer makes the statement for the purpose of establishing a record on the video-recording of their observation or realization. If the interviewer observes that the student used their fingers in a particular way during a solution, for example, the interviewer may comment on this in a non-committal fashion, for example 'I saw you raise four fingers'. This technique should be used in such a way that it causes no disruption to the student and little or no interruption to the flow of the interview.

Saying too much

A final point to realize is that, when first learning this approach to assessment, as teachers we have a tendency to say too much rather than too little. Keep in mind that the interview involves an extended one-to-one interaction with the student and this is quite different in nature from an interaction with a group or class.

Summary guidelines for conducting assessment interviews

1. Present the task groups and tasks according to the order indicated in the schedule.
2. Avoid re-posing the task unless you are sure it is necessary.
3. Verbal instructions may be rephrased if it is likely to help the student understand the task.
4. Tasks may be revisited in situations where the student is thought to have made a random error.
5. Give students sufficient time to focus on solving the tasks.
6. Avoid temptations to talk to the student when they are engaged in solving a task.
7. Watch closely for lip, finger, head and body movements that might provide insight into the student's thinking.
8. As a general rule, do not comment on the correctness of the student's response.
9. Be sensitive to the student's state of ease and comfort during the course of the interview and use motivation and encouragement sparingly.
10. Use the technique of 'talking to the camera' if it is likely to be particularly useful to record an observation or realization.

Video-recording assessment interviews

Adapted from the Blue Book:

> Wright et al. (2006a). *Early Numeracy: Assessment for Teaching and Intervention* (2nd edn). London: Sage, Chapter 9 (pp. 146–8).

You do not need an additional person to operate the camera, nor do you need specialist video equipment. You only need a device that can record video, and a tripod on which you can mount the device; then you can press start and stop yourself. It is important to think carefully about the room you will use for assessment interviews, and if necessary to negotiate with the school administration. Positioning of the camera, desk and assessment materials needs to be planned and tested. As well, you should endeavour to learn as much as possible about camera operation, and download and storage of your video files.

It is common for teachers initially to be somewhat daunted by the prospect of video-recording their assessment interviews. At the same time, the vast majority of teachers quickly gain a level of expertise and the process of video-recording their assessment interviews becomes routine. No doubt this process is helped by the fact that, after conducting and reviewing a series of interviews, teachers begin to appreciate the power of the video-recording process for learning about students' numerical knowledge and strategies.

Specific guidelines for video-recording assessment interviews are now presented under the following subheadings:

- Setting up the interview room and camera
- Operating the camera
- Recording the interview
- Storing and labelling video files.

Setting up the interview room and camera

- To enable administration and recording of the interview, certain conditions are necessary. These relate to power, lighting, acoustics and space.
- The space can be small, either a very small room or the corner of a larger room, but it does need to be quiet, and screened from distraction.
- Check beforehand that mains power supply is available and conveniently located. An extension lead is useful. Most cameras have a battery-operation feature that can be used if necessary.
- The camera should be pointed away from any outside light source such as windows and glass doors.
- Position the furniture and camera away from devices such as air-conditioners or lights to minimize interference.
- Obtaining high-quality sound recording is very important. The interviewer should attempt to ensure that the student's voice is audible and is recorded as clearly as possible.
- Place a notice on the door to indicate recording is in progress.
- The teacher and student are to be seated on the same side of the table and the camera placed to face the teacher and student (see Figure 2.1).
- Angle the seating so the student and interviewer can see one another.
- Mount the camera on a tripod and be sure to remove the lens cap.
- Position the camera approximately 2 metres from the table.
- Raise the camera to look down on the subjects and the tabletop.
- Space should be sufficient to allow both the teacher and the student to be included in the video frame.
- Use a wide-angle setting (i.e. the 'W' button) to enable locating the camera as closely as possible to the interview table.
- Adjust the zoom lens facility (i.e. 'W' and 'T' buttons) so that the video picture includes the student, the teacher and the tabletop on which the tasks are presented.

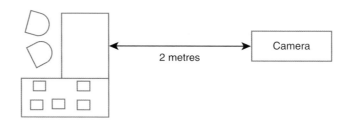

Figure 2.1   Setting up for video-recording assessment interviews

Operating the camera

- There are now a range of devices that can record digital video, including video cameras or camcorders, digital cameras with a video mode, computers, tablets, pods and mobile phones. A digital video camera is ideal, but most devices will produce sufficiently clear audio and video: test your device.
- Digital video-recordings are large files: a 10-minute recording may be 300MB–1GB or more. You may be able to adjust the settings of your camera to record at a lower but still sufficient quality, making smaller files. Get to know the size of the files on your camera, and ensure that your camera has sufficient storage capacity to record all the interviews you will do in one day.
- You will need a tripod, and an attachment for connecting your camera to the tripod. Most dedicated cameras have a lug to fit the standard screw on a tripod. Tablets, pods and phones will need an extra attachment device.

- Ensure that you are familiar with the ON/OFF and STANDBY features of the camera. Some cameras automatically switch to a STANDBY setting during periods when they are not being used.
- Some cameras may be supplied with a remote control device that enables you to switch the recording function on and off. Use of such devices is not particularly important in recording the interview.

Recording the interview

- Ensure you have parental or guardian permission before you video-record the student.
- Prior to commencing the assessment interview, complete the required information at the top of the assessment schedule.
- Press the RECORD button prior to commencing the interview. When the RECORD button is activated a symbol should appear on the recording screen such as 'REC' or a flashing red light.
- When conducting the interview, do not write on the assessment schedule! Let the camera do the recording.

Storing and labelling video files

- Learn how to connect your camera to a computer, using a USB cable for example, and to import your video-recordings onto a computer for storage and viewing.
- Create a filing system for organizing your video files on your computer. Given the large size of video files, you may want to store the video on a dedicated external hard-drive.
- Develop a protocol for labelling your video files. For example, the following file name refers to teacher Tom at Happy Valley School interviewing Chelsea on Assessment 3B on 24 October 2017:

    HAPPYVALLEY_Tom_Chelsea_Ass3B_2017_10_24.m4v

- Import and label video files as soon as possible. A useful technique is to commence the interview video session by stating or asking the student's name and other relevant particulars, such as class teacher's name and school name. This helps to ensure accuracy of this kind of information.
- Storing a backup copy of each of your video files is very important. This is best done by using a separate storage device external to your computer which is located remotely from your main storage device.

Summary guidelines for video-recording interviews

1. Ensure you have parental or guardian permission to record the student.
2. Ensure you have a power supply or sufficient battery charge on your camera.
3. Ensure your camera has sufficient storage capacity for the recording planned.
4. Seat the student beside the teacher on the same side of the table.
5. Position the camera on a tripod facing them, close (~2m) and high.
6. Adjust the frame to capture the student, the teacher beside them and the desk in front.
7. Take care with lighting: light the faces, and avoid light shining into the camera.
8. Take care with sound quality: ensure the student's voice is audible, and minimize noise from air-conditioning, other people, etc.
9. Remember to press RECORD at the beginning, and press STOP at the end.
10. Import video files promptly, and label with school name, student's name and interview date.

Coding and analysis

Adapted from the Blue Book:

Wright et al. (2006a). *Early Numeracy: Assessment for Teaching and Intervention* (2nd edn). London: Sage, Chapter 9 (pp. 149–51).

The process of coding and analysis involves using a paper copy of the assessment schedule while reviewing the video of the interview, and includes:

a. notating the student's responses, strategies, teacher directions, etc.;
b. describing insights into the student's number knowledge; and
c. using the relevant models of learning progressions to determine the student's levels, thus characterizing the student's number knowledge.

Determining levels from the LFIN models in this way generates what we refer to as a *profile*. This is complemented by the *portrait*, that is the rich description of the student's knowledge portrayed in written notes on the assessment schedule. The coding and analysis results in three levels of information about the student's knowledge. The most detailed level is the actual video of the assessment interview. Next is the annotated assessment schedule which constitutes a written summary of the interview. The briefest level is the student's profile based on the models.

Coding system

The coding system enables the teacher to notate detailed information from a student's responses during the assessment interview. The codes indicate both how the student responded as well as the answers given. The codes can also indicate how the interview was conducted. The codes are listed in the Coding Sheet (see below).

LFIN Coding Sheet

✓	correct
✓✓	correct with certitude
——	pause/thinking time
_____✓	long pause then correct
8 ×	incorrect (noting answer) – also note strategy if possible
SC	student self-corrects
8 × SC ✓	initially incorrect, then self-corrects
Λ	omission of a number in FNWS or BNWS
IDK	student says 'I don't know'
REV	assessor revisits an item
REP	assessor re-poses an item
TTA	assessor asks 'Try that again'
KF	known fact
fgs	using fingers
subv	sub-vocal speech
' '	indicates the words used
C ×1s pr	counting-by-ones (using perceptual replacements)
C ×1s npr	counting-by-ones (not using perceptual replacements)
CF1 -3×	counting forward from 1 (three counts)
CF1 -1×	counting forward from 1 (one count)
CUF	counts up from
CUT	counts up to
CDF	counts down from
CDT	counts down to

The Coding Sheet is self-explanatory but it may be useful to give examples for particular features.

- The interviewer wants to know not only the answer the student gives but also the student's level of fluency or certitude. Correct answers are ticked but two ticks can be given indicating a swift, confident response.
- When the student takes a long pause or thinking time before producing an answer, this can be indicated with the code line ____. A longer line can indicate a longer pause.
- If the student makes an error it is advisable to write down the student's response. In this way the interviewer can see the response was incorrect, but might also be able to detect patterns among the incorrect responses. For example, on **numeral identification** tasks students frequently reverse the digits saying 'fifty-one' for 15 and 'thirty-one' for 13.
- Sometimes students answer incorrectly and then self-correct. Where the student has corrected an answer without any prompting from the interviewer we use the code 'SC'.
- Recording students' omissions or repetitions when they are saying number word sequences is also important.
- Often students say 'I don't know' and 'IDK' is recorded.

We want to give the students every opportunity to respond, so tasks can be rephrased, re-posed and revisited.

- Where an error may be an oversight or slip, the assessor can revisit the task later in the interview, to see if the student gives the same incorrect answer. In this case, the code 'REV' is written beside the task, and the student's response to the revisited task can be noted.
- When a student's answer is incorrect it is sometimes appropriate to re-pose the task immediately, which is coded as 'REP'. This is particularly useful when the student uses a counting strategy and is just one away from a correct answer. Since this may be due to inaccurate counting it is helpful to re-pose the task.
- Where the student has understood the question but given an incorrect response, 'TTA' can be used to indicate that the teacher asked the student if they would like to try that one again.

It is advisable, particularly on tasks that involve significant computation for the student, to record the explanations the student gives about their computation strategy.

- A rough transcription of the student's words can be indicated with quotation marks.
- Finger movements and specific non-verbal gestures often reveal the strategies a student is using and these should be noted.
- Lip movements may reveal the student using sub-vocal speech, to do some counting for example, and this can be indicated with the code 'subv'.
- If the interviewer determines the strategy during the interview, she can use the technique of talking to the camera described earlier, so that this information can be accessed during coding and analysis. For example, the interviewer might code the student's count-down-from (CDF) strategy.

The counting strategies listed in the Coding Sheet are described in Chapter 4. Many other non-counting computation strategies can arise, such as adding-through-ten, near-doubles, compensation, jump, split, skip-counting, and so on. Common strategies relevant to each task group are listed in the commentaries on the assessment schedules. If a student's strategy is recognized, it should be noted in the coding.

Comprehensive application of coding will allow:

- the strengths and weaknesses of a student to be determined;
- the identification of patterns in the student's responses;
- the correct identification and allocation of levels and stage; and
- an accurate, concise description of the student's knowledge and strategies.

Coding the assessment video also allows the interviewer to reflect on their administering of the task items. For example, one might check whether certain tasks could have been re-posed or revisited. Reviewing the video, especially with colleagues, enables refinement of the coding process.

Analysing the student's stage and levels

Determining the student's stage or level on one or more of the models of learning progressions is an important outcome of the assessment. While the video-recording provides rich data, and the coding produces a comprehensive overview of the student's responses, the stage and levels provide a succinct summary of the relative sophistication of the student's knowledge of number and whole number arithmetic. The stage and levels are useful for documenting the student's knowledge and summarizing the student's progress over a period of several weeks or months. Figure 2.2 shows an example profile of stage and levels.

Model	Stage/Level	
Stage of Early Arithmetical Learning	③	Initial number sequence
Forward Number Word Sequences	④	Facile FNWS to 'thirty'
Backward Number Word Sequences	③	Facile BNWS to 'ten'
Numeral Identification	③	Identify numerals to 100
Structuring Numbers to 20	②	Small doubles, small partitions of 10
Conceptual Place Value	②	Inc/decrementing flexibly by 10s and 1s, with materials, in range to 100
Addition and Subtraction to 100	①	Add-up-from/subtract-down-to decuple

Figure 2.2   Example profile of a grade 3 student

Learning to identify stages and levels, and developing skills in video-recording and editing, has allowed many teachers to compile libraries consisting of illustrative video excerpts. The LFIN models can be used to generate video-based exemplars of high-, average- and low-attainers. Compilations of exemplars can show the range of student responses and patterns within students' responses. Video excerpts can also highlight frequently occurring non-standard responses.

3

Assessment Schedules

Assessment schedules are one of the three types of pedagogical tools presented in this book. The LFIN incorporates nine assessment schedules, one for each domain. The schedules serve as refined sets of tasks for posing to students in assessment interviews, to assess knowledge of each domain.

The chapter begins with an overview of the nine assessment schedules, and a list of the materials needed to administer each of the schedules. A second section explains the printed format of the schedules, and a third section explains how to use the schedules for assessment interviews, coding and analysis. Following these introductory sections, the majority of the chapter consists of the nine schedules in order, accompanied by commentaries on each schedule.

Overview of the set of assessment schedules

Listed below are the titles of the nine assessment schedules:

2A Early Number Words and Numerals

2B Early Structuring

2C Early Arithmetical Strategies

3A Number Words and Numerals

3B Structuring Numbers 1 to 20

3C Conceptual Place Value

3D Addition and Subtraction to 100

3E Early Multiplication and Division

3F Multiplicative Basic Facts

The Assessment Schedules Overview Chart lists for each schedule:

a. the typical grade levels in which the schedule is used;
b. the associated model or models to be used in conjunction with the assessment schedule; and
c. the task groups in the schedule.

The set of assessment schedules is designed to assess all the domains and associated models in the LFIN. Note that some assessment schedules do not extend over the full range of levels of their associated models. Instead, two different schedules in the set assess lower and upper levels of the same model. For example, the FNWS and BNWS models extend from Level ⓪ to Level ⑦. However, Schedule 2A – Early Number Words and Numerals – has tasks to assess Levels ⓪ to ⑤ only, while Schedule 3A – Number Words and Numerals – assesses Levels ④ to ⑦ only. Similarly, for the Structuring Numbers 1 to 20 model, Schedule 2B assesses Levels ⓪ to ③ only, while Schedule 3B assesses Levels ② to ⑦ only.

Assessment Schedules Overview

	Schedule	Gr	Models and levels	Task groups
2A	**Early Number Words & Numerals**	K–1	FNWS/BNWS: ⓪–⑤... NID: ⓪–④...	*Number words:* FNWS, NWA, BNWS, NWB up to 100. *Numerals:* Identification and Writing of 1-, 2-, 3-digit numerals.
2B	**Early Structuring**	K–2	SN20: ⓪–③...	Making finger patterns, Regular configurations, Small doubles, Small partitions of 10, Partitions of 5, Five-plus facts.
2C	**Early Arithmetical Strategies**	K–1	SEAL: ⓪–⑤	*Additive:* Two screened collections, Missing addend, Partially screened, Get me. *Subtractive:* Removed items, Written subtraction, Missing subtrahend.
3A	**Number Words & Numerals**	1–4	FNWS/BNWS: ...④–⑦ NID: ...③–⑥	*Number words:* FNWS, NWA, BNWS, NWB up to 10,000. *Numerals:* Identification and Writing of 2-, 3-, 4-, 5-digit numerals.
3B	**Structuring Numbers 1 to 20**	1–5	SN20: ...②–⑦	Making finger patterns 6–10 *Combinations & partitions:* Small & big doubles, Five-plus, Ten-plus, Teen-plus, Partitions of 5 & of 10, Partitions in range 1 to 9, Partitions in range 11 to 20. *Formal addition & subtraction 1–20:* Range 2, Range 3, Range 4.
3C	**Conceptual Place Value**	1–4	CPV: ⓪–④	Incrementing & decrementing by 10, on & off the decuple (bundling sticks). Incrementing flexibly by 10s & 1s (bundling sticks). Incrementing by 100s on the hundred (100 squares). Jump of 10 more/less, 100 more/less, in range to 1000 (no materials).
3D	**Addition & Subtraction to 100**	2–5	A&S: ⓪–⑥	*Formal addition & subtraction:* Add/subtract a decuple, 2-digit tasks without/with regrouping, 3-digit tasks with regrouping. *Higher decade addition & subtraction:* to, from, and across a decuple.
3E	**Early Multiplication & Division**	3–5	EM&D: ⓪–⑥	*Tasks with equal groups:* Forming equal groups, Multiplication, Quotition. *Tasks with arrays:* Multiplication, Quotition. *Skip counting:* 2s, 5s, 3s. *Bare number tasks:* Basic facts Ranges 1, 2, 3; Using multiplicative relations.
3F	**Multiplicative Basic Facts**	3–5	MBF: ①abcd–⑤abcd	*Formal tasks:* Four × facts and four ÷ facts for each of Ranges 1, 2, 3 and 4. Two × facts and two ÷ facts for Range 5.

Learning Framework in Number © Wright & Ellemor-Collins, 2018 (Sage)

LFIN Assessment Kit

	Schedule	Task group	Task cards / Materials
2A	**Early Number Words & Numerals**	**3. Numeral identification**	28 numeral cards
		4. Writing numerals	Pen and paper
2B	**Early Structuring**	**2. Regular configurations**	5 dice pattern cards
2C	**Early Arithmetical Strategies**	**1–5, 7. Add and sub tasks**	Red and blue counters, screens
		6. Written subtraction	2 task cards
3A	**Number Words & Numerals**	**1. Numeral identification**	26 numeral cards
		2. Writing numerals	Pen and paper
3B	**Structuring Numbers 1 to 20**	**10–13. Formal add & sub**	13 task cards
3C	**Conceptual Place Value**	**1–4. Inc/dec by 10s**	15 bundles of bundling sticks
		8. Incrementing by 100s	13 of 100-dot squares
		5–7. 10 more/less	19 numeral cards
3D	**Addition & Subtraction to 100**	**1–5. Formal add & sub**	10 task cards
		6–10. Higher decade add & sub	10 numeral cards, decuple line
3E	**Early Multiplication & Division**	**1, 3. Equal groups tasks**	Counters and screen
		2. Mult with equal groups	Four 3-dot cards, screen
		4–6. Arrays tasks	Arrays: 6×4, 5×3, 5×6, 6×2, 3×4
		8–9. Basic facts tasks	8 task cards
		10. Using relations tasks	4 task cards
3F	**Multiplicative Basic Facts**	**1–5. Ranges 1 to 5**	36 task cards

LFIN Assessment Kit

The LFIN Assessment Kit Chart lists the materials needed to administer each of the nine assessment schedules. Materials include simple task cards printed with, for example, specific numerals or sums needed for tasks in a schedule. These task cards need to be prepared in advance of using the schedules. Masters for the task cards in the LFIN Assessment Kit are included on the book's website. We recommend using coloured cards to match the colour-coding of the schedules, for ease of organization. A few instructional settings are also used, such as counters and **bundling sticks** – see Appendix 1 for descriptions of these settings.

Format of the assessment schedules

Task groups

An assessment schedule is organized as a sequence of task groups. Each task group has the purpose of evoking students' responses on a specific topic in mathematics. A task group is constructed as a graduated sequence of similar tasks, which typically differ only in the numbers involved. Each task might reveal particular levels of knowledge and strategy. The interviewer can work through one or more tasks in a task group. By carefully observing the student's responses as the level of challenge increases, the interviewer can assess the student's most sophisticated level of reasoning in the topic addressed by the task group.

In an assessment interview, the interviewer proceeds task group by task group. Within each task group, some tasks may be skipped, as described above. Also, some schedules indicate a point at which to stop if the student has not indicated a particular level of knowledge. In this case the subsequent task groups are likely to be too difficult and unlikely to reveal additional information. Thus, task groups and schedules are pedagogical tools from which to select tasks to pose. Not every task need be posed!

Shading

On the schedules, a system of graduated shading indicates the relative difficulty of the tasks within each task group. Darker shading indicates more challenging or unfamiliar tasks. An interviewer can begin with the lightest shade – the easiest task – and proceed with subsequent tasks until she decides she has reached the student's limit. Alternatively, an interviewer can choose to start at the middle shade tasks. If the student is unsuccessful, the interviewer would go back to the lightest shade, while if the student is successful, the interviewer would go ahead to the darkest shade, thus skipping over the easiest tasks.

Models and level indicators

Each assessment schedule is designed to assess levels on an associated model or models. Each schedule displays the associated model or models at the top of the first page, for reference.

Beside most tasks or rows of tasks, a level indicator (e.g. ④) is displayed. This number indicates the level on the relevant model that this task serves to inform. For example, on Assessment Schedule 3B, Task Group 6 – Partitions in the range 1 to 9 – has the level indicator ④. This indicates that the tasks in this row are relevant to Level ④ – Facile structuring of numbers 1 to 10 – on the associated model of Structuring Numbers 1 to 20. Some tasks do not have a single associated level, because they inform several levels, and the association is not straightforward. Other tasks are not associated with any model, but are included on the schedule as broader informative assessment tasks.

Using assessment schedules

Using assessment schedules in an assessment interview

Each schedule requires 10–15 minutes to administer in an assessment interview. A typical assessment interview involves administering two or three assessment schedules, to address several domains. The LFIN Progressions across K to 5 Chart (in Chapter 1) shows the progression of domains across grades K to 5. This chart can guide which schedules would be appropriate for an assessment interview at different grades. Common groupings include:

K–1	2A, 2B and 2C	Early number learning
1–3	3A, 3B and 3C	Development of non-counting strategies
2–4	3B, 3C, 3D	Addition and subtraction
3–5	3E and 3F	Multiplication and division

Using assessment schedules for coding and analysis

When reviewing an assessment interview, a printed copy of the schedule is used for coding the student's responses. There is room at the top for recording basic administrative information about the assessment. It is easy to skip this – save yourself later grief, and complete it diligently. There is room in each task group for writing basic codes and describing strategies, and along the margins for various annotations. Finally, once the assessment has been analysed, the model levels or stages can be marked directly on the model/s at the top of the schedule sheet. If two or three schedules were assessed together, the coded sheets can be stapled and filed together.

Learning to assess with assessment schedules

Learning to assess involves learning the general approach to conducting and analysing VIBA assessment interviews, which is described in Chapter 2. The present chapter builds on Chapter 2 by providing specific and detailed information about each of the nine assessment schedules. Developing expertise in a schedule involves learning the words and actions associated with presenting each assessment task. Furthermore, expertise involves coming to know the range of students' responses in each task group, and how different tasks might elicit different levels of sophistication in the student's thinking. The schedule commentaries in this chapter offer detailed information on each task group. Also important is learning the models of learning progressions associated with each schedule, which are described in Chapter 4.

Assessment schedules and commentaries

Each assessment schedule consists of two pages of task groups, except for 2B which has one page only and 3E. Following each schedule is a section of explanatory notes, which we refer to as the *commentary*. The purpose of the commentary is to provide detailed information about the task groups in the schedule, on topics such as:

- the specific purpose of the task group;
- how to present tasks;
- guidance on observing students' responses; and
- typical student responses, difficulties and errors.

2A. Early Number Words and Numerals

Assessment Schedule

MATERIALS: TASK CARDS, PAPER AND PEN

Student Name: ....   Interview Date: ....

DoB: .... Age: .... (yrs) .... (mths)   Interviewer: ....

Number Word Sequences Models (FNWS and BNWS)

Forward Number Word Sequences	**Backward Number Word Sequences**
⓪ Emergent FNWS	⓪ Emergent BNWS
① Initial FNWS up to 'ten'	① Initial BNWS up to 'ten'
② Intermediate FNWS up to 'ten'	② Intermediate BNWS up to 'ten'
③ Facile FNWS up to 'ten'	③ Facile BNWS up to 'ten'
④ Facile FNWS up to 'thirty'	④ Facile BNWS up to 'thirty'
⑤ Facile FNWS up to 'one hundred'	⑤ Facile BNWS up to 'one hundred'
⑥ Facile FNWS up to 'one thousand'	⑥ Facile BNWS up to 'one thousand'
⑦ Facile FNWS up to 'ten thousand'	⑦ Facile BNWS up to 'ten thousand'

Numeral Identification Model (NID)
⓪ Emergent numeral identification
① Numerals to 10 – Identify
② Numerals to 20 – Identify
③ Numerals to 100 – Identify
④ Numerals to 1000 – Identify & write
⑤ Numerals to 10,000 – Identify & write
⑥ Numerals to 100,000—Identify & write

---

1. Forward number word sequences (FNWS)

Start counting from ___ and I'll tell you when to stop.

①-④	**1.1)** 1 (to 32)	
⑤	**1.2)** 68 (to 83)	
⑤+	**1.3)** 97 (to 112)	

2. Number word after (NWA)

The number that comes just after 1 is 2. What is the next number after ___?

②-③	**2.1)** 4	9	7	3	6
④	**2.2)** 16	12	19	23	29
⑤	**2.3)** 67	43	50	79	88

Learning Framework in Number © Wright & Ellemor-Collins, 2018 (Sage)

3. Numeral identification (NID)

[NUMERAL CARDS]

Show each card in turn, asking, *What number is this?*

①	5	3	9	4	8	6	7	
②	10	18	12	19	11	14	16	13
③	47	50	21	66	72	81	38	29
④	100	251	680	109	417			

START HERE → ②

4. Writing numerals

Provide PAPER and PEN. *Write the number that I say.*

	7	6	3	9
	12	18		
	21	30	89	92
④	513	270	306	

5. Backward number word sequences (BNWS)

Count backwards from ___ and I'll tell you when to stop.

①	**5.1)** 5 (to 1)	
①–③	**5.2)** 10 (to 1)	
①–③	**5.3)** 12 (to 1)	
④	**5.4)** 35 (to 17)	
⑤	**5.5)** 72 (to 58)	

START HERE → ①–③ (5.3)

6. Number word before (NWB)

The number that comes just before 2 is 1. What number comes before ___?

②–③	**6.1)** 6	3	9	5	7
④	**6.2)** 24	17	30	13	21
⑤	**6.3)** 67	38	73	80	51

START HERE → ④ (6.2)

Commentary on Assessment Schedule 2A

The purpose of Assessment Schedule 2A is to determine:

a. the student's early levels on the models of Forward Number Word Sequences – Levels ⓪ to ⑤; Backward Number Word Sequences – Levels ⓪ to ⑤; and Numeral Identification – Levels ⓪ to ④;

b. a portrait of the student's knowledge of these three sub-domains.

Early Number Words and Numerals is the first of three important domains of early number learning. This domain focuses on becoming **facile** with forward and backward number word sequences and learning to identify (read) numerals in the range to about 100. This domain is continued in Domain 3A, and the schedule overlaps with Schedule 3A.

1. Forward number word sequences (FNWS)

If the student cannot say the sequence from 1 to 32, do not present the tasks in the second and third rows.
    Look for:
- Errors, omissions, hesitations, and repetitions.
- Can't say the sequence beyond 10, 12 or 29.
- Says the sequence of **decuples** (30, 40, … 90, 20) instead of the teen numbers.
- Can't say what comes after 69 or 79.
- Says '… 107, 108, 109, 200'.

2. Number word after (NWA)

Look for:
- *Drops back*, that is, says the FNWS from a lower number word to figure out the next number word. For example, drops back to say the FNWS from 'one' to 'twelve', to figure out what comes after 'twelve'.
- Number words with 'nine' in the ones (e.g. seventy-nine) are often more difficult because they involve bridging a decuple – students might have difficulty in producing the decuple.

3. Numeral identification (NID)

These tasks assess facility in identifying (reading) 1-, 2- and 3-digit numerals.
    Look for:
- Says the sequence from 'one' to generate the name of a numeral.
- Has difficulty identifying '12'. Might name '12' as 'twenty' or 'twenty-one'.
- Because they have learned to read numerals in the teens from right to left ('17' is read as 'seven–teen'), look for reversing the order of the **digits** when reading numerals beyond 20, for example, '47' is read as 'seventy-four'.
- Has difficulty reading 3-digit numerals with '1' in the tens column; or '0' in the ones or tens column (e.g. 680, 109, 417).

4. Writing numerals

Look for:
- When writing teen numbers, for example 'eighteen', writes the '8' first and then writes '1' to the left (resulting in the correct answer '18'). We suppose that this results from being unable to visualize the numeral '18' prior to commencing to write it. Because the number word 'eight' comes first in 'eighteen', the student commences by writing the digit '8'.
- Confuses writing 'twelve' and 'twenty-one'.
- Writes 'two hundred and seventy' as '20070', and 'three hundred and six' as '3006'.

5. Backward number word sequences (BNWS)

Look for:
- Drops back, that is, says the FNWS from a lower number to determine the next number word in a BNWS. For example, says the FNWS from 'one' to 'twelve' to find what comes before 'twelve'.
- Omits a decuple or says the incorrect decuple, typically the decuple before, for example 'seventy-two, seventy-one, sixty, sixty-nine, sixty-eight'. We suppose students reason from the FNWS (seventy-eight, seventy-nine, then comes the next decuple 'eighty', eighty-one, eighty-two, …). Hence for the BNWS (seventy-two, seventy-one, then comes the next decuple going backwards 'sixty', sixty-nine, sixty-eight, …).

6. Number word before (NWB)

Look for:
- Drops back to figure out the number word before a given number word. For example, drops back to say the FNWS from 'one' to 'thirteen' to figure out what comes before 'thirteen'.

2B. Early Structuring

Assessment Schedule

2B

MATERIALS: DICE PATTERN CARDS

Student Name: ....   Interview Date: ....

DoB: .... Age: .... (yrs) .... (mths)   Interviewer: ....

Structuring Numbers 1 to 20 Model (SN20)
⓪ Emergent spatial patterns and finger patterns   ④ Facile structuring numbers 1 to 10
① Finger patterns 1–5 and spatial patterns 1–6   ⑤ Formal addition (parts ≤ 10)
② Small doubles and small partitions of 10   ⑥ Formal addition & subtraction (parts ≤ 10)
③ Five-plus and partitions of 5   ⑦ Formal addition & subtraction (whole ≤ 20)

Note: For Levels ①-⑦, student has to use facile strategies, that is, not counting by ones.

In each task group, if student uses counting, ask *Can you do it without counting?*

1. Making finger patterns

Show me a number on your fingers, as quickly as you can. Show me ___.

①	3	5	2	4		
	10	8	7	9	6	6 *another way?*

2. Regular configurations

[DICE PATTERN CARDS]

I am going to quickly show you a card with some dots on it. Ready? How many?

Flash each pattern card to the student for ½ second.

①	3	5	2	4	6

3. Small doubles

②	2 & 2	5 & 5	3 & 3	4 & 4

If student is not facile to this point → END ASSESSMENT HERE.

- -

4. Small partitions of 10

I'll say a number, and you say how many more to make 10.

For example, I say '5', you say ___ (Can prompt '5').

②	9	7	8	6

5. Partitions of 5

I'll say a number, and you say how many more to make 5.

For example, I say '4', you say ___ (Can prompt '1').

③	2	1	3

6. Five-plus facts

③	5 plus 2	5 plus 4	5 plus 1	5 plus 3

Learning Framework in Number © Wright & Ellemor-Collins, 2018 (Sage)

Commentary on Assessment Schedule 2B

The purpose of Assessment Schedule 2B is to determine:

a. early levels on the Structuring Numbers 1 to 20 model – Levels ⓪ to ③;

b. a portrait of the student's knowledge of Early Structuring.

Early Structuring is the second of three important domains of early number learning. This domain focuses mainly on additive structure in the range 1 to 10.

1. Making finger patterns

Developing facile finger patterns in an arithmetical context can support students' learning of structuring numbers (Task Group 1). Look for:

- Raises fingers simultaneously or sequentially.
- Looks at their fingers.
- Counts by ones to make the pattern or to check the pattern.

The student is facile with finger patterns in the range 1 to 5 if they raise fingers simultaneously without needing to look at their fingers.

2. Regular configurations

Flash for half of a second. Assess whether the student takes a few seconds to answer, rather than answering immediately. We suppose this indicates that the student counts the dots while visualizing the pattern. The student is facile if they answer quickly and correctly for all configurations. Ascribing number to **regular spatial configurations** can provide a basis for structuring numbers.

3. Small doubles

a. Raises an equal number of fingers on each hand and then counts from one; or

b. Counts on (e.g. counts on from 4 to solve 4 + 4); or

c. Answers quickly without counting or raising fingers.

4. Small partitions of 10

A small partition has the unknown number 5 or smaller. Look for:

a. Builds a finger pattern for the number given by counting out fingers from one, and then counts their remaining fingers; or

b. Builds a finger pattern for the number given and then reads the pattern on their remaining fingers without counting by ones; or

c. Answers quickly without counting or raising fingers.

5. Partitions of 5

a. Counts by ones to build the number given on one hand and then counts by ones to determine the number of fingers remaining; or

b. Raises fingers simultaneously to build the number given and then reads the pattern on their remaining fingers without counting by ones; or

c. Answers quickly without counting or raising fingers.

6. Five-plus facts

a. Counts by ones from one and uses fingers to keep track of the second **addend**;

b. Counts on from 5, with fingers keeping track of the second addend;

c. Counts on from 5, without using fingers to keep track; or

d. Answers quickly without counting or raising fingers.

2C. Early Arithmetical Strategies

Assessment Schedule

MATERIALS: TASK CARDS, COUNTERS OF TWO COLOURS, TWO SCREENS

Student Name: ....   Interview Date: ....

DoB: .... Age: .... (yrs) .... (mths)   Interviewer: ....

Stages of Early Arithmetical Learning Model (SEAL)
⓪ Emergent counting
① Perceptual counting
② Figurative counting
③ Initial number sequence – Counting-on- and -back
④ Intermediate number sequence – Counting-down-to
⑤ Facile number sequence – Non-count-by-ones strategies

Additive tasks

1. Two screened collections [COUNTERS – TWO COLOURS]

There are 5 red counters under here, and 3 blue counters under here.
How many counters are there altogether?
[Possible strategies include: CF1-3x   CF1-1x   COF   Non-counting   Known Fact]

1.1	5 & 3
1.2	9 & 2
1.3	12 & 4

2. More advanced task: Missing addend [COUNTERS – TWO COLOURS]

There are 8 red counters under here. I put some blue counters under here, and now there are 11 counters altogether. How many blue counters did I put under here?

8 & ? = 11

IF COUNTING-ON   → **TASK 5**

IF NOT YET COUNTING-ON   → **TASK 3 and 4, then END ASSESSMENT.**

3. Partially screened addition [COUNTERS – TWO COLOURS]

3.1	9 & 5	*9 red counters under here, 5 blue here. How many altogether?*
3.2	7 & 4	*7 red counters here, 4 blue under here. How many altogether?*

4. 'Get me' task [COUNTERS – ONE COLOUR]

Put out a pile of about 30 counters of one colour. Then say:
Get me 13 counters from this pile of counters please.

	STOP HERE

Subtractive tasks

5. Removed items [COUNTERS – ONE COLOUR]

There are 7 counters under here. I'm taking 2 counters away.
How many counters are left?

5.1	7 r 2
5.2	12 r 3
5.3	**Optional supplementary task** 15 r 4

IF UNSUCCESSFUL with 5.1 and 5.2 → STOP HERE.

6. More advanced: Written subtraction [CARDS – NUMBER SENTENCES]

Read this to me. (If read incorrectly, e.g. – as +, correct the student.)
Work that out please.
[Possible strategies include: CDF   CDT   CUT   Non-counting]

6.1	15 – 12
6.2	22 – 18

7. Missing subtrahend [COUNTERS – ONE COLOUR]

There are 19 counters under here. I'm taking some counters away.
There are 17 left. How many counters did I take away?

19 r ? = 17

Commentary on Assessment Schedule 2C

The purpose of Assessment Schedule 2C is to determine:

a. the student's stage on the Stages of Early Arithmetical Learning model (SEAL);

b. a portrait of the student's knowledge of Early Arithmetical Strategies.

Early Arithmetical Strategies is the third of three important domains of early number learning. This domain focuses on learning to solve simple addition and subtraction tasks through the development of increasingly sophisticated counting strategies, that is, counting-by-ones. Although both Domain 2C and Domain 3C are important, they are not necessarily strongly linked (unlike 2A and 3A, and 2B and 3B).

The first section of the assessment schedule focuses on additive tasks, and the second section focuses on subtractive tasks. The numbers involved in these tasks (5 and 3, 9 and 2, etc.) are chosen so that the first addend is significantly larger than the second, and the second addend is typically in the range 2 to 5.

Additive tasks

1.1 Two screened collections: 5 & 3

Look for:

a. Can't solve the task;

b. Builds a finger pattern for 5 on one hand and a finger pattern for 3 on the other hand and then counts their fingers from one, by ones – indicative of *perceptual counting*;

c. Counts their fingers on one hand by ones from one, and then continues counting by ones to count their fingers on the other hand – indicative of **figurative counting**;

d. Counts on by ones from 5 (or from 3), perhaps using fingers to keep track – referred to as **counting-up-from**; or

e. Answers quickly and correctly without counting by ones – referred to as a **non-count-by-ones strategy**.

1.2 Two screened collections: 9 & 2

Look for:

a. Students who solved Task 1.1 by building a finger pattern for 5 and a finger pattern for 3 might similarly attempt to build a finger pattern for 9 and a finger pattern for 2 and then reach an impasse.

b. Counts from 1 to 9, and then counts by ones keeping track of two counts. As for Task 1.1 above, this is indicative of figurative counting.

c. A more advanced strategy is to count on from 9, keeping track of two counts – counting-up-from.

d. More advanced still is to answer without counting by ones.

1.3 Two screened collections: 12 & 4

Similarly, the likely strategies for Task 1.3 are figurative counting, counting-up-from and non-count-by-ones.

2. More advanced task: Missing addend

Present Task 2 only if the student is successful on Tasks 1.1–1.3.

Look for:

a. Students who solved Tasks 1.1–1.3 by counting-up-from might solve Task 2 by another advanced counting-by-ones strategy, referred to as **counting-up-to**. This strategy involves starting from 8 and counting by ones to 11, keeping track of the number of counts required to reach 11 (three counts).

b. Misinterprets the missing addend task as an addition task, that is, on Task 2, they will attempt to add 8 and 11.

As indicated on the Assessment Schedule, if the student's strategies on Tasks 1 and 2 are less sophisticated than counting-on (that is, the strategies are figurative, perceptual, or unsuccessful), then pose the less advanced Tasks 3 and 4, and end the assessment. On the other hand, if the student has used counting-on or more sophisticated strategies, then Tasks 3 and 4 are not presented, and the assessment continues from Task 5.

3. Partially screened addition

Because one of the two collections is unscreened, these tasks are less demanding than Tasks 1.1–1.3.

Look for:

- 9 & 5, with 9 screened, says the number word sequence from 'one' to 'nine' and then continues to count the second (unscreened) collection.

- 7 & 4, with 4 screened, counts the unscreened counters from 'one' and attempts to continue to count the second (screened) collection and keep track of four counts.

4. 'Get me' task

Task 4 is presented to establish whether the student has a perceptual counting strategy, that is, whether the student can count out 13 counters for example, from a collection of 30 or more counters. Students may not be able to coordinate number words and counters.

Look for:

- Says one number word for two counters;
- Says two number words for one counter;
- Omits counters;
- Counts some counters twice; or
- Does not stop at 'thirteen'.

Subtractive tasks

5. Removed items

Look for:

- Used a counting-on strategy on the additive tasks, and uses a counting-back strategy to solve these subtractive tasks.
- For Task 5.1, for example, starts at 7 and makes two counts backwards while keeping track of the two counts. Referred to as *counting-back-from*, one of the advanced counting-by-ones strategies.
- Uses a non-count-by-ones strategy to solve these tasks.

As indicated on the Assessment Schedule, if the student is unsuccessful on Tasks 5.1 and 5.2 the assessment is discontinued. If the student's strategy on Tasks 5.1 and 5.2 is not apparent, present Task 5.3.

6. More advanced: Written subtraction

Tasks 6.1 and 6.2 are each presented in the form of a written expression and typically are more difficult than Tasks 5.1 and 5.2. Students who solved Tasks 5.1 and 5.2 by counting-back-from or Tasks 1.1–1.3 by counting-up-from, solve Tasks 6.1 or 6.2 by any of the following advanced counting-by-ones strategies.

Look for:

a. *Counts-up-to*, that is, begins at 12, and counts up to 15 while keeping track of the number of counts (i.e. three);

b. *Counts-down-to*, that is, begins at 15, and counts down to 12 while keeping track of the number of counts (i.e. three); or

c. *Counts-down-from*, that is, begins at 15 and make 12 counts backwards while keeping track of the number of counts. Counting-down-from on such tasks is regarded as the least advanced of these three strategies because the student is apparently unable to anticipate that 12 is a stopping point. Nevertheless, it is very common for students to count-down-from rather than count-down-to, and thereby undertake a long count backwards which involves the difficulty of keeping track of 12 counts.

7. Missing subtrahend

Task 7 is somewhat similar to Tasks 6.1 and 6.2. In this case, the task is presented in a setting of counters rather than as a written expression. The numbers in Task 7 are chosen so that the **minuend** is significantly larger than the unknown difference and the difference is in the range 2 to 5. Similar to Tasks 6.1 and 6.2, students who counted on or back to solve additive and subtractive tasks, solve Task 7 by counting-up-to, counting-down-to, or counting-down-from.

As a general rule, presenting these additive and subtractive tasks in a setting of a screened collection (or collections) is designed to and can evoke particular advanced counting-by-ones strategies. Thus the addition tasks involving two screened collections (Task Group 1) are likely to evoke counting-up-from. The **Missing Addend** task (Task 2) is likely to evoke counting-up-to. The **Removed Items** tasks (Task Group 5) are likely to evoke counting-down-from. And finally, the **Missing Subtrahend** task (Task 7) is likely to evoke counting-down-to.

3A. Number Words and Numerals

Assessment Schedule

MATERIALS: TASK CARDS, PAPER, MARKER PEN

Student Name: ....   Interview Date: ....

DoB: .... Age: .... (yrs) .... (mths)   Interviewer: ....

Number Word Sequences Models (FNWS and BNWS)

Forward Number Word Sequences	Backward Number Word Sequences
⓪ Emergent FNWS	⓪ Emergent BNWS
① Initial FNWS up to 'ten'	① Initial BNWS up to 'ten'
② Intermediate FNWS up to 'ten'	② Intermediate BNWS up to 'ten'
③ Facile FNWS up to 'ten'	③ Facile BNWS up to 'ten'
④ Facile FNWS up to 'thirty'	④ Facile BNWS up to 'thirty'
⑤ Facile FNWS up to 'one hundred'	⑤ Facile BNWS up to 'one hundred'
⑥ Facile FNWS up to 'one thousand'	⑥ Facile BNWS up to 'one thousand'
⑦ Facile FNWS up to 'ten thousand'	⑦ Facile BNWS up to 'ten thousand'

Numeral Identification Model (NID)

⓪ Emergent numeral identification
① Numerals to 10 – Identify
② Numerals to 20 – Identify
③ Numerals to 100 – Identify
④ Numerals to 1000 – Identify & write
⑤ Numerals to 10,000 – Identify & write
⑥ Numerals to 100,000 – Identify & write

Numerals

1. Numeral identification (NID) [CARDS – NUMERALS]

Show each card in turn, asking, *What number is this?*

③	12	15	47	21	66	83
④	101	275	400	517	730	306
⑤	1000	8245	1006		3406	6032
	4820	3010	1300		40,000	
⑥	10,235	12,500	59,049		80,402	64,004

START HERE → ④

2. Writing numerals

Provide PAPER and PEN. *Write the number that I say.*

③	6	12	18	92
④	517	270	306	
⑤	1000	6005	2020	4940
⑥	10,000	15,625	34,700	50,050

Learning Framework in Number © Wright & Ellemor-Collins, 2018 (Sage)

Number word sequences

3. Backward number word sequence (BNWS)

Count backwards from ___. I'll tell you when to stop.

④	**3.1)** 15 (to 10)	
	3.2) 23 (to 17)	
⑤	**3.3)** 52 (to 38)	
	3.4) 103 (to 96)	
⑥	**3.5)** 303 (to 296)	
	3.6) 1003 (to 987)	
⑦	**3.7)** 2203 (to 2187)	

START HERE → (points to 3.3)

4. Number word before (NWB)

Example: *The number that comes just before 2 is 1.*

Say the number that comes just before ___.

START HERE → (points to row ⑤)

④	8	13	17	20	14	25	30
⑤	55	41	80	100			
⑥	170	201	300	1000			
⑦	1100	2000	5050	10,000			

5. Forward number word sequences (FNWS)

Count forwards from ___. I'll tell you when to stop.

④	**5.1)** 8 (to 17)	
	5.2) 15 (to 33)	
⑤	**5.3)** 57 (to 68)	
	5.4) 95 (to 113)	
⑥	**5.5)** 197 (to 210)	
	5.6) 995 (to 1010)	
⑦	**5.7)** 1095 (to 1103)	
	5.8) 6595 (to 6612)	

START HERE → (points to 5.3)

6. Number word after (NWA)

(Example if needed: *The number that comes just after 1 is 2.*)

Say the number that comes just after ___.

START HERE → (points to row ⑤)

④	6	12	17	25	22	19	29
⑤	50	39	65	77	89		
⑥	144	109	1000	359	610	999	
⑦	1699	1728	2099	8999			

Commentary on Assessment Schedule 3A

The purpose of Assessment Schedule 3A is to determine:

a. the student's levels on the models of Forward Number Word Sequences – Levels ④ to ⑦; Backward Number Word Sequences – Levels ④ to ⑦; and Numeral Identification – Levels ③ to ⑥;

b. a portrait of the student's knowledge of these three sub-domains.

Schedule 2A is used to assess Levels ⓪ to ③ on the FNWS and BNWS models, and Levels ⓪ to ② on the Numeral Identification model. The tasks on Schedule 2A overlap with those on Schedule 3A.

Numerals

1. Numeral identification (NID)

Determine the student's facility in identifying (reading) 2-, 3-, 4- and 5-digit numerals.

The assessment can begin on the Level ④ row (3-digit numerals). Depending on the facility with Level ④, progress to the ⑤ and ⑥ rows, or drop back to the ③ row. Important numerals to pose include decuples (730), **centuples** (1300) and powers of ten (1000).

Look for:

- Has difficulty identifying '12'. Misnames '12' as 'twenty' or 'twenty-one'.
- Identifies '21' as 'twelve'.
- Identifies teen numbers as decuples, for example, '15' is read as 'fifty'.
- For 3-digit numerals, has difficulty identifying numerals that have a '1' or a '0' in the tens place, for example '517' or '306'.
- For 4- and 5-digit numerals, has difficulty with numerals with '0s', for examples, '1006', '3406', '3010, '64,004'.

2. Writing numerals

Determine the student's facility in writing 2-, 3-, 4- and 5-digit numerals.

The assessment can begin on the Level ④ row (3-digit numerals). Depending on the facility with Level ④, progress to the ⑤ and ⑥ rows, or drop back to the ③ row.

Look for:

- For teen numbers, writes the ones digit first. We presume that the student is unable to visualize the numeral (e.g. '18') prior to starting to write it. When asked to write 'eighteen' the student will write '8', and after a pause write '1'. Thus it takes the student a few seconds to figure out on which side of '8' to write '1'. Students might write the '1' on the right-hand side which results in '81' instead of '18'.
- For 'twelve' writes '21'.
- For 3-, 4- and 5-digit numerals, has difficulties writing numerals with '0s'.
- For 'two hundred and seventy' writes '20070'.
- For 'three hundred and six' writes '3006'.
- For 'six thousand and five' writes '60005'.
- Powers of ten (1000, 10,000) are important numerals to pose.

Number word sequences

3. Backward number word sequences (BNWS)

Determine the student's facility with Backward Number Word Sequences. Of particular interest is the student's facility in crossing **'hurdles'** such as decuples, centuples and thousands. The assessment can begin on 3.3 and 3.4 (2-digit numerals). Depending on the facility with 3.3 and 3.4, progress to 3.5–3.7, or drop back to 3.1 and 3.2.

Look for:

- Drops back, that is, counts forwards from a lower number to determine the next number in a BNWS. For example, drops back to say the FNWS from 'one' to 'fourteen' to figure out what comes before 'fourteen'.
- When saying the sequence from 'fifteen' back to 'ten', omits 'thirteen'.
- Confuses teens and decuples, for example, 'twenty-three, twenty-two, twenty-one, twenty, ninety, eighty, seventy, …'.
- Says the next lowest decuple, for example, 'fifty-two, fifty-one, forty, forty-nine, forty-eight, …'.

- Omits a decuple, for example, 'fifty-two, fifty-one, forty-nine, forty-eight, ….'.
- Omits a repeated-digit number word, for example, '… forty-seven, forty-six, forty-five, forty-three, forty-two', etc.
- Says the next lowest centuple, for example, '303, 302, 301, 200, 299, 298, …'.

4. Number word before (NWB)

Determine the student's facility with Number Word Before. The assessment can begin on the Level ④ row (2-digit numerals). If the student is facile with Levels ④, ⑤ and ⑥, progress to the Level ⑦ row.

Students' errors on number word before tasks might or might not correspond with errors on backward number word sequence tasks. For example, a student might correctly name the number word before 'thirty-one' (thirty) but might omit 'thirty' when saying a backward number word sequence.

Look for:

- 'Drops back', that is, says the sequence forwards from a lower number to determine the number word. For example, drops back to say the FNWS from 'ten' to 'fourteen' to figure out what comes before 'fourteen'.

5. Forward number word sequences (FNWS)

Determine the student's facility with Forward Number Word Sequences. Of particular interest is the student's facility in crossing hurdles such as decuples, centuples and thousands. The assessment can begin on 5.3 and 5.4 (2-digit numerals). Depending on the facility with 5.3 and 5.4, progress to 5.5–5.7, or drop back to 5.1 and 5.2.

Look for:

- Says: '… 107, 108, 109, 200, …'.
- Says: '… 1007, 1008, 1009, 2000, …'
- Says: '… 1097, 1098, 1099, 2000, …'

6. Number word after (NWA)

Determine the student's facility with Number Word After. The assessment can begin on the Level ④ row. If facile with Level ④, progress to the Level ⑤, ⑥ and ⑦ rows.

Look for:

- Attempts to visualize a numeral sequence in order to determine the number word after a given number.

3B. Structuring Numbers 1 to 20

Assessment Schedule

3B

MATERIALS: TASK CARDS

Student Name:	Interview Date: ....
DoB: .... Age: .... (yrs) .... (mths)	Interviewer: ....

Structuring Numbers 1 to 20 Model (SN20)

⓪ Emergent spatial patterns and finger patterns   ④ Facile structuring numbers 1 to 10
① Finger patterns 1–5 and spatial patterns 1–6   ⑤ Formal addition (parts ≤ 10)
② Small doubles and small partitions of 10   ⑥ Formal addition & subtraction (parts ≤ 10)
③ Five-plus and partitions of 5   ⑦ Formal addition & subtraction (whole ≤ 20)

Note: For levels 1–7, student has to use facile strategies, that is, not counting by ones.

In each task group, if student uses counting, ask *Can you do it without counting?*

If student can only solve by counting, no need to pose remainder of task group.

1. Making finger patterns (6–10)

Show me a number on your fingers, as quickly as you can. Show me ___.

10	8	7	9	6	6 *another way?*

If not facile, pose Tasks 1 and 2 from Schedule 2B (fingers 1–5, configurations 1–6).

2. Small doubles

② 2 & 2	5 & 5	3 & 3	4 & 4

3. Partitions of 10

I'll say a number, and you say how many more to make 10.
For example, I say '5', you say … (Can prompt '5').

② **3.1) Small partitions**	9	7
④ **3.2) Big partitions**	2	4

4. Partitions of 5

I'll say a number, and you say how many more to make 5.
For example, I say '4', you say … (Can prompt '1').

③ 2	1	3

5. Five-plus facts

③ 5 plus 2	5 plus 4	5 plus 1
5 plus 3	1 plus 5	3 plus 5

6. Partitions in range 1 to 9

I am going to give two examples. 3&1 add up to 4, yes? Also, 2&2 add up to 4.
Now, can you tell me two numbers that add up to ___? Can you tell me another two numbers?

④ 6	9

7. Partitions in range 11 to 20

Can you tell me two numbers that add up to ___?...Another two?

⑦ 12	19

8.1 Ten-plus facts

⑤ 10 plus 4	10 plus 8	10 plus 2
7 plus 10	5 plus 10	1 plus 10

8.2 Teen plus 10

16 plus 10	12 plus 10

9. Big doubles

⑤ 10 & 10	6 & 6	8 & 8	9 & 9	7 & 7

If student only uses counting-by-ones in Task Groups 1–9 → END ASSESSMENT HERE.

Formal addition & subtraction 1–20

[ADDITION AND SUBTRACTION CARDS]

Show the card: *Read this please … What is the answer?*
Generally, enquire about strategy. If the student counts, ask: *Can you do it without counting?*

10. Range 2 (Whole ≤ 10): Addition

④ 4 + 3	3 + 6	2 + 7

11. Range 3 (Parts ≤ 10): Addition

⑤ 6 + 5	9 + 6	8 + 7

12. Range 3 (Parts ≤ 10): Subtraction

⑥ 14 − 7	11 − 4	17 − 9

13. Range 4 (Whole ≤ 20): Addition and subtraction

⑦ 13 + 3	11 + 8	17 − 15	19 − 13

Commentary on Assessment Schedule 3B

The purpose of Assessment Schedule 3B is to determine:

a. the student's level on the model of Structuring Numbers 1 to 20 – Levels ② to ⑦;

b. a portrait of the student's knowledge of the domain of Structuring Numbers 1 to 20.

Schedule 2B is used to assess Levels ⓪ to ③ on the model, overlapping with Schedule 3B. Each task group on Schedule 3B consists of several tasks.

1. Making finger patterns (6–10)

To determine facility in making finger patterns for numbers in the range 6 to 10.

Look for:

- Raises fingers simultaneously or sequentially.
- Looks at fingers while building a pattern.
- Builds 8 as 5 & 3, and 6 as 5 & 1; rather than 4 & 4 and 3 & 3.

When asked to build 6 another way, students who have built 6 as 5 & 1 either maintain the pattern while swapping the positions of their hands; or swap the numbers of fingers on their hands. If necessary, ask if they can build 6 using numbers different from the numbers they have used.

Task Groups 2–9: Key combinations and partitions

Task Groups 2–9 assess knowledge of the key combinations and partitions:

- Small doubles (1 + 1 up to 5 + 5) and Large doubles (6 + 6 up to 10 + 10);
- Partitions of 5 and partitions of 10;
- Five-pluses and ten-pluses.

Assess whether the student answers quickly, without using counting or fingers.

2. Small doubles

Look for:

a. Raises an equal number of fingers on each hand and then counts from one;

b. Counts on; or

c. Answers quickly without counting or raising fingers.

3. Partitions of 10

A small partition has the unknown number 5 or smaller.

Look for:

a. Builds a finger pattern for the number given by counting out fingers from one, and then counts the remaining fingers;

b. Builds a finger pattern for the number given and then reads the pattern on their remaining fingers without counting by ones; or

c. Answers quickly without counting or raising fingers.

4. Partitions of 5

Look for:

a. Counts by ones to build the number given on one hand and then counts by ones to determine the number of fingers remaining;

b. Raises fingers simultaneously to build the number given and then reads the pattern on the remaining fingers without counting by ones; or

c. Answers quickly without counting or raising fingers.

5. Five-plus facts

Look for:

a. Counts by ones from one and uses fingers to keep track of the second addend;

b. Counts on from 5 using fingers to keep track of the second addend;

c. Counts on from 5 without using fingers to keep track of the second addend;

d. Answers quickly without counting or raising fingers.

6. Partitions in range 1 to 9

Look for:

- Answers 'five and one' (for 6) and 'eight and one' (for 9), that is, routinely determines 'one' to be the second addend.
- Takes more time to answer these tasks compared with the time taken to answer previous tasks.

7. Partitions in range 11 to 20

Look for:

- For 12, answers '11 and 1', '10 and 2' or '6 and 6'.
- For 19, answers '18 and 1' or '10 and 9'.

- Students who answer '18 and 1' can't give a second answer.
- Takes more time to answer these tasks compared with the time taken to answer previous tasks.

8.1 Ten-plus facts

Look for:

a. Counts by ones from one using fingers to keep track of the second addend;

b. Counts on from '10' by ones using fingers to keep track;

c. Counts on from '10' by ones without using fingers to keep track; or

d. Answers quickly without counting or raising fingers.

These tasks typically are easier for students than the partition tasks (Task Groups 6 and 7).

8.2 Teen plus 10

These tasks are not used to determine the student's level but can provide useful information for planning instruction. For example, not readily knowing that 16 plus 10 is 26, might indicate that the student cannot regard 16 as a ten and six ones. These tasks typically are more difficult than those in Task Group 8.1.

9. Big doubles

Look for:

a. Counts by ones from one using fingers to keep track of the second addend;

b. Counts on from the first addend by ones with or without using fingers to keep track; or

c. Answers quickly without counting or raising fingers.

These tasks typically are more difficult for students than the Ten-plus tasks (Task Group 8.1).

Task Groups 10–13: Formal addition and subtraction 1 to 20

As indicated on the assessment schedule, if the student uses only counting-by-ones strategies on Task Groups 1–9 then end the assessment here. Also, if the student is not successful on Task Groups 10 and 11, then do not go on to the darker shaded Task Groups 12 and 13.

Observe very closely how the student responds to each task. After the student has attempted to solve a task, enquire about the strategy used. Questions should be closely informed by one's observations of the student's attempt to solve the task. Observe closely whether the student counts by ones, and if so, try to determine whether the student counts from one, counts on (for addition), counts back (for subtraction), or uses fingers to keep track of all or part of their count. If the student does not count by ones, try to determine their strategy as precisely as possible. Look for use of doubles or adding or subtracting using 5 or 10.

10. Range 2 (Whole ≤ 10): Addition

These tasks assess facility on Range 1 ($4 + 3$) and Range 2 ($3 + 6$, $2 + 7$) addition facts. Facile strategies include:

a. for $4 + 3$, using $3 + 3$, or $4 + 4$, or adding though 5;

b. for $3 + 6$, adding 3 to 6 using multiplicative structure ($3 + 6$ is the same as 3×3);

c. for $2 + 7$, using $3 + 7$.

11. Range 3 (Parts ≤ 10): Addition

Facile strategies include:

a. for $6 + 5$, using $5 + 5$, or $6 + 6$, or adding through 10 ($6 + 5$ as $6 + 4 + 1$);

b. for $9 + 6$, counting by threes ($9 + 6$ is the same as $9 + 3 + 3$);

c. for $8 + 7$, using $7 + 7$, or $8 + 8$, or adding through 10 from 8, or adding through 10 from 7, or using fives ($8 + 7$ as $5 + 3$ and $5 + 2$).

12. Range 3 (Parts ≤ 10): Subtraction

Facile strategies include:

a. for $14 - 7$, using $7 + 7 = 14$ or $14 - 4 = 10$;

b. for $11 - 4$, using $11 - 1 = 10$ or $10 - 4 = 6$;

c. for $17 - 9$, using $17 - 10$, $18 - 9$, $9 + 9$, or $8 + 8$.

13. Range 4 (Whole ≤ 20): Addition and subtraction

Facile strategies include:

- for $13 + 3$, using $3 + 3$; and for $17 - 15$, using $7 - 5$; referred to as using the *ten structure* of teen numbers.

For $17 - 15$ and $19 - 13$, could use different counting-by-ones strategies:

a. two counts from 17 back to 15 (**Count-back-to**);

b. two counts from 15 forwards to 17 (Count-up-to); or

c. 15 counts from backwards from 17, which should reach 2 (Count-back-from).

3C. Conceptual Place Value

Assessment Schedule

MATERIALS: TASK CARDS, 15 X 10-STICK BUNDLES, 13 X 100-DOT SQUARES, COVER

Student Name: ....   Interview Date: ....

DoB: .... Age: .... (yrs) .... (mths)   Interviewer: ....

Conceptual Place Value Model (CPV)
- ⓪ Emergent incrementing & decrementing by 10
- ① Incrementing & decrementing by 10, with materials, in range to 100
- ② Incrementing & decrementing flexibly by 10s and 1s, with materials, in range to 100
- ③ Incrementing & decrementing by 10, without materials, in range to 100
- ④ Incrementing & decrementing by 10, without materials, in range to 1000

1. Incrementing by 10s ON the decuple [BUNDLING STICKS]

①
- Establish there are 10 sticks in each bundle.
- Place one bundle under cover. *How many sticks are under there?* (10)
- Continue placing bundles under cover. *Now how many sticks are under there?*

| 20 | 30 | 40 | 50 | 60 | 70 |

- At 70 ask *How many sticks? How many bundles?*
- Continue incrementing, asking *How many sticks?*

| 80 | 90 | 100 | 110 | 120 |

2. Incrementing by 10s OFF the decuple [BUNDLING STICKS]

①
- Place out four sticks. *How many sticks?* (4)
  After answer, place sticks under the cover.
- Place a bundle beside the cover.
  If I add this bundle under the cover, how many sticks will that be? (14)
  After answer, place bundle under the cover.
- Continue adding bundles. *Now how many sticks are under there?*

| 24 | 34 | 44 | 54 | 64 | 74 | 84 |

IF STUDENT IS NOT SUCCESSFUL ON TASK 2 → SKIP TASKS 3 and 4.

3. Decrementing by 10s OFF the decuple [BUNDLING STICKS]

① Place out 147 sticks: a big bundle of 10 bundles, 4 more bundles, and 7 sticks.

- Explain that the big bundle has 100 sticks.
- Ask *How many sticks are there altogether?*
  If the student doesn't establish how many, just tell him/her there are 147.
- Cover the sticks. *Okay, there are 147 sticks under there.*
  Remove a bundle. *Now how many sticks are there?* (137)
- Continue removing bundles. *Now how many are there?*

| 127 | 117 | 107 | 97 | 87 | 77 |

Learning Framework in Number © Wright & Ellemor-Collins, 2018 (Sage)

4. Incrementing flexibly by 10s and 1s [BUNDING STICKS]

② • Place out one bundle. *How many sticks?* (10)

    After answer, place bundle under the cover.

  • Place the indicated bundles (**B**) and/or sticks (**s**) beside the cover.

    If I put this under the cover, how many sticks will that be?

    After answer, place added amount under the cover.

  • Present each task in turn:

  | 1**B** (10) | 4**s** (14) | 2**B** (34) | 4**s** (38) | 2**s** (40) | 1**B** (50) | 2**s** (52) | 2**B** (72) |

  If successful without counting-by-ones, continue with the next sequence:

  | 5**s** (5) | 1**B** (15) | 2**B** (35) | 1**B** 3**s** (48) | 2**B** 1**s** (69) |

5. Jump of 10 more [NUMERAL CARDS]

Show number on card. *Which number is ten **more** than this?*

③
| 40 | 90 | 79 | 44 |

If jumping without counting-by-ones is OK, try tasks in the 3-digit range:

④
| 356 | 306 | 195 |

If the 3-digit range is OK, try a task across 1000:

④
| 999 |

6. Jump of 10 less [NUMERAL CARDS]

Show number on card. *Which number is ten **less** than this?*

③
| 40 | 79 | 44 | 101 |

If jumping without counting-by-ones OK, try tasks in the 3-digit range:

④
| 356 | 306 |

If the 3-digit range is OK, try a task across 1000:

④
| 1005 |

7. Jump of 100 [NUMERAL CARDS]

Show number on card. *Which number is…?*

one hundred more than this? (50)	*one hundred more than this?* (306)
one hundred more than this? (973)	*one hundred **LESS** than this?* (108)

8. Incrementing by 100s on the hundred [100-DOT SQUARES]

  • Establish there are 100 dots on each 100-square.
  • Place one square under cover. *How many dots are under there?* (100)
  • Continue placing squares under cover. *Now how many dots are under there?*

  | 200 | 300 | 400 | 500 | 600 |

  • At 600 ask *How many dots? How many squares?*
  • Continue incrementing, asking *How many dots?*

  | 700 | 800 | 900 | 1000 | 1100 | 1200 | 1300 |

Commentary on Assessment Schedule 3C

The purpose of Assessment Schedule 3C is to determine:

a. the student's level on the model of Conceptual Place Value;

b. a portrait of the student's knowledge of this domain.

Task Groups 1–4: Tasks with bundling sticks

Task Groups 1–4 involve using a setting of bundling sticks bundled into tens and ones.

1. Incrementing by 10s ON the decuple

Look for:

- After the second bundle is placed under the screen, counts on from 10 or immediately answers 'twenty'.
- Does not keep track of the number of sticks.
- Can regard 70 sticks as alternatively seven bundles.
- At each step, incorrectly states the corresponding teen number ('thirteen, fourteen, … nineteen, twenty') rather than the decuple ('thirty, forty, …').
- Has difficulty saying the decuples after 'one hundred'.

2. Incrementing by 10s OFF the decuple

Look for:

- At the first increment from 4, whether the student counts on by ones from 4; or at the increment from 14, whether the student counts on by ones from 14.
- If the student uses counting by ones for the initial increments, do they begin to count by 10s for later increments.

If the student is unsuccessful on Task Group 2 the assessment is discontinued.

3. Decrementing by 10s OFF the decuple

Look for:

- Has difficulty decrementing by 10 from 127, 117 and 107. Decrementing by 10 from 127 involves generating a teen number name ('17') which does not conform to the sound pattern of '157, 147, 137, …'). Decrementing by 10 from 117 involves generating 'one hundred and seven' which can be difficult for students. Decrementing by 10 from 107 involves bridging the centuple (100).

4. Incrementing flexibly by 10s and 1s

Student may have success incrementing and decrementing by single 10s using settings (materials) such as bundling sticks, but have difficulty with:

a. incrementing with more than one bundle (*multiple units*);

b. switching between incrementing by 10s and incrementing by 1s (*switching units*); or

c. incrementing by 10s and 1s combined (*mixing units*).

Being facile with multiple units, switching units and mixing units is referred to as *incrementing flexibly by 10s and 1s*.

Task Groups 5–7: Bare number tasks

These task groups are presented using **numeral cards**. Because these task groups do not involve settings such as bundling sticks, we refer to them as ***formal arithmetic***.

When presenting these tasks, show the numeral card but do not say the number and do not ask the student to say the number.

- Task Groups 5 and 6 involve single jumps – 10 more and 10 less.
- Task Group 7 involves single jumps – 100 more and 100 less.

For each of Task Groups 5–7, if the student is not successful on the first row, then do not present the second or third rows.

5. Jump of 10 more

These tasks provide insight into whether the student has difficulty in stating the number that is 10 more than a given number (presented on a numeral card).

Look for:

- Counts 10 forwards by ones.
- Confuses this task with the task of jumping forward to the next decuple. For example, incorrectly says 10 more than 44 is 50.

6. Jump of 10 less

These tasks provide insight into whether the student has difficulty in stating the number that is 10 less than a given number (presented on a numeral card).

Look for:

- Attempts to count 10 backwards by ones.
- Confuses this task with the task of jumping backward to the next decuple, for example, incorrectly says 10 less than 44 is 40.
- For the task of 10 less than 306, attempts to make 10 counts backwards by ones from 306 but can't do so because they can't keep track of the number of counts or have difficulty decrementing by 1s through 300.

7. Jump of 100

Task Groups 7 and 8, involving incrementing by 100s, do not correspond to a level on the model. Nevertheless, students' responses to these tasks are of interest and contribute to the portrait of the student's knowledge.

8. Incrementing by 100s on the hundred

This task group involves using a setting of 100-dot squares (a 10×10 array of dots).

When determining the level on the model we do not take this task group into account. Nevertheless, these tasks can provide interesting insights into the students' reasoning, for example:

a. Can the student regard six 100-dot squares alternatively as 600 ones and as six 100s? and
b. Can the student bridge 1000 when incrementing by 100s?

3D. Addition and Subtraction to 100

Assessment Schedule

3D

MATERIALS: TASK CARDS

Student Name:	Interview Date: ....
DoB: .... Age: .... (yrs) .... (mths)	Interviewer: ....

Addition and Subtraction to 100 Model (A&S)

⓪ Emergent addition & subtraction to 100
① Add-up-from/subtract-down-to decuple
② Add-up-to/subtract-down-from decuple – small
③ Add-up-to/subtract-down-from decuple – large

④ Add/subtract across a decuple
⑤ 2-digit addition with regrouping
⑥ 2-digit addition & subtraction with regrouping

Note: For Levels ①–⑥, student has to use facile strategies, that is, not counting by ones.

Formal addition and subtraction

Present each task on a CARD. *Read this please ... What is the answer?*

Generally need to enquire about strategy used.

1. Add/subtract a decuple

1.1) 61 + 30	**1.2)** 87 – 50

2. 2-digit addition/subtraction without regrouping

2.1) 36 + 22	**2.2)** 65 – 13

3. 2-digit addition with regrouping

⑤	**3.1)** 58 + 24	**3.2)** 43 + 19

4. 2-digit subtraction with regrouping

⑥	**4.1)** 51 – 25	**4.2)** 82 – 39

If unsuccessful on Task Groups 3 and 4 → Go back and pose Task Groups 1 and 2 as well.

5. 3-digit addition & subtraction with regrouping

⑥	**5.1)** 386 + 240	**5.2)** 705 – 698
+		

Learning Framework in Number © Wright & Ellemor-Collins, 2018 (Sage)

Higher decade addition and subtraction

Preliminaries

Show a sample DECUPLE LINE (a simple number line with only 10, 20, 30 … 100 marked).

What do you call these numbers? (Tens, whole tens, round numbers, tens, decades …?)

I'm going to turn this card over, and then ask you some questions about decuples.

(Use the name that the student uses for decuples.)

Remove the decuple line. Show the NUMERAL CARD for each task.

6. Decuple after/before a number

① **58** *What's that number?* *What is the decuple after 58?* *What is the decuple before 58?*	**40** *What's that number?* *What is the decuple after 40?* *What is the decuple before 40?*

7. Add-up-from/subtract-down-to a decuple

① **20** *What's that number?* *What's 3 more than 20?*	**36** *What's that number?* *What is the decuple before 36?* *How far is it back to 30?*

8. Add-up-to/subtract-down-from a decuple (small 1–5)

② **46** *What's that number?* *What is the decuple after 46?* *How far is it up to 50?*	**60** *What's that number?* *What is 2 less than 60?*

9. Add-up-to/subtract-down-from a decuple (large 6–9)

③ **53** *What's that number?* *What is the decuple after 53?* *How far is it up to 60?*	**80** *What's that number?* *What is 8 less than 80?*

10. Add/subtract across a decuple

④ **37** *What's that number?* *What is 6 more than 37?*	**63** *What's that number?* *What is 8 less than 63?*

Commentary on Assessment Schedule 3D

The purpose of Assessment Schedule 3D is to determine:

a.   the student's level on the model of Addition and Subtraction to 100;

b.   a portrait of the student's knowledge of this domain.

Task Groups 1–5: Formal addition and subtraction

Tasks are presented on cards as written expressions. Because these task groups do not involve settings such as bundling sticks we refer to them as formal arithmetic. Of interest are the mental computation strategies and reasoning used. (Further reading: Red Book, pp. 99–109.) In general, look for:

* Use of counting-by-ones, or non-counting strategies;
* What number relationships and reasoning are used;
* How flexible and facile any non-counting strategies are; and
* Which non-counting strategies are used: jump, split, or other alternatives.

Examples of the range of possible non-counting strategies are given in the notes on each task group below.

1. Add/subtract a decuple

Commence the assessment at Task Group 3.

Possible strategies:

Count by ones:	counting on from 61 by 30 counts
Split:	$61 + 30$ as $60 + 30 \rightarrow 90 + 1 \rightarrow 91$
Jump (three steps):	$61 + 30$ as $61 + 10 \rightarrow 71 + 10 \rightarrow 81 + 10 \rightarrow 91$
Jump (one step):	$87 - 50$ as $87 - 50 \rightarrow 37$

2. 2-digit addition/subtraction without regrouping

Possible strategies:

Split (right to left):	$36 + 22$ as $6 + 2 = 8$, $30 + 20 = 50 \rightarrow 8 + 50 = 58$
Jump:	$65 - 13$ as $65 - 10 \rightarrow 55 - 3 \rightarrow 52$

3. 2-digit addition with regrouping

Possible strategies:

Count by ones:	starts at 58 and attempts to keep track of 24 counts
Split (left to right):	$58 + 24$ as $50 + 20 = 70$, $8 + 4 = 12$, $\rightarrow 70 + 12 = 82$
Jump:	$43 + 19$ as $43 + 10 \rightarrow 53 + 7 \rightarrow 60 + 2 \rightarrow 62$
Over-jump:	$43 + 19$ as $43 + 20 \rightarrow 63 - 1 \rightarrow 62$
Compensation:	$58 + 24$ as $60 + 24 \rightarrow 84 - 2 \rightarrow 82$
Transformation:	$58 + 24$ as $58^{+2} + 24^{-2} \rightarrow 60 + 22 \rightarrow 82$

4. 2-digit subtraction with regrouping

Possible strategies:

Count by ones:	starts at 51 and attempts to keep track of 25 counts backward
Split-jump:	$51 - 25$ as $50 - 20 \rightarrow 30 + 1 \rightarrow 31 - 5 \rightarrow 26$
Jump:	$82 - 39$ as $82 - 30 \rightarrow 52 - 2 \rightarrow 50 - 7 \rightarrow 43$
Over-jump:	$82 - 39$ as $82 - 40 \rightarrow 42 + 1 \rightarrow 43$
Compensation:	$51 - 25$ as $50 - 25 \rightarrow 25 + 1 \rightarrow 26$

A common error with the **split strategy** is to take smaller from larger in the ones column rather than use regrouping (e.g. for $51 - 25$, take 1 from 5, answer: 34).

5. 3-digit addition & subtraction with regrouping

Tasks 5.1 and 5.2 are relatively difficult mental computations. Nevertheless, students use a range of interesting strategies when attempting to solve these tasks.

Possible strategies:

Split-jump: $386 + 240$ as $300 + 200 \rightarrow 500 + 86 \rightarrow 586 + 20 \rightarrow 606 + 20 \rightarrow \textbf{626}$

Complementary addition: $705 - 698$ as $698 + 2 \rightarrow 700 + 5 \rightarrow 705.\ 2 + 5 = \textbf{7}$

Task Groups 6–10: Higher decade addition and subtraction

These tasks involve a 1-digit number added to or subtracted from a 2-digit number. Developing facile strategies for these kinds of tasks provides a foundation for developing facile jump and split strategies for addition and subtraction involving two 2-digit numbers. Solving these tasks without counting by ones involves knowledge of the partitions of numbers from 2 to 10.

6. Decuple after/before a number

Some students have difficulty working out the decuple before or after a given number, for example, the decuple after 47 is 50 and the decuple before 82 is 80. Students will confuse the decuple after a given number with 10 more than the number, and the decuple before a number with 10 less than the number. For example, students will say incorrectly that the decuple after 34 is 44 and the decuple before 34 is 24. This error can occur, in part, because when the number in question is a decuple, then the decuple after is the same as 10 more and the decuple before is the same as 10 less. For example, the decuple after 60 is 70 which is 10 more than 60 and the decuple before 60 is 50 which is 10 less than 60.

7. Add-up-from/subtract-down-to a decuple

An example of add-up-from a decuple is to work out $40 + 6$. This involves starting with the decuple 40 and adding a 1-digit number to obtain a non-decuple number. An example of subtract-down-to a decuple is to work out the number that, when subtracted from 72, results in the decuple before 72, that is, 70. A necessary part of subtract-down-to is to generate the decuple before the given number (in this case, 70 is the decuple before the given number 72). Thus we can say that subtract-down-to has two steps. The first is to determine that 70 is the decuple below the given number (72) and the second is to figure out how far it is from the given number to the decuple below (70). Thus the answer is 2. The two cases just described are generally easier for students than add-up-to and subtract-down-from (see Task Groups 8 and 9).

8. Add-up-to/subtract-down-from a decuple (small 1–5)

Add-up-to has two steps. The first is to generate the decuple after the given number – in this case, that 60 is the decuple after 57 – and the second is to figure out how far it is from the given number to the decuple – in this case, that 57 to 60 is 3. An example of subtract-down-from a decuple is to work out $40 - 2$ (38). Thus subtract-down-from a decuple involves subtracting a 1-digit number from a decuple.

Both add-up-to and subtract-down-from involve a 1-digit number. In this task group the 1-digit number is in the range 1 to 5. In Task Group 9 the 1-digit number is in the range 6 to 9.

9. Add-up-to/subtract-down-from a decuple (large 6–9)

These tasks are like the tasks in Task Group 8, except the 1-digit number involved is now in the range 6 to 9, not 1 to 5. Students can find these larger jumps more challenging.

10. Add/subtract across a decuple

$37 + 6$ can be solved by first adding up to a decuple ($37 \rightarrow 40$) which involves a jump of 3 and leaves 3. Then add-up-from involves adding 3 to 40, resulting in 43. Thus, adding across a decuple may involve adding-up-to a decuple, then adding-up-from the decuple. Students might use other strategies. For example, using $7 + 6$ is 13; or using $36 + 6$ is 42. Similarly, subtracting across a decuple can involve subtracting-down-to and subtracting-down-from a decuple. $63 - 8$ can be solved by first subtracting 3 to reach 60, and then subtracting the remaining 5 from 60, resulting in 55.

3E. Early Multiplication and Division

Assessment Schedule

3E

MATERIALS: TASK CARDS, COUNTERS, SCREEN

Student Name:	Interview Date: ....
DoB: .... Age: .... (yrs) .... (mths)	Interviewer: ....

Early Multiplication and Division Model (EM&D)

⓪ Emergent grouping
① Perceptual items, counted by ones
② Perceptual items, counted in multiples
③ Figurative items, counted in multiples

④ Abstract groups, items counted in multiples
⑤ Abstract groups, facile repeated addition
⑥ Multiplicative strategies

Tasks with equal groups

1. Forming equal groups: 4 × 5 [COUNTERS]

	1.1) Present a pile of more than 30 counters. *Using these counters, make groups of 5.* Stop the student at **four** groups of 5.	
① ②	**1.2)** Move the excess counters aside. *How many groups of five have you made?* *How many counters did you use altogether?*	

2. Multiplication with equal groups [3-DOT CARDS]

③	**2.1) 4 × 3** Show a 3-dot card. *Each card has three dots.* Place four 3-dot cards face down and screen the four cards. *There are four cards under here. How many dots altogether?*	
③ ③ ②	**2.2)** If unsuccessful → unscreen the four cards. **2.3)** If still unsuccessful → flash one card. **2.4)** If still unsuccessful → turn up all cards.	

If successful with 2.1–2.4, pose extension task:

⑥	**2.5) Extension: 8 × 3** *Can you use that to work out eight 3s?*	

3. Quotition division with equal groups: ? × 4 = 20 [COUNTERS]

④	Present a pile of 20 counters. *There are 20 here.* Screen all the counters. *I am putting them into groups of four* (briefly show one group of four). *How many groups of four can I make?*	

Tasks with arrays

4. Introductory array task [ARRAYS]

Present arrays. *Have you seen these before in class work?* *What do you call them? We can call it an array.*	
Present the 6×4 array. Place a ruler under the first row. *How many dots in the top row?* Move ruler down a row. *How many in the next row?* Move ruler down a row. *How many in the next row?* (If hasn't shown awareness that rows are equal: *What do you notice?*)	
Finally, ask *How many rows?*	

5. Multiplication with an array

③	**5.1) 5 × 3** [5×3 ARRAY] Briefly show then screen the 5×3 array. *Five rows of 3. How many dots altogether?*	
②	**5.2)** If unsuccessful → unscreen top row. **5.3)** If still unsuccessful → unscreen whole array. Observe closely how student counts.	

If successful with 5.1–5.3, pose extension:

⑥	**5.4) Extension: 5 × 6** [5×6 ARRAY] *What about five rows of 6?* Briefly show then screen 5×6 array. *How many dots altogether?*	

6. Quotition division with an array
Briefly display array, then screen all but the top row.
There are 12 spots altogether. Here is one row. How many rows are there altogether?

④	**6.1) 12 ÷ 2** [6×2 ARRAY]	**6.2) 12 ÷ 4** [3×4 ARRAY]

Skip-counting

7. Skip-counting
Count by ___. I'll tell you when to stop.

7.1) by 2s (to 30)
7.2) by 5s (to 50)
7.3) by 3s (to 36)

Bare number tasks

8. Basic facts Ranges 1 and 2 [EXPRESSION CARDS]
Present on card. *Read this please. Can you work this out?*

④	**8.1)** 7 × 2	**8.2)** 10 × 8
	8.3) 5 × 4	**8.4)** 4 × 3

9. Basic facts Range 3 [EXPRESSION CARDS]
Present on card. If student uses counting-based strategies, ask
Can you find the answer without skip-counting? (Assesses levels ⑤ and ⑥.)

④ ⑤ ⑥	**9.1)** 3 × 8	**9.2)** 9 × 4
	9.3) 18 ÷ 3	**9.4)** 40 ÷ 5

10. Tasks using multiplicative relations [TASK CARDS]
Present the complete number sentence(s) on card. *Read this please.*
Present the incomplete number sentence below. *Can you use that, to help you do this?*

⑥	**10.1) Associativity/distributivity** 4 × 13 = 52 8 × 13 = ☐	**10.2) Inverse** 12 × 9 = 108 108 ÷ 9 = ☐
	10.3) Distributivity 10 × 15 = 150 9 × 15 = ☐	**10.4) Distributivity** 5 × 14 = 70 2 × 14 = 28 7 × 14 = ☐

Commentary on Assessment Schedule 3E

The purpose of Assessment Schedule 3E is to determine:

a. the student's level on the model of Early Multiplication and Division;

b. a portrait of the student's knowledge of this domain.

Assessment Schedule 3E consists of 10 task groups arranged in four sections: (a) Tasks with equal groups; (b) Tasks with arrays; (c) Skip-counting; and (d) Bare number tasks. For all tasks, the level of sophistication of the student's strategy is of interest. Observe closely whether fingers are used, whether the equal groups and array settings are used, whether counting is involved, how counting of different units is coordinated, and what multiplicative relations are used.

Task Groups 8 and 9, bare number basic facts, overlap with the tasks on Assessment Schedule 3F. These task groups are used in Schedule 3E to assess whether students have progressed to the highest level on the EM&D model, Level ⑥, Multiplicative strategies. Once students are achieving some success with these task groups, at Levels ④, ⑤, or ⑥, assessment with Schedule 3F becomes appropriate, to develop a more detailed assessment of the student's knowledge and strategies with multiplicative basic facts.

1. Forming equal groups

Look for:

a. Quickly forms successive groups of five;

b. Makes groups which do not have 5 counters;

c. Counts the counters incorrectly; or

d. Cannot state the number of groups or the number of counters.

2.1 Multiplication with equal groups: 4×3

Look for:

a. Quickly answers without counting;

b. Counts by 3s – 'three, six, nine, twelve!' – keeping track of four counts.

c. Counts by ones, keeping track of each set of three counts; or

d. Appears not to have a strategy.

In the case that the student is unsuccessful while the 3-dot cards are screened, look for what degree of unscreening they need before they can succeed:

2.2) the screen is removed (revealing four face-down cards);

2.3) one card is flashed (briefly showing three dots); or

2.4) all cards are turned up (showing four groups of three dots).

2.5 Extension: 8×3

If the student is successful with Task 2.1, 2.2, or 2.3, pose Task 2.5.

Given the higher multiplier of 8×3, the student might use a less sophisticated strategy than she used for 4×3. For example:

a. Solved 4×3 as a known fact, but solves 8×3 by skip counting by 3s;

b. Solved 4×3 by skip-counting by 3s, but solves 8×3 by counting by ones beyond 12, perhaps indicating a lack of facility with the number word sequence by 3s beyond 12.

Alternatively, the student uses a multiplicative strategy; in particular, the student could derive the answer from the previous task (e.g. eight 3s as double four 3s). This task cannot determine Level ⑥, Multiplicative strategies, as it is not a bare number task, however it can provide additional information about the student's strategies.

3. Quotition division with equal groups

Look for:

a. Uses $5 \times 4 = 20$ as a known fact;

b. Otherwise quickly answers without counting;

c. Counts by 4s keeping track of the number of fours;

d. Counts by ones keeping track of the number of fours; or

e. Appears not to have a strategy.

4. Introductory array task

This introductory task has the purpose of determining what the student knows about arrays and, if necessary, to introduce the notions of rows and columns.

Look for:

• Does not show awareness that each row has four dots;

• Misinterprets the final task *How many rows* as determining the number of dots altogether, or the number of dots in each row.

5.1 Multiplication with an array: 5 × 3

Look for:

a. Quickly answers without counting;

b. Counts by 3s – 'three, six, nine, twelve, fifteen';

c. Counts by 5s – 'five, ten, fifteen';

d. Counts by ones, keeping track of each set of three counts; or

e. Appears not to have a strategy.

In the case that the student is unsuccessful while the array is screened, look for what degree of unscreening they need before they can succeed, and observe closely how the student organizes her count:

5.2) the top row is unscreened (revealing one row of three dots);

5.3) the whole array is unscreened (revealing a 5×3 array). The student may count in rows, or count around the perimeter of the array, or use a less organized count.

5.4 Extension: 5 × 6

If the student is successful with Task 5.1 or 5.2, pose Task 5.4.

Given the higher factor in 5 × 6, the student might use a less sophisticated strategy than she used for 5 × 3. For example:

a. Solved 5 × 3 as a known fact, but solves 5 × 6 by repeated addition of 6s;

b. Solved 5 × 3 by skip-counting by 3s, but solves 5 × 6 by counting by ones, keeping track of the number of 6s, perhaps indicating she is not facile with the addition of 6s.

Alternatively, the student uses a multiplicative strategy; in particular, the student could derive the answer from the previous task (e.g. five 6s as double five 3s). As with the extension task 2.5, this extension task cannot determine Level ⑥, Multiplicative strategies, as it is not a bare number task, however it can provide additional information about the student's strategies.

6. Quotition division with an array

Look for:

a. Quickly answers without counting;

b. Relates to a known multiplication fact;

c. Uses skip-counting – for example, for 12 ÷ 2 counts by 2s 'two, four, six, eight, ten, twelve' keeping track of the number of 2s;

d. Uses counting by ones – for example, for 12 ÷ 4, counts 'one, two, three, four; five, six, seven, eight; nine, ten, eleven, twelve' keeping track of each set of four counts; or

e. Appears not to have a strategy.

7. Skip-counting

This task group has the purpose of determining the student's facility with skip-counting by 2s, by 5s and by 3s, each for at least 10 counts. This is important because students' initial strategies for multiplicative tasks frequently involve skip-counting by these units. If a student cannot skip-count then they are unlikely to use skip-counting to solve multiplicative tasks.

Students are typically familiar with skip-counting by 2s and 5s. Students may have much less facility with skip-counting by 3s, especially beyond 12. They may produce alternative patterns, such as '3, 6, 9, 13, 16, 19, 23, 26, 29'; or '3, 6, 9, 12, 14, 16, 18'.

8 and 9. Basic facts Ranges 1 to 3

These tasks involve presenting the student with multiplication and division tasks in standard written form. The tasks are from Ranges 1, 2 and 3. Descriptions of the multiplication ranges, and the Multiplication Ranges Grid, are in Chapter 1.

The Range 3 tasks in Task Group 9 are important for assessing Level ⑤ (Abstract groups with facile repeated addition) and Level ⑥ (Multiplicative strategies) on the model. If the student is using lower-level skip-counting strategies, ask whether she can find the answer without skip-counting.

Look for:

a. Knows the answer immediately;

b. Uses a multiplicative strategy;

c. Uses skip-counting; or

d. Uses counting-by-ones.

10. Tasks using multiplicative relations

When students answer these tasks, enquire about their strategies, which can indicate their awareness of important multiplicative relations. Some of the relations involved, when expressed formally, are referred to as *associativity*, *distributivity* and *inversion*. Students typically use these relations in their reasoning long before they can articulate them formally. Some students will use multiplicative relations in these tasks, though they did not use multiplicative relations in the earlier basic facts tasks in Task Groups 8 and 9. Students can also solve these tasks without using the expected relations.

3F. Multiplicative Basic Facts

Assessment Schedule

3F

MATERIALS: TASK CARDS

Student Name:...   Interview Date:.....................................

DoB:............   Age:................(yrs).............(mths)   Interviewer:...

Multiplicative Basic Facts Model (MBF)

Range	ⓐ Counting-based	ⓑ Mult've strategy	ⓒ Facile mult'n	ⓓ Facile division
1. 2s and 10s	⑴ₐ	⑴ᵦ	⑴ᵧ	⑴𝒹
2. Low × low	⑵ₐ	⑵ᵦ	⑵ᵧ	⑵𝒹
3. Low × high	⑶ₐ	⑶ᵦ	⑶ᵧ	⑶𝒹
4. High × high	⑷ₐ	⑷ᵦ	⑷ᵧ	⑷𝒹
5. Factor > 10	⑸ₐ	⑸ᵦ	⑸ᵧ	⑸𝒹

Present on cards. Assess strategies by enquiring about reasoning, even for known facts.

If student uses counting-based strategies (e.g. finds 2 × 6 by skip-counting by 2 six times), ask *Can you do it without counting?*

1. Range 1: 2s and 10s

① ...	2 × 6	5 × 10	8 × 2	10 × 7
	90 ÷ 10	14 ÷ 7	18 ÷ 2	80 ÷ 8

2. Range 2: Low × low (low 3s, 4s and 5s)

② ...	3 × 4	5 × 3	3 × 3	4 × 5
	15 ÷ 5	16 ÷ 4	25 ÷ 5	12 ÷ 3

Learning Framework in Number © Wright & Ellemor-Collins, 2018 (Sage)

3. Range 3: Low × high (high 3s, 4s and 5s)

③ ...	6 × 3	4 × 7	3 × 9	5 × 7
	21 ÷ 3	32 ÷ 8	30 ÷ 6	45 ÷ 5

4. Range 4: High × high (high 6s, 7s, 8s and 9s)

④ ...	6 × 6	8 × 7	9 × 8	7 × 6
	48 ÷ 8	63 ÷ 9	54 ÷ 6	49 ÷ 7

5. Range 5: Factor > 10

⑤ ...	3 × 12	15 × 7	65 ÷ 5	96 ÷ 4

Commentary on Assessment Schedule 3F

The purpose of Assessment Schedule 3F is to determine:

a. the student's levels on the model of Multiplicative Basic Facts;

b. a portrait of the student's knowledge of this domain.

The model of Multiplicative Basic Facts is distinctive in assigning multiple levels simultaneously: we can determine the student's strategy level, for each of Ranges 1 to 5. The strategy levels are: (a) counting-based; (b) multiplicative strategy; (c) facile multiplication; and (d) facile division. These are described in Chapter 4.

Schedule 3F is a successor to Schedule 3E on Early Multiplication and Division. While a student is assessed on the Early Multiplication and Division model at lower levels – Levels ⓪ to ③, perceptual and figurative counting strategies – there is no need to assess the student on Schedule 3F. Once a student is working at higher levels – Levels ④ to ⑥, reasoning with abstract groups and multiplicative strategies – it becomes appropriate to assess the student on Schedule 3F.

Schedules 3E and 3F overlap in posing basic facts tasks. Schedule 3E includes only eight basic facts tasks. These tasks are used to assess whether the student can reason at the higher levels on the EM&D model – abstract groups and multiplicative strategies. Schedule 3F, by contrast, includes 32 basic facts tasks. These tasks are used to more thoroughly assess the student's knowledge and strategies for both multiplication and division in each of the four ranges of basic facts.

Assessment Schedule 3F consists of five task groups, one for each of the five Multiplication Ranges (see the Multiplication Ranges Grid in Chapter 1).

Range 1	2s and 10s:	Multiples of 2 and multiples of 10
Range 2	Low × low:	Low multiples of 3, 4 and 5
Range 3	Low × high:	High multiples of 3, 4 and 5
Range 4	High × high:	High multiples of 6, 7, 8 and 9
Range 5	Factor > 10:	Products with one factor greater than 10
		Range 5 tasks are beyond the basic facts.

Ranges 1 to 4 are the traditional basic facts of multiplication and division. For each of these ranges, the schedule includes four multiplication and four division tasks. Between them, these eight tasks assess many of the multiplicative combinations in the range, enabling a determination of the student's knowledge and strategy level for each range in the basic facts. For Range 5, the schedule includes two multiplication and two division tasks. These tasks enable an assessment of the kinds of reasoning and facility the student uses for multiplicative tasks beyond the basic facts.

Commence the assessment at Range 1, and progress through each row in turn. Of interest are the mental computation strategies and reasoning used in each task. If a student is limited to counting-based strategies for one range, then there is no need to continue the assessment of the later ranges.

Range 1: 2s and 10s

Range 1 basic facts, involving doubles and multiples of 10, are among the earliest multiples learned, as they are already important combinations for addition.

Look for:

- Which factor is regarded as the multiplier, which the **multiplicand**. For example, is 2 × 6 calculated as double 6, or as six 2s.
- Uses known multiplication fact to solve division task.
- Alternatively, does not recognize relationship of a known multiplication fact to a division task, for example, knows 2 × 9 is 18, but solves 18 ÷ 2 by counting how many 2s make 18.
- Achievement of grounded habituation of all tasks.

Range 2: Low × low

Range 2 basic facts, with factors of only 3, 4 and 5, can be visualized as small arrays. There is limited need or opportunity to use multiplicative strategies with Range 2 multiplication tasks. For example, 3 × 4 is reasonably solved by skip-counting by 3 four times: 'three, six, nine, twelve'. An alternative strategy 'double 3 and double again' can be regarded as multiplicative, however it can be difficult to distinguish the latter strategy from the former strategy in assessment. So, with multiplication tasks, beyond counting-based strategies, the focus is on assessing students' progress with habituation. With division tasks, assess students' use of related multiplication facts.

Range 3: Low × high

Range 3 basic facts, the higher multiples of 3, 4 and 5, are not so readily habituated. Also, students' strategy level may differ for the multiples of 3, the multiples of 4, and the multiples of 5.

For higher multiples of 3 and 4, skip-counting becomes more long-winded, and students' knowledge of skip-counting by 3 or 4 may not extend far enough. For example, 4×7 might be attempted by skip-counting by 4 seven times, but the skip-counting sequence by 4 is slow and uncertain. So, the higher multiples of 3 and 4 are typically the first tasks requiring the development of efficient multiplicative computation strategies. Multiplicative strategies include:

×3 as *Double plus another*	e.g. 6×3 as double $6 + 6 \rightarrow 12 + 6 \rightarrow$ **18**
×4 as *Double-double*	e.g. 4×7 as 7 doubled $\rightarrow$ 14 doubled $\rightarrow$ **28**
Nearby multiple	e.g. 4×7 as five 4s + two 4s $\rightarrow 20 + 8 \rightarrow$ **28**

By contrast, students are typically facile with the sequence by 5s. As a consequence, they may persist longer with using skip-counting strategies for the higher multiples of 5, such as 5×7 and $45 \div 5$. Multiplicative strategies include:

×5 as *Times 10 halved*	e.g. 5×7 as half $(10 \times 7) \rightarrow$ half $(70) \rightarrow$ **35**
Neighbouring multiple	e.g. 5×7 as $5 \times 6 + 5 \rightarrow 30 + 5 \rightarrow$ **35**

For division tasks, assess whether the student relates to known multiplication facts. If not, does the student regard the task as *quotition* or *partition*? For example, for $21 \div 3$, does the student try to find how many 3s make 21 (quotition), or how to divide 21 into three equal parts (partition)?

Range 4: High × high

Range 4 basic facts, with all high factors, include the most demanding basic facts to calculate and learn. For some students, the squares are habituated earlier: for example, 6×6, and $49 \div 7$. For some students the higher multiples of 9 are learned earlier, perhaps because they make a memorable pattern: 45, 54, 63, 72, 81.
Possible multiplicative strategies for multiplication tasks include:

×6 as *Times 5 plus another*	e.g. 7×6 as $7 \times 5 + 7 \rightarrow 35 + 7 \rightarrow$ **42**
×6 as *Times 3 doubled*	e.g. 7×6 as $7 \times 3 \rightarrow 21 \times 2 \rightarrow$ **42**
×8 as *Double-double-double*	e.g. 9×8 as $9 \times 2 \rightarrow 18 \times 2 \rightarrow 36 \times 2 \rightarrow$ **72**
×9 as *10 times minus one time*	e.g. 9×8 as $10 \times 8 - 8 \rightarrow 80 - 8 \rightarrow$ **72**
Nearby multiple	e.g. 8×7 as $8 \times 5 + 8 + 8 \rightarrow 40 + 8 + 8 \rightarrow$ **56**

Note how all these strategies derive from knowledge of Range 1, 2 and 3 basic facts. Assess the student's facility with using these earlier facts. Also note how all these strategies rely on facility with addition and subtraction involving 2-digit numbers. The examples above include the following additions and subtractions:

$$21 + 21; \qquad 80 - 8; \qquad 36 + 36; \qquad 40 + 8 + 8$$

Assess how the student's facility with addition and subtraction affects their success with multiplication and division.
For Range 4 division tasks, using repeated addition is long-winded and demanding. Students may struggle to solve these tasks, unless they can relate the tasks to known multiplication facts. Thus, the division tasks can inform an assessment of students' knowledge of multiplication facts.

Range 5: Factor > 10

Range 5 tasks involve a 2-digit factor. These products are generally not habituated; rather, they require well-organized multiplicative computation strategies, which build on knowledge of all the previous ranges.
Possible multiplicative strategies include:

3×12 as $2 \times 12 + 12 \rightarrow 24 + 12 \rightarrow$ **36**

3×12 as $3 \times 10 + 3 \times 2 \rightarrow 30 + 6 \rightarrow$ **36**

15×7 as $10 \times 7 + 5 \times 7 \rightarrow 70 + 35 \rightarrow$ **105**

$65 \div 5$ as 50 is 10 fives, 15 is 3 fives $\rightarrow 10 + 3 = $ **13** fives

$96 \div 4$ as 96 halved $\rightarrow$ 48 halved $\rightarrow$ **24**

$96 \div 4$ as 100 is 25 fours $\rightarrow$ 96 is **24** fours

4

Models of Learning Progressions

The models of learning progressions constitute one of the three types of pedagogical tools presented in this book. The LFIN incorporates nine models, which set out progressions in number learning in each of the domains. As explained in Chapter 2, these models are used in conjunction with completed assessment schedules, to determine the stage and levels of a student's number knowledge.

The chapter begins with an overview of the set of models, which includes the LFIN Models Chart. Following this overview we present each of the nine models. For each model, we give brief descriptions of the levels or stages, followed by a commentary. The purpose of the commentary is to provide more detailed information about each stage or level, and issues that can arise when assigning a stage or level.

Overview of the set of models

LFIN Models Chart

The LFIN Models Chart presented on the next page is also reproduced in Appendix 2. The Models Chart displays all nine models in summary form. The chart is a major reference for assessment and instruction with the LFIN.

Linking models and domains

Recall the LFIN Chart introduced in Chapter 1 (and also reproduced in Appendix 2). The LFIN Chart indicates how the models are linked with the domains of the LFIN. The three models Forward Number Word Sequence, Backward Number Word Sequence and Numeral Identification are all associated with both Domains 2A and 3A. The lower levels of these three models correspond with Domain 2A, while the higher levels correspond with Domain 3A. Similarly, the model for Structuring Numbers 1 to 20 is associated with both Domains 2B and 3B. Finally, each of the other five models – Stages of Early Arithmetical Learning, Conceptual Place Value, Addition and Subtraction to 100, Early Multiplication and Division and Multiplicative Basic Facts – is associated with one domain only.

Progressions in the models

Each model is characterized by a distinctive form of progression in the learning of number and early arithmetic. The model for Stages of Early Arithmetical Learning (SEAL) involves a progression of conceptual reorganizations in students' early arithmetic. SEAL is the only model described in terms of *stages*. All of the other models are described in terms of *levels*. The reason for this is explained in the commentary for the SEAL model.

For the FNWS and BNWS models, the progression from Level ⓪ to Level ③ relates to the student becoming more fluent with FNWSs and BNWSs in the range up to 10, whereas the progression from Level ③ to Level ⑦ reflects a progression in the range of the sequences up to 10, up to 30, up to 100 and so on. For the Numeral Identification model, the progression from Level ⓪ onward is a progression in the range in which the student can identify numerals, and from Level ④ onward, the model includes progression in writing numerals as well as identifying numerals.

LFIN Models Chart

Models of Learning Progressions

2A–3A   Number Word Sequences

Forward (FNWS)

⓪ Emergent FNWS
① Initial FNWS to 'ten'
② Intermediate FNWS to 'ten'
③ Facile FNWS to 'ten'
④ Facile FNWS to 'thirty'
⑤ Facile FNWS to '100'
⑥ Facile FNWS to '1000'
⑦ Facile FNWS to '10,000'

Backward (BNWS)

⓪ Emergent BNWS
① Initial BNWS to 'ten'
② Intermed. BNWS to 'ten'
③ Facile BNWS to 'ten'
④ Facile BNWS to 'thirty'
⑤ Facile BNWS to '100'
⑥ Facile BNWS to '1000'
⑦ Facile BNWS to '10,000'

2A–3A   Numeral Identification (NID)

⓪ Emergent numeral ID
① Numerals to 10 – Identify
② Numerals to 20 – Identify
③ Numerals to 100 – Identify
④ Numerals to 1000 – ID & write
⑤ Numerals to 10,000 – ID & write
⑥ Numerals to 100,000 – ID & write

2B–3B   Structuring Numbers 1 to 20 (SN20)

⓪ Emergent spatial patterns and finger patterns
① Finger patterns 1–5 and spatial patterns 1–6
② Small doubles and small partitions of 10
③ Five-plus and partitions of 5
④ Facile structuring numbers 1 to 10
⑤ Formal addition (parts ≤ 10)
⑥ Formal addition & subtraction (parts ≤ 10)
⑦ Formal addition & subtraction (whole ≤ 20)

2C   Stages of Early Arithmetical Learning (SEAL)

⓪ Emergent counting
① Perceptual counting
② Figurative counting
③ Initial number sequence – Counting-on and -back
④ Intermediate number sequence – Counting-down-to
⑤ Facile number sequence – Non-count-by-ones strategies

3C   Conceptual Place Value (CPV)

⓪ Emergent inc- & decrementing by 10
① Inc- & decrementing by 10, with materials, in range to 100
② Inc- & decrementing flexibly by 10s and 1s, with materials, in range to 100
③ Inc- & decrementing by 10, without materials, in range to 100
④ Inc- & decrementing by 10, without materials, in range to 1000

3D   Addition & Subtraction to 100 (A&S)

⓪ Emergent addition & subtraction to 100
① Add-up-from/subtract-down-to decuple
② Add-up-to/subtract-down-from decuple – small
③ Add-up-to/subtract-down-from decuple – large
④ Add/subtract across a decuple
⑤ 2-digit addition with regrouping
⑥ 2-digit addition & subtraction with regrouping

3E   Early Multiplication & Division (EM&D)

⓪ Emergent grouping
① Perceptual items, counted by ones
② Perceptual items, counted in multiples
③ Figurative items, counted in multiples
④ Abstract groups, items counted in multiples
⑤ Abstract groups, facile repeated addition
⑥ Multiplicative strategies

3F   Multiplicative Basic Facts (MBF)

Range	(a) Count-based	(b) Mult've strategy	(c) Facile mult'n	(d) Facile div'n
1. 2s and 10s	(1a)	(1b)	(1c)	(1d)
2. Low × low	(2a)	(2b)	(2c)	(2d)
3. Low × high	(3a)	(3b)	(3c)	(3d)
4. High × high	(4a)	(4b)	(4c)	(4d)
5. Factor > 10	(5a)	(5b)	(5c)	(5d)

The model for Structuring Numbers 1 to 20 is more elaborate than the FNWS, BNWS and Numeral Identification models because progression across the levels involves an interweaving of progressions in four dimensions of mathematization – range, setting, complexity and orientation. This is explained in more detail in the commentary for this model. The model for Conceptual Place Value involves an interweaving of progressions in three dimensions – range, setting and complexity.

In the model for Addition and Subtraction to 100, Levels ⓪ to ④ encapsulate progression in the sub-domain of Higher Decade Addition and Subtraction, while Levels ⑤ and ⑥ refer to facility with general additive tasks in the range to 100.

The model for Early Multiplication and Division involves a progression in the sophistication of students' early strategies for multiplicative tasks. This involves a progression in distancing the setting, alongside a progression in unitization, toward advanced multiplicative reasoning with composite units. The Early Multiplication and Division model provides for multiplicative tasks that the SEAL model provides for additive tasks. Both models feature cognitive reorganizations from a numerical composite to an abstract composite unit. Cognitive reorganizations are described below in the commentary on the SEAL model.

Finally, the model for Multiplicative Basic Facts involves a progression through the five Multiplication Ranges, and within each of those ranges, a progression through the development of multiplicative strategies toward facile habituation of basic facts.

Models of learning progressions and commentaries

Below we present the nine models of learning progressions. Following each model is a section of explanatory notes, which we refer to as the commentary. The purpose of the commentary is to provide detailed information about:

- links between levels or stages on the model and task groups on the assessment schedule;
- the progressions of learning that characterize each stage or level;
- the significance of the model in terms of learning and teaching of number.

Model for Stages of Early Arithmetical Learning (SEAL)

Stage ⓪: Emergent counting

Cannot count visible counters. The student either does not know the number words or cannot coordinate the number words with counters.

Stage ①: Perceptual counting

Can count perceived counters but not those in screened (that is concealed) collections. This may involve seeing, hearing or feeling counters.

Stage ②: Figurative counting

Can count the counters in a screened collection but counting typically includes what adults might regard as a redundant activity. For example, when presented with two screened collections, told how many in each collection, and asked how many counters in all, the student will count from 'one' instead of counting-on.

Stage ③: Initial number sequence – Counting-on and -back

To solve addition tasks, the student uses counting-on rather than counting from 'one' (e.g. 5 + 3 as 5, 6, 7, 8 – answer 8), and to solve removed items tasks, the student uses a count-down-from strategy (e.g. 17 – 3 as 16, 15, 14 – answer 14). The student may use a count-up-to strategy to solve missing addend tasks (e.g. 6 + □ = 9 as 6, 7, 8, 9, – answer 3), but the student does not yet use a count-down-to strategy to solve missing subtrahend tasks (e.g. 17 – 14 as 16, 15, 14 – answer 3).

Stage ④: Intermediate number sequence – Counting-down-to

The student counts-down-to to solve missing subtrahend tasks (for example 17 – 14 as 16, 15, 14 – answer 3). The student can choose the more efficient of count-down-from and count-down-to strategies.

Stage ⑤: Facile number sequence – Non-count-by-ones strategies

The student uses a range of what are referred to as non-count-by-ones strategies. These strategies involve procedures other than counting-by-ones but may also involve some counting-by-ones. Thus, in additive and subtractive situations, the child uses strategies such as compensation, using a known result, adding to 10, commutativity, subtraction as the inverse of addition, awareness of the '10' in a teen number.

Commentary on Model for Stages of Early Arithmetical Learning (SEAL)

Blue Book reference: pp. 21–2. The stages are discussed in depth in Chapter 4 (pp. 51–74), with further examples in Chapter 5 (pp. 75–91).

The Stages of Early Arithmetical Learning (SEAL) model resulted from research by Steffe and colleagues into young children's development of counting when solving additive and subtractive tasks (Steffe, Cobb & von Glasersfeld, 1988). The goal of these researchers was to develop a psychological model of the emergence of counting and early arithmetical strategies in young children's solutions of additive and subtractive tasks, where the tasks were based on collections of counters and involved simple arithmetic, typically in the range 1 to 20. The researchers identified in students' solutions, several major cognitive shifts called reorganizations. These reorganizations satisfied several criteria for being labelled as stages, such as involving cognitive reorganization to progress to the subsequent stage. For this reason, the learning progressions are referred to as stages, whereas in the other models, the learning progressions are regarded as involving students' attainment of levels, which by and large do not satisfy the criteria for being regarded as stages.

In this context, we use the term 'counting' to describe strategies that involve coordinating number words and conceptual items, that is, imagined items that are generated in the act of counting. Important to remember is that, in describing students' counting, the reference to an item is a reference to a mental symbol rather than a material object.

We use the term 'counting' in a broader sense than that in which it is typically used. Counting as used here can refer to students' strategies when solving several kinds of tasks. These are described briefly here: counting a collection of objects (e.g. counters), counting to figure out how many altogether in two screened (hidden) collections of counters, and counting to figure out how many counters remain when some counters are removed from a screened collection. Detailed descriptions of these kinds of tasks appear in Assessment Schedule 2C.

Also important is the distinction between, on the one hand, 'counting', and, on the other hand, the act of merely reciting a number word sequence. The latter is the focus of the FNWS and BNWS models (see below). Task groups in Assessment Schedule 2A focus on students' facility with FNWSs and BNWSs, whereas task groups in Assessment Schedule 2C focus on students' use of counting and non-counting strategies to solve additive and subtractive tasks.

The SEAL model encompasses a progression of strategies from emergent counting to non-count-by-ones strategies. All but the last of these involve counting-by-ones strategies. The following descriptions serve to illustrate this progression of strategies. Consider the following task – referred to as an additive task with two screened collections:

> *There are 8 red counters under this screen and 5 blue counters under that screen. How many counters in all?*

Below is a range of solutions to this task. Note that, for Stage 4, there is no description of a solution to the task, because Stage 4 is only evident in students' solutions of subtractive tasks, not additive tasks.

Stage ⑤: Facile number sequence

This student solves the task using a non-count-by-ones strategy such as adding through 10, that is 8 and 2 more are 10, and 10 and 3 more are 13. The student knows what goes with 8 to make 10, referred to as the tens complement of 8. And the student can determine 10 + 3 without counting, using what we call the ten-plus-ones structure of a teen number.

Stage ③: Initial number sequence

This student solves the task by counting-on from 8 and keeping track of 5 counts. The student stops at 13 because she knows that she has made 5 counts, because, for example, she recognizes reaching a pattern for 5 on her fingers. This strategy is referred to as counting-up-from. The student counts up 5 from 8 and answers 13.

Stage ②: Figurative counter

This student solves the task by first saying the number word sequence from 1 to 8, and then keeping track of five further counts from 8 to 13. For this student, saying the number word 8 does not stand for a count. The student 're-presents' the act of counting the 8 screened counters. Only after saying the words from 1 up to 8 does 8 stand for a count. From an adult perspective, the count from 1 to 8 is unnecessary but, from the student's perspective, it is necessary in order for 8 to stand for a count.

Stage ①: Perceptual counter

This student is unable to solve the task. If the teacher then removes the screens, the student can count all of the counters from 1, and answers 13. This student apparently has to see the counters in order to solve the task. Hence this student is referred to as a perceptual counter.

Stage ⓪: Emergent counter

This student, like the Stage ① student, is unable to solve the task. Furthermore, if the teacher removes the screens, the student still cannot solve the task. The student attempts to count the counters but cannot coordinate the number words with the counters or perhaps does not know the number words.

Stages ③ and ④ elaborated

Together, these two stages encompass the four advanced counting-by-ones strategies – counting-up-from, counting-down-from, counting-up-to and counting-down-to. A student who counts-up-from to solve an additive task, and counts-down-from to solve a removed items task, is considered to be Stage 3. The student might also count-up-to to solve missing addend tasks, though this is not necessary to be considered Stage 3. Counting-down-to is distinctive. It is used to solve tasks such as 17 – 14 presented in horizontal written format. Stage ④ students solve this task by counting from 17 down to 14 and keeping track of the counts, that is, three counts. By way of contrast, Stage ③ students will typically attempt to count down 14 counts from 17. Thus while Stage ③ students can count-up-from and count-down-from, and might count-up-to, the count-down-to strategy arises at Stage ④.

We have found the SEAL model to be particularly useful for identifying and understanding the additive and subtractive strategies of pre-numerical students, that is, students who have not reached Stage ③. Stages ⓪, ① and ② are collectively referred to as pre-numerical because at Stage ② and lower – as described above (Stage ②: Figurative counter) – a single number word does not stand for a count. Further, teachers with whom we work continually assess their students to be at any of the stages from Stage ⓪ to Stage ⑤. Thus we find the SEAL model to be very useful for application to both assessment and instruction.

Models for Number Word Sequences	
Forward (FNWS)	**Backward (BNWS)**
Level ⓪: Emergent FNWS	**Level ⓪: Emergent BNWS**
Cannot produce the FNWS from 'one' to 'ten'.	Cannot produce the BNWS from 'ten' to 'one'.
Level ①: Initial FNWS to 'ten'	**Level ①: Initial BNWS to 'ten'**
Can produce the FNWS from 'one' to 'ten'. Cannot produce the number word just after a given number word in that range.	Can produce the BNWS from 'ten' to 'one'. Cannot produce the number word just before a given number word in that range.
Note: Students at Levels ①, ② and ③ may be able to produce FNWS beyond 'ten'.	Note: Students at Levels ①, ② and ③ may be able to produce BNWS beyond 'ten'.
Level ②: Intermediate FNWS to 'ten'	**Level ②: Intermediate BNWS to 'ten'**
Can produce the FNWS from 'one' to 'ten'. Can produce the number word just after a given number word in that range, but drops back to generate a running count when doing so.	Can produce the BNWS from 'ten' to 'one'. Can produce the number word just before a given number word in that range, but drops back to generate a running count when doing so.
Level ③: Facile FNWS to 'ten'	**Level ③: Facile BNWS to 'ten'**
Can produce the FNWS from 'one' to 'ten'. Can produce the number word just after a given number word in that range, without dropping back. Has difficulty producing the number word just after a given number word, for numbers beyond ten.	Can produce the BNWS from 'ten' to 'one'. Can produce the number word just before a given number word in that range, without dropping back. Has difficulty producing the number word just before a given number word, for numbers beyond ten.
Level ④: Facile FNWS to 'thirty'	**Level ④: Facile BNWS to 'thirty'**
In the range to 'thirty', can produce the FNWS, and can produce the number word just after a given number without dropping back.	In the range to 'thirty', can produce the BNWS, and can produce the number word just before a given number without dropping back.
Level ⑤: Facile FNWS to 'one hundred'	**Level ⑤: Facile BNWS to 'one hundred'**
In the range to 'one hundred', can produce any FNWS, and can produce the number word just after a given number without dropping back.	In the range to 'one hundred', can produce any BNWS, and can produce the number word just before a given number without dropping back.
Level ⑥: Facile FNWS to 'one thousand'	**Level ⑥: Facile BNWS to 'one thousand'**
As for Level ⑤, with range extended up to and including 1000.	As for Level ⑤, with range extended up to and including 1000.
Level ⑦: Facile FNWS to 'ten thousand'	**Level ⑦: Facile BNWS to 'ten thousand'**
As for Level ⑤, with range extended up to and including 10,000.	As for Level ⑤, with range extended up to and including 10,000.

Commentary on Model for Forward Number Word Sequences

Blue Book reference: pp. 23–4; Red Book reference: pp. 26–8, 36–7.

Becoming fluent with FNWSs is an important milestone in early number learning. One aspect of this is that learning FNWSs is closely interrelated with, and typically pre-empts, learning BNWSs, learning about numeral sequences and developing counting strategies. Thus becoming facile with FNWSs provides an important basis for all of that interrelated learning.

Levels ⓪ to ③

The model serves to elaborate the earliest learning about FNWSs, that is, in the range up to ten. It is not unusual to find some students in the first year of school who cannot say the number words from one to ten, that is they are Level ⓪. In some cases students can state the sequence from one to beyond ten, but cannot state the number word after a given number, allowing even for dropping back. This constitutes Level ①. Level ② focuses on students' responses that involve dropping back to an earlier number word to find the number word after a given number word. For example, when asked to state the number after six, students might say the FNWS from one: 'one, two, three, four, five, six, seven!' perhaps saying 'seven' twice, with emphasis the second time. Level ③ students are facile with FNWSs in the range one to ten and possibly beyond ten but are not facile to thirty.

Levels ④ to ⑦

After Level ③ the model extends to being facile to thirty (Level ④); to 100 (Level ⑤); to 1000 (Level ⑥); and to 10,000 (Level ⑦). Common errors in these higher ranges include saying 'thirty, forty …' instead of 'thirteen, fourteen …' and omitting repeated-digit numbers (e.g. forty-four, sixty-six). Bridging decuples (e.g. 30, 40, 50), centuples (e.g. 100, 200, 900) and multiples of 1000 (1000, 2000, etc.) and 10,000, can present significant difficulties. These are referred to as hurdles. In most cases the student stops at the number before the hurdle, that is, the student stops at 29, 39, 99, 109, 199, 999, and so on.

Commentary on Model for Backward Number Word Sequences

For simplicity and ease of application the BNWS model has a parallel construction with the FNWS model. In both models, Levels ⓪ to ③ apply to progressively acquiring facility in the range one to ten, with the occurrence or non-occurrence of dropping back being significant. From Level ④ onward the ranges extend to 30, to 100, to 1000 and to 10,000. As to be expected, students' knowledge of and facility with BNWSs typically is one to three levels behind that for FNWSs.

Levels ⓪ to ③

Some students can say the FNWS from one to beyond ten but not the BNWS from ten to one. This corresponds to Level ⓪. Some students can say the BNWS from ten to one but cannot say the number word before a given number, even allowing for dropping back. This corresponds to Level ①. As in the case of FNWSs, students will drop back to generate a number word before a given number word. Thus when asked to state the number before nine, students might say the forward number sequence from one as follows: 'one, two, three, four, five, six, seven, eight, nine; eight!' This corresponds to Level ②. At Level ③ students can say the BNWS from ten to one without difficulty and say the number word before a given number word in the range one to ten without hesitation.

Model for Numeral Identification (NID)

Level ⓪: Emergent numeral identification
Cannot identify some or all of the numerals in the range 0 to 10.

Level ①: Numerals to 10 – Identify
Can identify numerals in the range 0 to 10.

Level ②: Numerals to 20 – Identify
Can identify numerals in the range 0 to 20.

Level ③: Numerals to 100 – Identify
Can identify 1- and 2-digit numerals.

Level ④: Numerals to 1000 – Identify & write
Can identify and write 1-, 2- and 3-digit numerals.

Level ⑤: Numerals to 10,000 – Identify & write
Can identify and write 1-, 2-, 3- and 4-digit numerals.

Level ⑥: Numerals to 100,000 – Identify & write
Can identify and write 1-, 2-, 3-, 4- and 5-digit numerals.

Levels ④ to ⑦

Becoming facile with BNWSs in the range one to thirty involves significant new learning for students and this corresponds with Level ④. Common errors include omitting 'twenty', omitting 'thirteen', and saying the decuples back from ninety ('ninety, eighty, seventy, … twenty') instead of the teens (nineteen, eighteen, …). Thus Level ④ corresponds to students who have moved beyond the troublesome teens and can properly connect BNWSs in the twenties with BNWSs in the teens. Levels ⑤, ⑥ and ⑦ correspond to facility with BNWSs extending to the 100s, 1000s and 10,000s respectively.

Commentary on Model for Numeral Identification

Blue Book reference: p. 24; Red Book reference: pp. 29–30, 35–6.

Students' knowledge of numerals is an important but typically under-emphasized sub-domain of early arithmetical learning. This developing knowledge includes not only identifying numerals but also knowledge of numeral sequences, writing requested numerals and recognizing numerals, that is, being able to select a named numeral from a collection of numerals. As can be seen, the relevant model and task groups on the assessment schedule focus on identification and writing of numerals. Numeral identification tasks can be administered relatively quickly and provide a useful index for the broad development of number knowledge. Note that Levels ①, ② and ③ of the model focus on identification only, whereas from Level ④ onward the criteria include writing numerals as well as identifying numerals. The initial focus on identification only is warranted given that, initially, learning to identify numerals pre-empts learning to write numerals.

Model for Structuring Numbers 1 to 20 (SN20)

Levels ① to ⑦ indicate facile strategies: not counting by ones or using fingers.

Levels ② to ⑦ require facility in the absence of settings.

Level ⓪: Emergent spatial patterns and finger patterns

Not yet at Level ①.

Level ①: Finger patterns 1–5 and spatial patterns 1–6

Can build the finger patterns for numbers 1 to 5, raising fingers simultaneously. Can name the domino patterns for 1 to 6 (pattern flashed for ½ second).

Level ②: Small doubles and small partitions of 10

Facility with small doubles and small partitions of 10.

Level ③: Five-plus and partitions of 5

Beyond Level ②, facility with 5-plus and partitions of 5.

Level ④: Facile structuring numbers 1 to 10

Facility on all combination and partition tasks in the range 1 to 10.

The tasks beyond Level ③ include: big partitions of 10, and partitions of 6 to 9. Addition tasks may be written, but written subtraction is not yet expected.

Level ⑤: Formal addition (parts ≤ 10)

Facility with addition tasks with addends in the range 1 to 10.

The tasks beyond Level ④ include: regular ten-plus tasks, big doubles and written addition tasks which cross over 10, such as $6 + 5$, $9 + 6$, $8 + 7$.

Level ⑥: Formal addition & subtraction (parts ≤ 10)

Facility with addition and subtraction tasks with parts in the range 1 to 10.

The tasks beyond Level ⑤ include: written subtraction tasks with parts < 10, such as $8 - 5$, $14 - 7$, $11 - 4$, $17 - 9$.

Level ⑦: Formal addition & subtraction (whole ≤ 20)

Facility with addition and subtraction tasks with whole in the range 1 to 20.

The tasks beyond Level ⑥ are: partitions of teen numbers, and written addition and subtraction tasks with one part >10, such as $13 + 3$, $11 + 8$, $17 - 15$, $19 - 13$.

Commentary on Model for Structuring Numbers 1 to 20

Red Book reference: pp. 53, 62–7.

This model focuses on students' developing facility with non-counting strategies for addition and subtraction in the range 1 to 20. This facility can be understood as knowledge of the additive structure of numbers in the range

1 to 20: how numbers combine to make larger numbers; and partition into smaller numbers. We think of the learning progression in structuring numbers to 20 as involving four interrelated progressions:

a. a progression in *range*, from smaller numbers to larger numbers;
b. a progression in *complexity*, from key combinations, such as doubles and partitions of 10, through to all combinations;
c. a progression in *orientation*, from addition to subtraction, since subtraction usually takes more time to master; and
d. a progression in *distancing the setting*, from tasks in settings, through to bare number tasks, and formal written tasks.

Learning typically involves a somewhat circuitous route, recursively working through each of these progressions, several times. Constructing a model of this learning progression as a single hierarchy of levels is artificial. We have developed the seven levels of the model to work practically for informing instruction: the levels indicate priorities for instruction, and recognize important milestones. The levels are mainly organized by range. The progressions in complexity, orientation and setting are also involved, as explained further below.

Progression in ranges

In this model, and in the instruction in Structuring Numbers 1 to 20, we organize the progression in range using the scheme of four addition ranges (see Addition Ranges Grid in Chapter 1).

	Range	Examples			
Range 1	Parts ≤ 5	2 + 2	8 − 3	1 + □ = 5	10 − □ = 5
Range 2	Whole ≤ 10	3 + 6	9 − 7	2 + □ = 8	10 − □ = 4
Range 3	Parts ≤ 10	7 + 8	16 − 8	10 + □ = 16	11 − □ = 4
Range 4	Whole ≤ 20	13 + 3	19 − 11	15 + □ = 17	19 − □ = 13

Progression to bare number tasks

From Level ② onward the levels refer to facility with bare numbers, that is, in the absence of settings. Settings such as five- and ten-frame cards and the arithmetic rack are important for instruction in early structuring. In instruction, the purpose of these settings is to support students' development of additive reasoning and knowledge of particular number relationships. Nevertheless, the goal is for students to progress to such knowledge with bare number tasks. When students exhibit such reasoning in the absence of settings their knowledge can be regarded as 'adult-like' and characteristic of formal reasoning. By pitching each of Levels ② to ⑦ at bare number facility, we expect to nest within each level a small instructional progression from settings to bare number. The progression to bare numbers is discussed further in Chapter 6, in explaining the teaching charts.

Level ①

Level ① indicates facility with ascribing number to regular spatial configurations (dice patterns in this case) and building finger patterns, in Range 1. This constitutes important early knowledge of additive structure. Facility with these tasks requires not counting: with the dice patterns, the student associates the number word with the dot pattern without counting the dots; with the finger patterns, the student can build the pattern as a single movement, without counting the fingers. This facility does not involve making combinations or partitions as such, but it is an important precursor. For example, learning the dice pattern for 6 may support learning that 3 and 3 makes 6; while learning the finger pattern for 5 may support learning the pattern for 8 as 5 and 3.

Levels ② and ③

Levels ② and ③ are basically key combinations in Range 1. Level ② does include learning the small partitions of 10, which are formally in Range 2, since the first addend is greater than 5, but these are such an important set of combinations that we promote them early in instruction. The large partitions of 10 are also important, but we find facility with these often lags behind the small partitions significantly, so we leave requiring this accomplishment until Level ④.

Level ④

Level ④, Facile structuring numbers 1 to 10, marks facility with non-counting strategies for all of Range 2, that is, any additive or subtractive task in the range to 10. The progression from Levels ①–③ through to Level ④ can be seen as a progression from the key combinations to all combinations, in the range 1 to 10. It is a significant achievement for students, and underpins all further progress in arithmetic. Facility with formal written tasks is not yet required at this level. Written addition is typically not problematic at this level, but written subtraction may still be problematic.

Level ⑤

Levels ⑤, ⑥ and ⑦ require facility with formal written tasks, hence the term *formal* in the level names. Level ⑤ marks the progression to Range 3, parts ≤ 10. Range 3 introduces tasks involving crossing 10, that is, regrouping. This is the major arithmetic challenge in the range 1 to 20. Facility with these tasks typically requires the development of a range of mental computation strategies, such as adding-through-ten and compensation. There are key combinations in this range which are important in instruction, such as ten-pluses and big doubles, but we do not isolate a level to mark them.

Level ⑥

Level ⑥ continues in Range 3, and marks a progression in orientation, from facility with addition tasks only (Level ⑤), to facility with subtraction as well (Level ⑥). Level ⑥ is the first level to require facility with written subtraction tasks. For many students, subtraction tasks, especially written subtraction tasks, are significantly more challenging than addition tasks.

Level ⑦

Level ⑦ marks the final progression to Range 4. The shift from Range 3 (parts ≤ 10) to Range 4 (whole ≤ 20, one part possibly ≥ 10) does not involve a major increase in arithmetic challenge. For example, 8 + 5 (Range 3) is typically harder than 12 + 5 (Range 4). Nevertheless, there are new tasks to master in Range 4. The final achievement of Level ⑦, a facility with non-counting strategies for all addition and subtraction tasks in the range to 20, is a major accomplishment in a student's school mathematics, worthy of dedicated aspiration, and happy celebration.

Model for Conceptual Place Value (CPV)

Levels ① to ④ indicate facile strategies, that is, not counting by ones or using fingers.

Level ⓪: Emergent incrementing & decrementing by 10

Not yet at Level ①.

Level ①: Incrementing & decrementing by 10, with materials, in range to 100

Facility with incrementing by 10, on and off the decuple, with tasks in a setting of base-ten materials, in the range 1 to 100.

Level ②: Incrementing & decrementing flexibly by 10s and 1s, with materials, in range to 100

Facility with incrementing and decrementing *flexibly by 10s and 1s* (involving multiple units, switching units and mixing units) with tasks in a setting of base-ten materials, in the range 1 to 100.

Level ③: Incrementing & decrementing by 10, without materials, in range to 100

Facility with both incrementing and decrementing by 10, on and off the decuple, *in the absence of settings*, in the range 1 to 100.

Level ④: Incrementing & decrementing by 10, without materials, in range to 1000

Facility with both incrementing and decrementing by 10, on and off the decuple, in the absence of settings, *in the range 1 to 1000*.

Commentary on Model for Conceptual Place Value

Red Book reference: pp. 83–8.

This model refers to students' developing facility to increment and decrement numbers flexibly by 1s, 10s and 100s. The learning progression in CPV involves three main interrelated dimensions of progression:

a.   a progression in range, from the range to 100, to the range to 1000.

b.   a progression in complexity of the increments, from incrementing by 10 on the decuple, to incrementing and decrementing by mixtures of 100s, 10s and 1s;

c.   a progression in distancing the setting, from using base-ten materials such as bundling sticks through to bare numbers.

In learning and instruction these dimensions of progression are intertwined. For the model, we have singled out four levels that mark identifiable milestones in this intertwined learning progression.

Level ⓪

At Level ⓪, students might increment in the range 1 to 100 on the decuple and in a setting of base-ten material, for example, bundling sticks. Thus students might name three bundles of 10 as 30, and then when one bundle is added they answer 40, or when one bundle is subtracted they answer 20. But they cannot yet increment or decrement *off the decuple*. For example, when shown 24 in bundling sticks, and another bundle of 10 is added, they might sub-vocally make 10 counts before answering 34.

Level ①

Levels ① to ③ all mark progressions within the range to 100. Level ① marks the first important progress in complexity, to facility with incrementing and decrementing by 10 off the decuple. Teachers can be surprised to discover that students cannot achieve Level ①, instead adding 10 by counting on by 1s. Note that many students, when asked a sequence of increments by 10 off the decuple, will recognize the pattern emerging, and begin to answer later tasks without counting by 1s. This recognition is good, but it is not sufficient to achieve Level ①. Level ① indicates the student knows *from the first increment* a way to add 10 off the decuple without counting.

Level ②

Level ② continues in the range to 100, and with materials, and indicates a more complete progression in complexity, to managing any kind of increment or decrement involving 10s and 1s. Ways of making increments more complex include incrementing by multiple units, switching units and mixing units. Examples of these complexities are included in Assessment Schedule 3C, Task 4, and described in the notes on instruction in CPV in Chapter 6.

Level ③

Level ③ continues in the range to 100, and indicates progress in distancing the setting, to facility in bare numbers. At this point, we let go of assessing facility with flexible or complex increments and decrements. While such tasks are productive in instruction, they can be cumbersome in assessment and in level descriptions. Instead, for Levels ③ and ④ without materials, simple 10 more and 10 less tasks are sufficient to indicate facility.

Model for Addition and Subtraction to 100 (A&S)

Levels ① to ⑥ indicate facile strategies, that is, not counting by ones or using fingers.

Level ⓪: Emergent addition and subtraction to 100
Not yet at Level ①.

Level ①: Add-up-from/subtract-down-to decuple
Facility with tasks of adding a 1-digit number going up from a decuple (20 + 3), and with the complementary tasks of subtracting a 1-digit number down to a decuple (23 – □ = 20).

Level ②: Add-up-to/subtract-down-from decuple – small
Facility with tasks of adding a small 1-digit number (1–5) to reach a decuple
(46 + □ = 50), and with the complementary tasks of subtracting a small 1-digit number from a decuple (50 – 4).

Level ③: Add-up-to/subtract-down-from decuple – large
Facility with tasks of adding a large 1-digit number (6–9) to reach a decuple
(53 + □ = 60), and with the complementary tasks of subtracting a large 1-digit number from a decuple (60 – 7).

Level ④: Add/subtract across a decuple
Facility with tasks of adding or subtracting a 1-digit number across a decuple (37 + 6, 63 – 8).

Level ⑤: 2-digit addition with regrouping
Facility with written tasks with two 2-digit numbers which involve regrouping (58 + 24, 43 + 19).

Level ⑥: 2-digit addition and subtraction with regrouping
Facility with written addition and written subtraction tasks with two 2-digit numbers, which involve regrouping (51 – 25, 82 – 39).

Level ④

Level ④ indicates progress in extending the range, reaching to 1000. Instruction in this range is likely to include progressions in the complexity of increments, and in distancing the setting, but we find less need to mark these progressions with levels in the model. Indeed, much of the instruction in the range beyond 100 with materials may occur *before* the student achieves facility with formal tasks in the range up to 100.

Note that facility with decrementing may generally lag behind facility with incrementing, but this is usually not a long lag. For simplicity, we include both in each level of the model.

Commentary on Model for Addition and Subtraction to 100

Red Book reference: pp. 109, 120–4.

Domain 3D, Addition and Subtraction to 100, can be regarded as the culmination of the development of additive reasoning in Band 3, that is, Middle Number knowledge. The domain builds on students' developing knowledge of Domain 3B, Structuring Numbers 1 to 20, and Domain 3C, Conceptual Place Value. As well, Domain 3D includes the sub-domain of Higher Decade Addition and Subtraction, involving adding 1-digit numbers to 2-digit numbers, and subtracting 1-digit numbers from 2-digit numbers. This sub-domain, along with Domains 3B and 3C, constitute the three foundations from which mental strategies can develop for multi-digit addition and subtraction.

Level ⓪

Students at Level ⓪ are likely to use strategies that involve counting-by-ones in the 1s place and the 10s place, or perhaps long counts by ones. For example, a student solves 43 + 19 by counting on 19 from 43.

Levels ① to ④

Levels ① to ④ address the sub-domain of Higher Decade Addition and Subtraction. Each level involves facility in a different type of task. Level ① encompasses the two simplest task types: adding from a decuple, for example 'what's 3 more than 20?'; and subtracting to a decuple, for example, 'how far from 23 back to 20?' Levels ② and ③ involve two more difficult task types: adding to a decuple, for example, 'what do I add to 46 to get to the next decuple?'; and subtracting from a decuple, for example, 'what is 60 minus 7?' In the case of Level ②, the jump in question is in the range 1 to 5, referred to as a *small jump*, whereas in the case of Level ③, the jump in question is in the range 6 to 9, referred to as a *large jump*. These tasks essentially involve an extension of knowledge of partitions of 10, to the higher decades.

The tasks at Level ④ involve the most challenging tasks of higher decade addition and subtraction: adding or subtracting *across* a decuple. Solving these task types typically involves solving two sub-tasks of the types described above. Thus adding across a decuple, for example, 'what is 6 more than 37?' might be solved by adding to a decuple followed by adding from a decuple:

$$37 + 3 \rightarrow 40 + 3 \rightarrow 43$$

Likewise, subtracting across a decuple, for example, 'what is 8 less than 63?', might be solved by subtracting to a decuple followed by subtracting from a decuple:

$$63 - 3 \rightarrow 60 - 5 \rightarrow 55$$

Levels ⑤ and ⑥

Finally, Levels ⑤ and ⑥ involve full 2-digit addition and subtraction, including tasks involving regrouping. Note that there are no levels to indicate success with **non-regrouping tasks**: these are not regarded as a significant accomplishment in the learning progression. Level ⑤ indicates facility with any addition task in the range 1 to 100. Level ⑥ indicates facility with subtraction as well as addition. Achieving these levels requires the development of some successful non-counting mental computation strategies, such as jump, split, compensation, and so on. Note that, while instruction to develop these strategies may initially involve use of base-ten materials, the goal is to progress to facility with bare number tasks, so this is what is required in the model levels. Be aware that developing these strategies for subtraction is often more challenging for students, so students who have achieved Level ⑤, addition, but are not yet succeeding with Level ⑥, subtraction, may need significant instructional support, including using base-ten materials, to properly understand the subtraction tasks. As with the final level of the structuring numbers model, the achievement of Level ⑥, a facility with mental strategies for all addition and subtraction tasks in the range to 100, should be regarded as another major accomplishment in a student's school mathematics.

Model for Early Multiplication and Division (EM&D)

Level ⓪: Emergent grouping

Not yet at level ①.

Level ①: Perceptual items, counted by ones

To count items arranged in equal groups, needs visible items, and counts by ones.

Level ②: Perceptual items, counted in multiples

To count items arranged in equal groups, needs visible items, and uses a multiplicative count, such as rhythmic counting, double counting, or skip-counting.

Level ③: Figurative items, counted in multiples

To count items arranged in equal groups, can count screened items, and uses a multiplicative count.

Level ④: Abstract groups, items counted in multiples

Can calculate bare multiplication and division tasks using a multiplicative count, requiring the counting of abstract composite units.

Level ⑤: Abstract groups, facile repeated addition

Can calculate bare multiplication and division tasks using facile repeated addition (or subtraction), which requires counting one factor as an abstract composite unit.

Level ⑥: Multiplicative strategies

Can calculate bare multiplication and division tasks using multiplicative strategies more sophisticated than repeated addition, involving multiplicative reasoning to derive answers from known facts. Such multiplicative reasoning requires coordinating both factors as abstract composite units.

Commentary on Model for Early Multiplication and Division

Blue Book reference: pp. 117–25; Red Book reference: pp. 142–6, 155–62.

This model describes a progression in the sophistication of students' early strategies for solving multiplicative tasks, toward more advanced multiplicative reasoning and strategies. The model is based on research by Steffe (1992b) and Mulligan (1998). The model makes a progression on the dimension of distancing the setting, as students progress from needing perceptual markers for counting, through figurative counting, to computations with bare numbers. The model also incorporates a progression in students' reasoning with composite units.

In Levels ②, ③ and ④ of the model, we observe students' use of distinctive forms of counting which we refer to as *multiplicative counting*. Three forms of multiplicative counting are described:

- *Rhythmic counting* involves counting all the items contained in several equal groups by ones and emphasizing the number word reached after each group is counted. For example, when counting four groups of three: 'one, two, **three**; four, five, **six**; seven, eight, **nine**; ten, eleven, **twelve**'.
- *Double counting* involves counting all the items by ones, in coordination with counting the number of groups by ones: 'One, two, three – **one**; four, five, six – **two**; seven, eight, nine – **three**; ten, eleven, twelve – **four**.'
- *Skip-counting* involves counting by threes (or fours, etc.) when counting all the items contained in several equal groups: 'three, six, nine, **twelve**'.

The model has close links to the SEAL model since, naturally, a student's sophistication in counting in an equal groups task will depend in part on the sophistication of their counting in simple additive tasks. Level ① here requires perceptual counting, SEAL Stage ①. Levels ②, ③ and ④ here require multiplicative counting, which involves SEAL Stage ③. Level ⑤ here requires facile addition and subtraction, SEAL Stage ⑤. Level ⑥ here involves multiplicative reasoning, an important conceptual advance on the facile additive reasoning of SEAL Stage ⑤.

To characterize the levels of the model, we consider students' responses to the following four types of tasks, which are listed in order of conceptual difficulty. The examples are from Assessment Schedule 3E.

Task A	Multiplication with equal groups of visible items.	e.g. **2.4** Four 3-dot cards all visible *How many dots altogether?*
Task B	Multiplication with equal groups of screened items.	e.g. **2.1**, **2.2**, or **2.3** Four 3-dot cards face-down *How many dots altogether?*

| **Task C** | Division with screened items. | e.g. **3**
20 counters screened.
How many groups of four can I make? |
| **Task D** | Bare number tasks in Range 3 to 4 (one factor > 5). | e.g. **9.1, 9.2**
3 × 8   9 × 4 |

⓪ Emergent grouping

The student cannot solve Task A, multiplication with visible items. They may be able to form equal groups, but cannot count up the total.

① Perceptual items, counted by ones

The student can solve Task A, and counts the dots by ones. They cannot solve Task B, multiplication with screened items. They apparently need to see the dots to be able to count them. For example, Beau, Blue Book, p. 121.

② Perceptual items, counted in multiples

The student solves the same task as Level ①, but uses a more advanced strategy. They solve Task A, and count the dots using a multiplicative count, such as rhythmic counting, double counting, or skip-counting, indicating an awareness that the numbers are multiples. They cannot solve Task B, multiplication with screened items – they need to see the dots. For example, Delise, Blue Book, p. 122.

③ Figurative items, counted in multiples

The student solves a more advanced task than Level ②. They can solve Task B, multiplication with screened items. They need to use some form of multiplicative counting to generate the count of equal groups. The student may or may not need perceptual markers for the groups. That is, they may be able to solve a task like 2.1 on the schedule, where the four 3-dot cards are screened, or they may need the cards to be unscreened (though still face down), like Tasks 2.2 or 2.3. For example, Jenna, Blue Book, p. 123.

④ Abstract groups, items counted in multiples

The student solves a more advanced task than Level ③. They can solve Task C, division with screened items, which requires an abstract construction of the groups as units to count. Their calculation involves counting-by-ones to keep track of the total of dots. They may solve Task D, a bare number task, similarly using a multiplicative count-by-ones. For example, Jamal, Blue Book, p. 124, who is asked to imagine sharing 12 cakes, four to each child, and concludes there would be three children, by reasoning: 'one two three four (pause) five six seven eight (pause) nine ten eleven twelve … counting one, two, three fours'.

⑤ Abstract groups, facile repeated addition

The student solves the same tasks as Level ④, using a more advanced strategy. They can solve Task C, division with screened items, and Task D, a bare number task, and their calculation involves facile repeated addition or skip-counting, that is, not counting-by-ones. For example, Jamal, Blue Book, p. 124, who is asked to share 20 counters, putting five in each piggy bank, and concludes he would need four piggy banks, saying: 'Four! – like that was one five, ten, fifteen, twenty'.

⑥ Multiplicative strategies

The student solves the same tasks as Levels ④ and ⑤, using more advanced strategies. They can solve Task C, division with screened counters, and Task D, a bare number task, deriving answers from known basic facts using multiplicative reasoning. For example, Aimee, Blue Book, p. 125.

The distinction of Level ⑥ is the use of more efficient, sophisticated multiplicative strategies than repeated addition or skip-counting. Their reasoning involves the coordination of all numbers involved as abstract composite units. Note that simply using a known fact is not conclusive for Level ⑥: for example, on Task B with four 3-dot cards all screened 'Oh, four 3s is 12' is not considered necessarily Level ⑥. What is distinctive about Level ⑥ is using a known fact to derive the answer for a different fact: for example, reasoning 'four 3s is 12, so eight 3s must be 24'.

The multiplicative reasoning at Level ⑥ is an important development in a student's number learning. However, while a student may use some multiplicative strategies, they may still often use lower level strategies, and not have habituated many basic facts. There is an important body of further learning to establish good strategies and habituation across *all* basic facts of multiplication and division. This is the focus of Domain 3F.

Model for Multiplicative Basic Facts (MBF)

Range	ⓐ Counting-based	ⓑ Mult've strategy	ⓒ Facile mult'n	ⓓ Facile division
1. 2s and 10s	⑴ₐ	⑴ᵦ	⑴ᵪ	⑴ᵤ
2. Low × low	⑵ₐ	⑵ᵦ	⑵ᵪ	⑵ᵤ
3. Low × high	⑶ₐ	⑶ᵦ	⑶ᵪ	⑶ᵤ
4. High × high	⑷ₐ	⑷ᵦ	⑷ᵪ	⑷ᵤ
5. Factor > 10	⑸ₐ	⑸ᵦ	⑸ᵪ	⑸ᵤ

Level ⓐ: Counting-based strategies

Student solves tasks in the given range using counting and skip-counting-based strategies, indicative of levels below Level ⑥ on the model for Early Multiplication and Division.

Level ⓑ: Multiplicative strategy

Student can solve tasks in the given range using efficient multiplicative strategies, deriving facts from known facts, indicative of Level ⑥ on the model for Early Multiplication and Division. Student may not yet use multiplicative strategies spontaneously, but when challenged to think of efficient strategies for given tasks, they can do so.

Level ⓒ: Facile multiplication

Student can answer multiplication tasks in the given range as known facts, with memorized or fluently habituated answers. This level also requires that students can explain their answers using multiplicative reasoning. Students who have merely memorized basic facts without understanding are not regarded as facile.

Level ⓓ: Facile division

Student can answer division tasks in the given range as known facts, as for Level ⓒ. Likewise, this level requires that students can explain their answers using multiplicative reasoning.

Commentary on Model for Multiplicative Basic Facts

This model does not present the learning progression in a single hierarchy of levels. Instead, the model is two-dimensional. The main progression is through the five multiplication ranges, which comprise four ranges of basic facts, and a fifth range beyond basic facts (see Multiplication Ranges Grid in Chapter 1).

	Range	Examples			
Range 1	2s and 10s	2×6	10×4	$10 \times \square = 70$	$18 \div 9$
Range 2	Low × low	3×4	5×5	$3 \times \square = 15$	$20 \div 4$
Range 3	Low × high	4×7	8×3	$5 \times \square = 45$	$24 \div 4$
Range 4	High × high	6×8	7×7	$9 \times \square = 54$	$42 \div 7$
Range 5	Factor > 10	12×4	5×36	$8 \times \square = 176$	$256 \div 4$

Within each range, the model indicates a progression through four levels of increasing knowledge, toward facile automatization of those basic facts:

ⓐ   Counting-based strategies
ⓑ   Multiplicative strategies
ⓒ   Facile multiplication
ⓓ   Facile division

A student can be assessed for a level *within each range*. So, a student can have five levels simultaneously, one for each range. Nevertheless, a less advanced student need not be assessed on higher ranges, while an advanced student who has reached facile division Level ⓓ in Range 4 can be assumed to have reached Level ⓓ in the earlier ranges. Figure 4.1 gives example profiles for these basic facts levels for three different students. The significance of the levels within each range is discussed further below.

Range 1

Level ⑴ᵦ: Multiplicative strategies can be elusive in Range 1. What multiplicative strategies are there for multiplication by 2, or by 10? However, some students clearly recognize that 8×2 and $14 \div 7$ can be solved using knowledge

Profile A: a student beginning to learn basic facts

Range	ⓐ **Counting**	ⓑ **Strategy**	ⓒ × **Facile**	**d̲. ÷ Facile**
1. 2s and 10s			ⓘⓒ	
2. Low × low	②ⓐ			
3. Low × high	③ⓐ			
4. High × high				
5. Factor > 10				

Profile B: a student making progress with basic facts

Range	ⓐ **Counting**	ⓑ **Strategy**	ⓒ × **Facile**	ⓓ ÷ **Facile**
1. 2s and 10s				①ⓓ
2. Low × low			②ⓒ	
3. Low × high		③ⓑ		
4. High × high	④ⓐ			
5. Factor > 10				

Profile C: a student who has developed good facility with basic facts

Range	ⓐ **Counting**	ⓑ **Strategy**	ⓒ × **Facile**	ⓓ ÷ **Facile**
1. 2s and 10s				①ⓓ
2. Low × low				②ⓓ
3. Low × high			③ⓒ	
4. High × high			④ⓒ	
5. Factor > 10		⑤ⓑ		

Figure 4.1   Three example profiles of levels for Multiplicative Basic Facts

of doubles rather than skip-counting, but they are not yet facile in answering the tasks. Such knowledge can be indicated by Level ⓘⓑ.

Level ⓘⓒ: The student now links tasks using the written × symbol, in either orientation (turn-around), to their facile knowledge of doubles and multiples of 10, rather than skip-counting by 2s or 10s. The significant challenge here is facility with the big doubles: 2 × 7, 2 × 8 and 2 × 9.

Level ⓘⓓ: Linking 7 × 2 to double 7 is one development; now linking 14 ÷ 7 with double 7 is a further development. Achieving facility with Range 1 division tasks is an early accomplishment in developing facility with using the ÷ sign.

Range 2

Level ②ⓑ: If a student does not have a Range 2 task, such as 3 × 3, as a known fact, there is little option more sophisticated than skip-counting. However, indications of more efficient, multiplicative thinking can emerge in this range. A student might indicate he is visualizing the 3 × 3 array, and then identify the answer as 9 without counting, but without consistent fluency. A student might solve 3 × 4 via double 6, and 4 × 4 via double 8.

Level ②ⓒ: The student can now answer any Range 2 multiplication task with facility, but is not yet facile on all the Range 2 *division* tasks. This is a common level for students to stop at, but it is important to work for facility with division as well.

Level ②ⓓ: The student has achieved facility on all Range 2 tasks. This is an important accomplishment, as knowledge of the Ranges 1 and 2 basic facts forms the basis for deriving the Ranges 3 and 4 facts.

Range 3

Level ③ⓑ: This is the first range where multiplicative strategies become important. Common strategies include:

×3 as *Double plus another*	e.g. 6 × 3 as double 6 + 6 → 12 + 6 → **18**
×4 as *Double-double*	e.g. 4 × 7 as 7 doubled → 14 doubled → **28**
×5 as *Times 10 halved*	e.g. 5 × 7 as half (10 × 7) → half (70) → **35**
Nearby multiple	e.g. 4 × 7 as five 4s + two 4s → 20 + 8 → **28**
Neighbouring multiple	e.g. 5 × 7 as 5 × 6 + 5 → 30 + 5 → **35**

Note that strategies for high multiples of 3 and 4 typically treat the 3 or 4 as a *multiplier*:

$$3 \times 8 \rightarrow 3 \text{ 8s} \rightarrow \text{double 8 plus 8 ...}$$

whereas strategies for high multiples of 5 often treat the 5 as a *multiplicand*:

$$5 \times 8 \rightarrow 8 \text{ 5s} \rightarrow 4 \text{ 10s...}$$

So, to achieve Level ③ⓑ, students need to develop a practice of turning the task around to suit their strategy. They may not be aware of doing this. Also, of course, a student can use a multiplicative strategy focused on a different factor than 3, 4, or 5: for example, solving

$$4 \times 9 \rightarrow 10 \times 4 - 4 \rightarrow 40 - 4 \rightarrow \mathbf{36}$$

Since skip-counting by 5s is typically easy, students can habitually skip-count to solve high multiples of 5. They may use a partial skip-count:

$$9 \times 5 \rightarrow 5 \text{ 5s is } 25, 30, 35, 40, \mathbf{45}$$

This is better than skip-counting from 5, but it is not regarded as an efficient multiplicative strategy. If students, when challenged, can think of an efficient multiplicative strategy, this is sufficient to achieve Level ③ⓑ.

Level ③ⓒ: To achieve Level ③ⓒ, students need to show facility with *any* task in Range 3. Students may well establish facility with their high multiples of 5, say, but still not with their high multiples of 3 or 4. Also, watch for some common confusions:

$$3 \times 9 = 27 \text{ and } 4 \times 7 = 28$$

$$3 \times 8 = 24 \text{ and } 4 \times 6 = 24 \text{ too}$$

Level ③ⓓ: Facility with Range 3 division tasks is not straightforward. Once the corresponding multiplication basic facts are known, then tasks dividing by 3, 4, or 5 can be readily recognized:

$$24 \div 3 \rightarrow 3 \text{ 8s are } 24 \rightarrow \mathbf{8}$$

$$35 \div 5 \rightarrow 7 \text{ 5s are } 35 \rightarrow \mathbf{7}$$

However, the other orientation is not so easy to recognize:

$$24 \div 8$$

$$35 \div 7$$

These can appear as tasks about those daunting 7s and 8s: how do you solve these tasks other than by adding up 7s or 8s? Students typically need to develop a recognition of all three numbers involved in each of these basic facts – such as 3, 8 and 24 – as a *multiplicative triple*. When any two of these numbers appear together in a task, the third related number is readily recalled.

Range 4

Level ④ⓑ : While there are only 10 distinct factor pairs in Range 4, there is a rich variety of possible multiplicative strategies for the tasks in this range. To achieve Level ④ⓑ, students need to be able to find an efficient multiplicative strategy for any task in the range, not just for, say, the 9s. Possible strategies include:

×6 as *Times 5 plus another*	e.g. 7×6 as $7 \times 5 + 7 \to 35 + 7 \to \mathbf{42}$
×6 as *Times 3 doubled*	e.g. 7×6 as $7 \times 3 \to 21 \times 2 \to \mathbf{42}$
×8 as *Double-double-double*	e.g. 9×8 as $9 \times 2 \to 18 \times 2 \to 36 \times 2 \to \mathbf{72}$
×9 as *10 times minus one time*	e.g. 9×8 as $10 \times 8 - 8 \to 80 - 8 \to \mathbf{72}$
Nearby multiple	e.g. 8×7 as $8 \times 5 + 8 + 8 \to 40 + 8 + 8 \to \mathbf{56}$

These strategies require facility with the basic facts in earlier ranges, and facility with addition and subtraction in the higher decades.

   Levels ④c and ④d: Range 4 completes the basic facts. Facility with all multiplication and division basic facts is a significant and empowering achievement, deserving celebration.

Range 5

Range 5 is beyond the basic facts. Solving these tasks requires well-organized multiplicative computation strategies. Possible strategies include:

3×12 as $2 \times 12 + 12 \to 24 + 12 \to \mathbf{36}$

3×12 as $3 \times 10 + 3 \times 2 \to 30 + 6 \to \mathbf{36}$

$65 \div 5$ as 50 is 10 fives, 15 is 3 fives $\to 10 + 3 = \mathbf{13}$ fives

$96 \div 4$ as 96 halved $\to$ 48 halved $\to \mathbf{24}$

$96 \div 4$ as 100 is 25 fours $\to$ 96 is $\mathbf{24}$ fours

Level ⑤b indicates a student who can solve the tasks with multiplicative strategies, but for whom this is a challenge. Levels ⑤c and ⑤d indicate a level of facility with multiplication and division tasks respectively. Unlike for the previous ranges, habituation of Range 5 tasks is certainly not expected.

5

Approach to Instruction

Chapter 5 describes our approach to instruction. We begin with a summary of our enquiry-based approach, and follow this with lists of nine guiding principles of instruction, and nine characteristics of children's problem solving, which together provide a basis for day-to-day instruction. We then elaborate on our approach to instruction over three sections, working from a broad scale down to a fine scale. The first of these sections sets our broad aim as the development of strong number knowledge, and describes our view of the broad progression of instruction as the ongoing development of mental computation, which in turn lays a basis for **written computation**. The next section recalls the framework of 10 dimensions of mathematization, introduced in Chapter 1, to help articulate the progressions in instruction, both on the broad scale and on the moment-to-moment scale. The final section describes a framework of 26 key elements of intensive one-to-one instruction, which are micro-instructional strategies used in moment-to-moment instruction.

An enquiry-based approach to instruction

Abridged extract from Chapter 2 of the Red Book:

> Wright et al. (2012). *Developing Number Knowledge: Assessment, Teaching, and Intervention with 7–11 Year-Olds.* London: Sage.

For day-to-day instruction, we advocate an intensive, interactive approach based on enquiry, that is, on posing and solving problems. We also advocate involving **rehearsal** to develop facility, that is, to increase familiarity and ease. The enquiry-based approach is summarized below in five points.

Assessment to inform instruction

Careful assessment is fundamental. Assessment involves attentive listening and observation of students solving significant mathematical tasks. Teachers make an initial assessment to develop a profile of students' knowledge across key domains of instruction, and to develop a portrait of students' particular strategies, misconceptions and difficulties. As well, teachers make ongoing assessment throughout the course of instruction. Regular assessment to inform instruction becomes an instructional norm.

Teaching just beyond the cutting edge

Based on their assessment of students' current levels of knowledge, teachers pitch instruction just beyond the cutting edge of students' learning. In this way, tasks are at a level that makes sense to the students in terms of their current knowledge, but typically to solve the task, students need to reorganize their approach, develop new strategies, or gain new insights. This activity beyond the cutting edge leads to learning. Teaching just beyond the cutting edge requires that, in moment-to-moment teaching, teachers closely observe students' activity and finely adjust tasks. Posing challenging tasks becomes an instructional norm.

Solving genuine problems

By pitching instruction just beyond the cutting edge of students' knowledge, students are regularly solving tasks that for them are genuine problems. That is, the tasks are challenging, but nevertheless there is a good likelihood that students will solve them given a supportive learning environment. To work on these tasks, students are given time for sustained, hard thinking. Students gain intrinsic satisfaction from thinking hard and solving genuine problems. Teachers gain satisfaction from making and upholding extended thinking time for students. Sustained thinking becomes an instructional norm.

Reflecting on problem solving

When students respond to tasks, it is students' responsibility to verify their answers. An individual can self-verify by using a less sophisticated strategy to check a solution; for example, by counting with materials to check the answer from a mental strategy. Also, students and teachers can discuss and determine as a group which solutions are justified. Teachers can notate students' solutions, creating a record that supports further reflection and discussion. Sustained reflection on solutions becomes an instructional norm.

Emphasizing mathematical thinking

Through all this instructional activity of assessment, posing tasks, solving tasks and reflecting on solutions, the teacher keeps activity oriented toward mathematization. Emphasizing thinking mathematically becomes an instructional norm.

Instruction: Principles and characteristics

Extract from Chapter 2 of the Green Book:

Wright et al. (2006b). *Teaching Number: Advancing Children's Skills and Strategies* (2nd edn). London: Sage.

We summarize nine guiding principles of instruction, and nine characteristics of children's problem solving. Together these provide a basis for our day-to-day enquiry-based instruction. Chapter 2 of the Green Book describes and illustrates each of these principles and characteristics in detail.

Guiding principles of instruction

1. Enquiry-based/problem-based teaching
2. Initial and ongoing assessment
3. Teaching just beyond the cutting edge
4. Selecting from a bank of teaching procedures
5. Engendering more sophisticated strategies
6. Observing the child and fine-tuning teaching
7. Incorporating symbolizing and notating
8. Encouraging sustained thinking and reflection
9. Aiming for children's intrinsic satisfaction

Characteristics of children's problem solving

1. Cognitive reorganization
2. Anticipation
3. Curtailment
4. Re-presentation
5. Spontaneity, robustness and certitude
6. Asserting autonomy
7. Child engagement
8. Child reflection
9. Enjoying the challenge

Guiding principles of instruction

1. **Enquiry-based/problem-based teaching.** The teaching approach is enquiry based, that is, problem based. Children routinely are engaged in thinking hard to solve numerical problems which, for them, are quite challenging.
2. **Initial and ongoing assessment.** Teaching is informed by an initial, comprehensive assessment and ongoing assessment through teaching. The latter refers to the teacher's informed understanding of the child's current knowledge and problem-solving strategies, and continual revision of this understanding.
3. **Teaching just beyond the cutting edge.** Teaching is focused just beyond the cutting edge of the child's current knowledge.
4. **Selecting from a bank of teaching procedures.** Teachers exercise their professional judgement in selecting from a bank of teaching procedures each of which involves particular instructional settings and tasks, and varying this selection on the basic of ongoing observations.
5. **Engendering more sophisticated strategies.** The teacher understands children's numerical strategies and deliberately engenders the development of more sophisticated strategies.
6. **Observing the child and fine-tuning teaching.** Teaching involves intensive, ongoing observation by the teacher and continual micro-adjusting or fine-tuning of teaching on the basis of his or her observation.
7. **Incorporating symbolizing and notating.** Teaching supports and builds on the child's intuitive, verbally-based strategies and these are used as a basis for the development of written forms of arithmetic which accord with the child's verbally-based strategies.
8. **Encouraging sustained thinking and reflection.** The teacher provides the child with sufficient time to solve a given problem. Consequently, the child is frequently engaged in episodes which involve sustained thinking, reflection on her or his thinking and reflecting on the results of her or his thinking.
9. **Aiming for children's intrinsic satisfaction.** Children gain intrinsic satisfaction from their problem solving, from their realization that they are making progress, and from the verification methods they develop.

Characteristics of children's problem solving

1. **Cognitive reorganization** refers to a qualitative change in the way the child regards the problem and generation of a strategy that was previously unavailable to the child.
2. **Anticipation** refers to a realization by the child prior to using a strategy that the strategy will lead to a particular result.
3. **Curtailment** refers to the mental process of cutting short an aspect of problem-solving activity when, prior to commencing the activity, the child has an awareness of the results of the activity and thus the activity becomes redundant.
4. **Re-presentation** refers to a kind of cognitive activity akin to a mental replay, during which the child presents again to herself or himself, a prior cognitive experience.
5. **Spontaneity, robustness and certitude.** A child's strategy is spontaneous when it arises without assistance. A child's strategy is robust when the child is able to use the strategy over a wide range of similar problems. Certitude refers to a child's assuredness about the correctness of their solution to a problem.
6. **Asserting autonomy.** Children sometimes assert their autonomy as problem-solvers, by imploring the teacher not to help them or to allow them sufficient time to solve a problem independently.
7. **Child engagement.** The ideal situation in the teaching sessions is for the child to apply herself or himself directly and with effort when presented with a problem, and to remain engaged in solving the problem for a relatively extended period if necessary.
8. **Child reflection** refers specifically to a child reflecting on their own prior thinking or the results of their thinking, which can lead to the child becoming explicitly aware of elements of their thinking that were not consciously part of their thinking prior to the period of reflection.
9. **Enjoying the challenge of problem solving.** There are many instances in the individualized teaching sessions where children seem to revel in challenging problem solving, and ultimately they can come to regard problem solving as an intrinsically satisfying and rewarding experience.

The broad progression of instruction in number

Abridged extract from Chapter 2 of the Red Book:

Wright et al. (2012). *Developing Number Knowledge: Assessment, Teaching, and Intervention with 7–11 Year-Olds.* London: Paul Chapman Publishing/Sage.

Aiming for strong number knowledge

Our aim is for students to develop strong integrated mathematical knowledge. We want students to know a lot about numbers. And we want students to be able to solve many kinds of number problems. Developing such mastery of numbers and arithmetic is within the grasp of every student. However, mastery may require years of working on challenging arithmetic problems, in the context of dedicated instruction.

A progression in mental computation and written computation

Many curricula emphasize the teaching of formal place value and formal written **algorithms**. Some curricula include instruction in mental computation, but treat it as a separate topic unrelated to written computation. In accordance with a growing consensus, we have a different approach to teaching computation. We envision the instruction as a single coherent development of computation knowledge, involving both mental and written strategies, as follows.

In most topics, we begin with tasks in settings that are common sense for students. The students solve these tasks using their informal strategies. Informal strategies are typically mental, but also make use of the settings – touching dots, looking at beads, making finger patterns, and so on.

Then we begin to distance the settings from the students, until we can pose tasks involving what are referred to as bare numbers, that is, involving formal written (or sometimes spoken) arithmetic devoid of any context or setting using materials. The purpose of this is for students to solve tasks mentally without using materials, fingers and so on. We also begin to introduce informal notations. Many students develop flexible and efficient mental strategies at this stage, and are able to notate their strategies. With mental strategies as a basis, students can then develop informal written computation strategies, and later, semi-formal and formal written computation methods.

Thus, developing strong mental strategies is considered important in its own right, and is also considered a basis for developing written strategies. Students ultimately develop a range of mental computation strategies, and a range of written strategies, and the development of all of these strategies can be closely interconnected. This broad progression in computation knowledge is central to the instructional approach.

Organizing instruction with domains

The LFIN is organized into domains of number learning. The progression of instruction within each domain, and from early domains to later domains, supports the broad progression in learning described above. The domains in the LFIN address the establishment of strong mental computation, providing a basis for students' development of written computation strategies.

Teachers organize instruction in arithmetic around addressing the domains of the LFIN. Choose two to four domains as a focus for a period of months. Assess students' knowledge of these focus domains. Then teach the focus domains alongside each other, including some time on each focus domain in most lessons. Over time, as instruction in an earlier domain is concluding, a new domain can be introduced. Thus, over the course of ages 5 to 10, the progression from early to late domains is staggered and overlapping.

Note that the domains are not seen as discrete topics. Rather, they are interrelated aspects of a coherent developing knowledge of arithmetic. Teachers seek to develop students' knowledge within each domain, and at the same time, teachers recognize how the domains connect, and are increasingly interwoven. For example, Domain 2B (Early Structuring) includes partitions of 10 in the context of finger patterns. Domain 3B (Structuring Numbers 1 to 20) includes knowledge of the partitions of 10 in a bare number context, such as solving $7 + \square = 10$. Then in Domain 3D (Addition and Subtraction to 100), this knowledge is extended to higher decades, to solve $47 + \square = 50$ for example. Instruction in the domains, and the interconnections between the domains, are described further in Chapter 6.

Dimensions of mathematization in instruction

For students, developing strong number knowledge is primarily a task of advancing in mathematical sophistication. Their learning can be described as the ***progressive mathematization*** of their activity, from context-dependent, verbal, inefficient activity, toward increasingly abstract, formal and well-organized reasoning. It is tempting to reduce instruction to memorizing facts or rehearsing procedures. However, such approaches lose sight of the advancement in mathematical thinking required, from the student's perspective. By contrast, we need an approach to instruction that emphasizes mathematical thinking. Invite students to visualize, notate, extend, invert, organize, generalize and explain – this is the kind of activity that is likely to help them advance mathematically.

Dimensions in the broad progression of instruction

In Chapter 1 we introduced a framework of 10 dimensions of mathematization:

- Extending the range
- Varying the orientation
- Increasing the complexity
- Distancing the setting
- Notating and formalizing
- Refining strategies
- Structuring numbers
- Unitizing
- Decimalizing
- Organizing and generalizing

These dimensions help articulate the progressions we need in instruction, to support students' progressive mathematization. The broad progression of instruction in arithmetic described above, from informal mental computation through to formal written computation, can be understood as a large advance along all 10 of these dimensions. The instruction within each of the domains of the LFIN can be described as an advance along a distinctive subset of the dimensions.

Dimensions in moment-to-moment instruction

In the shorter term, too, day-to-day and moment-to-moment interactive instruction can be directed along these dimensions. In our interactive instruction, we make our aim to encourage students to mathematize their arithmetic activity. We can elicit mathematization by commenting on a dimension in a student's response to a task, or by posing a new task with one dimension ratcheted up a level. The framework of dimensions can serve as a map of these possibilities at any given moment.

To illustrate, consider an example from instruction in Domain 3B, Structuring Numbers 1 to 20. A task has been posed:

8 + 5 with visible ten-frames

and the student has responded successfully. Below are possible follow-up tasks, directed along each of the dimensions. These are illustrated in Figure 5.1.

Extending the range:	28 + 5 with ten-frames
Varying the orientation:	8 + □ = 12 with ten-frames
Increasing the complexity:	8 + 14 with ten-frames
Distancing the setting:	8 + 4 with screened ten-frames
Notating and formalizing:	8 + 4 in standard written form
Refining strategies:	Compare a counting-on strategy (8, 9, 10, 11, 12, 13!) with an add-through-ten strategy (8 + 2 → 10 + 3 → 13!)
Structuring numbers:	How do you know there are 8 dots in that ten-frame?
Unitizing:	How many fives are there in 8 and 5? (One in the eight, and one in the five)
Decimalizing:	Draw attention to regrouping the numbers using 10
Organizing and generalizing:	Make all the pairs of numbers that sum to 13

Thus, drawing on the framework of dimensions, we can devise up to 10 ways to adjust an instructional task, with each adjustment directed toward significant mathematization. Interactive instruction can be conceived as a continual calibration, backwards as well as forwards, along small task adjustments like these, to keep challenging a student at the cutting edge of her reasoning.

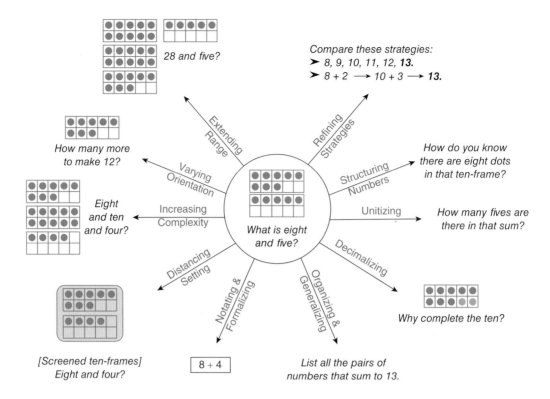

Figure 5.1 Adjusting a task along each of the ten dimensions of mathematization

Features of instruction with dimensions

Working with the dimensions of mathematization can help us understand important features of our instruction. We draw attention to three below.

Instruction works on several dimensions at once

Each domain, each lesson, even each task, involves challenging students on more than one dimension of mathematization. For example, a sequence of tasks in Domain 3B, Structuring Numbers 1 to 20, may involve a progression in the setting dimension from visible to screened ten-frames, a progression in the notation dimension, introducing an informal arrow sentence, and a progression in the orientation dimension, switching from addition to subtraction tasks.

Instruction along the dimensions is intertwined

Progression with one dimension can support instruction in another dimension. In the example above, the use of the ten-frame setting can support the student with organizing the switch of orientation from addition to subtraction. Likewise, the introduction of the informal notation can provide the student with another context for solving the tasks, which supports the distancing of the setting.

Progression along the dimensions is recursive

Students do not progress on the setting dimension in a single shift, from always needing visible materials at age 5 to always working in bare numbers at age 9. Even within a single domain, such as Structuring Numbers 1 to 20, there is not a simple progression from visible ten-frames to bare numbers. Indeed, not even within a single lesson is the progression achieved as a single shift. Instead, the instruction moves back and forth between visible settings, screened settings and bare numbers, over and over again. Likewise with all of the dimensions. We say that the progression along the dimensions is *recursive*: instruction needs to retreat and advance, return and extend, in a circuitous dance.

Key elements of intensive one-to-one instruction

This section draws from original research carried out by the authors: Tran, L. T. & Wright, R. J. (2017). Teachers' professional noticing from a perspective of Key Elements of intensive, one-to-one intervention. In E.O. Schack, M.H. Fisher, & J.A. Wilhelm (Eds.), *Teacher noticing: Bridging and broadening perspectives, contexts, and frameworks* (pp. 481–504). New York: Springer. Reproduced with permission of Springer.

The *key elements* of one-to-one instruction are micro-instructional strategies used by a teacher when interacting with a student in posing and solving an arithmetical task. The Key Elements Chart below presents a framework of 26 key elements, developed from the work of Wright et al. (2006b) and Tran (2016). The framework is organized into four stages of a teacher's working through a task:

- Before posing a task
- Posing a task
- During work on a task
- After a task

Each of the 26 key elements is described briefly below. We believe this set of key elements provides a sound basis for critical observation and analysis of one-to-one instruction.

Before posing a task
1. Stating a goal

The teacher summarizes the student's recent progress and describes what needs to be practised more or what needs to be done next. This has the purpose of motivating and guiding the student toward a goal.

2. Pre-formulating a task

The teacher makes comments or gestures, prior to presenting a task to the student, that have the purpose of orienting the student's thinking to the coming task. Pre-formulating might draw the student's attention to the setting, or direct the student's thinking to related tasks solved earlier in the teaching session or in an earlier session. Pre-formulating also has the purpose of providing a cognitive basis for a new task or sequence of tasks that the teacher intends to pose.

3. Introducing a setting

The teacher introduces a setting new to the student, which might involve letting the student examine the materials, asking the student about features in the materials, and introducing basic terms in the setting. The student gains some orientation to the setting, while the teacher gains insight into how the student might think about tasks presented in the setting.

4. Referring to an unseen setting

Before posing a task, the teacher reminds the student about a setting that has been distanced, that is, a setting that was used at an earlier time in the teaching segment but is currently not being used. Referring to an unseen setting has the purpose of focusing the student's thinking on how the teacher uses the setting when posing a task.

5. Linking settings

The teacher makes a connection between two or more settings. Linking settings has the purpose of enabling the student to regard an arithmetical problem from two or more perspectives. For example, base-ten dot material could be linked to bundling sticks; or a partitioned ten-frame could be linked to an arithmetic rack.

6. Directly demonstrating

When commencing a new sequence of tasks, the teacher demonstrates how a task can be solved, to help explain the tasks.

7. Scaffolding before

Prior to presenting the task or in the act of presenting the task, the teacher provides **scaffolding** support to the student, that is, a partial support that can be gradually withdrawn, such as suggesting the initial part of a strategy, or revealing part of a screened setting.

Posing a task
8. Colour-coding, screening and flashing

These are three techniques for presenting tasks in material settings. *Colour-coding* refers to using different colours for different parts of a setting, to draw attention to the mathematical organization. For example, a teacher uses

Key Elements of Intensive One-to-One Instruction

Stage of task	Key elements

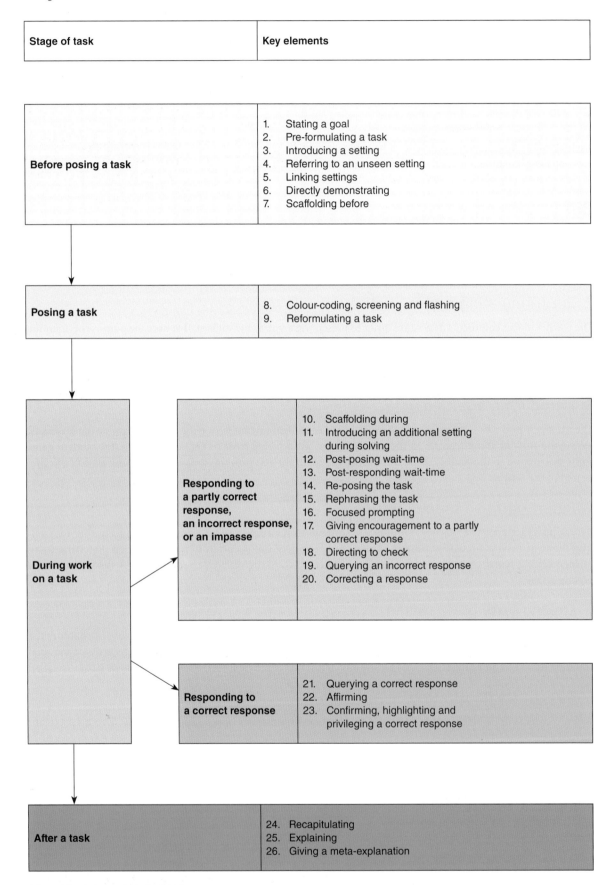

Before posing a task	1. Stating a goal 2. Pre-formulating a task 3. Introducing a setting 4. Referring to an unseen setting 5. Linking settings 6. Directly demonstrating 7. Scaffolding before
Posing a task	8. Colour-coding, screening and flashing 9. Reformulating a task

During work on a task		
	Responding to a partly correct response, an incorrect response, or an impasse	10. Scaffolding during 11. Introducing an additional setting during solving 12. Post-posing wait-time 13. Post-responding wait-time 14. Re-posing the task 15. Rephrasing the task 16. Focused prompting 17. Giving encouragement to a partly correct response 18. Directing to check 19. Querying an incorrect response 20. Correcting a response
	Responding to a correct response	21. Querying a correct response 22. Affirming 23. Confirming, highlighting and privileging a correct response

After a task	24. Recapitulating 25. Explaining 26. Giving a meta-explanation

Adapted from Tran and Wright (2017)

red and blue counters intending to highlight the partitions of 10 counters. *Screening* involves using a screen, such as a sheet of board or card, to conceal the material setting from the student. Screening has the purpose of challenging the student to visualize the setting, or to develop ways to solve the task that are less dependent on the setting. **Flashing** is an extension of screening. Flashing involves displaying the setting briefly, typically for about half a second, and then screening again. These three techniques are connected. A flashed view of a setting is more readily organized by the student when the setting is colour-coded. Also, after a student answers a screened task, the screen can be lifted to allow the student to check the materials, at which point colour-coding helps keep the parts of the task distinct.

9. Reformulating a task

The teacher makes further statements or actions after presenting a task and before the student commences solving the task. Reformulating has the purpose of refreshing the student's memory of some or all of the details of the task or providing the student with additional information about the task which is thought to be useful to the student.

Responding to a partly correct response, an incorrect response, or an impasse

10. Scaffolding during

The teacher provides scaffolding support in response to a student's unsuccessful attempt to solve a task. Thus this refers to scaffolding that is not provided during the presentation of the task.

11. Introducing an additional setting during solving

The teacher changes a material setting during the period when the student is attempting to solve a task, for example, flashing or unscreening the setting. This key element often occurs when the student apparently reaches an impasse, that is, when the teacher perceives that the student is unable to solve the task that they are currently attempting.

12. Post-posing wait-time

After posing a task, the teacher leaves extended uninterrupted time for a student to think about and solve the task.

13. Post-responding wait-time

After the student has responded to a task, the teacher leaves more uninterrupted time. Post-responding wait-time might occur when the student answers correctly, but shows a lack of certitude. In this case, the given wait-time might enable the student to self-check or confirm her answer. As well, post-responding wait-time might occur when the student answers incorrectly. In this case, after the wait-time, the student might be able to self-correct and thus solve the task; if not, the teacher might provide support to the student to solve the task.

14. Re-posing the task

The teacher restates the task to help the student fully understand the task or to remind the student of some details of the task. Re-posing typically arises after the student indicates that they cannot solve the task because they have lost track of some of the details of the task.

15. Rephrasing the task

The teacher expresses the task in an alternative way, with the purpose of making the meaning clearer to the student.

16. Focused prompting

The teacher asks, in an open-ended way, what the student is aware of or thinking of.

17. Giving encouragement to a partly correct response

When a student gives an incomplete or partly correct answer, the teacher confirms the correct part, and then provides scaffolding for the student to continue solving the task. The teacher shows little concern about the student's inadequate response; rather, the teacher's purpose is to keep the student on track and to give her confidence to continue.

18. Directing to check

The teacher asks or allows the student to check their last response.

19. Querying an incorrect response

After the student gives an incorrect answer, the teacher questions the student about her response. Typically, this has the purpose of helping the student to realize the errors in her solution method, so that she might find a way to solve the problem.

20. Correcting a response

After the student gives an incorrect answer, the teacher gives the correct answer directly. This can be useful in particular kinds of tasks such as answer-focused tasks. Overuse of this key element is likely to be counterproductive, particularly if it is used with a range of different kinds of tasks.

Responding to a correct response
21. Querying a correct response

After the student gives a correct answer, the teacher questions the student about her response. Typically, this has the purpose of either gauging the student's certitude or helping to determine the student's solution method.

22. Affirming

The teacher makes comments or gestures to affirm the student's effort or achievement, and to acknowledge that the student's answer is correct.

23. Confirming, highlighting and privileging a correct response

The teacher confirms the student's answer, particularly in cases when the student appears to lack certitude. Further, the teacher may make comments or gestures to highlight the correctness of the student's answer, in order to have the student reflect on their solution and thereby potentially increase their learning.

After a task
24. Recapitulating

The teacher reviews one or more strategies used during solving a task. This usually involves providing a brief summary of how the task was solved. Recapitulating allows the teacher to emphasize crucial features of the student's strategy or solution.

25. Explaining

The teacher engages the student in a conversation, seeking to explain some mathematical aspect of the current tasks.

26. Giving a meta-explanation

The teacher gives an explanation that is more general than the current tasks, addressing the whole topic they are currently learning, or where the learning can progress to.

Problematic teacher behaviours

We also identify nine problematic teacher behaviours. These are actions in one-to-one instruction that tend to be unhelpful in supporting students' learning. The nine problematic teacher behaviours are listed in Figure 5.2, and described briefly below. The list of problematic teacher behaviours complements the framework of key elements in helping teachers to refine their teaching practices. Teachers can develop their awareness to avoid the problematic behaviours, as well as encourage the key elements.

Flagging a task as being difficult

Before posing a task, the teacher advises the student that the coming task will be difficult or tricky. Such statements might make the student think he is not going to be able to solve the task, and this can hinder the student's attempt to solve the task and reduce the student's motivation.

Instructional context	Problematic teacher behaviours
Presenting a task	Flagging a task as being difficult Flagging a task as being easy Simultaneously making more than one request
Providing support	Interrupting the student Rushing or indecent haste Inappropriately re-posing Miscuing Distracting the student
Giving feedback	Giving a 'back-handed' compliment

Figure 5.2   Nine problematic teacher behaviours

Adapted from Tran and Wright (2017)

Flagging a task as being easy

Before posing a task, the teacher advises the student that the coming task will be easy. Such statements are likely to put additional pressure on the student to solve the task. In the case that the student gives an incorrect answer, he might feel uncomfortable about his ability and might lose confidence in solving tasks.

Simultaneously making more than one request

The teacher poses a task, but in doing so asks the student an additional question, which has the effect of confusing the student in that they do not know which request to respond to.

Interrupting the student

The teacher interrupts the student when the student has already commenced solving the task and thus hinders his attempt.

Rushing or indecent haste

The teacher proceeds unnecessarily quickly to providing support to the student. In some cases, the teacher's haste is transferred to the student. In any event, the haste on the part of the teacher is likely to be counterproductive. This key element can be contrasted with the key elements of post-posing wait-time and post-responding wait-time.

Inappropriately re-posing

The teacher unnecessarily re-poses a task, apparently to ensure that the student fully understands the task, but in fact the student has already commenced solving the task.

Miscuing

After the student has commenced working on the task, the teacher provides a hint or a suggested strategy, but the teacher's comment serves to mislead the student.

Distracting the student

The teacher makes a statement which, from the student's perspective, does not seem to logically follow from or connect to the immediately prior discussion.

Giving a 'back-handed' compliment

The teacher compliments a student but in a way that tends to understate or underestimate the student's ability. An example is when, after the student has solved a task, the teacher says with a surprised tone: *That's great. I didn't think you would be able to do that.*

6

Teaching Charts

The teaching charts constitute one of the three types of pedagogical tools presented in this book. The LFIN incorporates 10 teaching charts: one for each of the nine domains, and a second chart for Domain 3B. The teaching charts are the basic reference for instruction in each domain, laying out all the teaching topics and procedures as a matrix of interrelated progressions. The charts serve as maps for developing targeted, responsive instruction through each domain.

The chapter begins with an overview of the 10 teaching charts, and a list of the teaching materials needed for each chart. A second section explains the format of the charts, and a third section describes how to use the charts to plan instruction, and to guide the ongoing progression of instruction. Following these introductory sections are the 10 teaching charts in order. A commentary is included with each chart.

Overview of the set of teaching charts

The 10 teaching charts are listed in Table 6.1. This section provides a brief overview of the instruction in each domain, as described by each teaching chart. The overview includes the topics addressed in the chart, the progression of instruction through the chart, and key instructional settings used in the chart.

Table 6.1 List of 10 teaching charts

Bands	Teaching charts
2. Early Number (EN)	2A. Early Number Words & Numerals
	2B. Early Structuring
	2C. Early Arithmetical Strategies
3. Middle Number (MN)	3A. Number Words & Numerals
	$3B_{10}$. Structuring Numbers 1 to 10
	$3B_{20}$. Structuring Numbers 1 to 20
	3C. Conceptual Place Value
	3D. Addition & Subtraction to 100
	3E. Early Multiplication & Division
	3F. Multiplicative Basic Facts

Early Number
2A. Early Number Words and Numerals

This domain comprises the three interrelated topics of forward number word sequences (FNWSs), backward number word sequences (BNWSs) and numerals. The teaching chart has a section addressing FNWSs and BNWSs, with a progression of ranges from 1 to 10, through to 1 to 100, and a progression from copying sequences through to answering number word before and number word after tasks. The separate section addressing numerals has a similar progression of ranges from 1 to 10, through to 1 to 100, with a variety of teaching procedures involving numeral identification, **numeral recognition** and numeral sequences. Important settings for the numerals instruction include: numeral cards, **digit cards**, **numeral tracks** and **numeral rolls**.

2B. Early Structuring

Early structuring develops knowledge of spatial configurations, such as dice patterns, and especially knowledge of finger patterns, making key combinations and partitions in the range 1 to 10. The first topic in the chart addresses spatial configurations. Remaining topics make a progression in knowledge of finger patterns, including patterns for numbers in the range 1 to 5, patterns for small doubles and near-doubles, five-plus patterns, and partitions of 10 fingers. The instruction also progresses from building patterns with fingers seen and raised sequentially, through to fingers unseen and raised simultaneously. Important settings include spatial configurations cards (e.g. dice patterns for 1 to 6), and fingers.

2C. Early Arithmetical Strategies

This domain focuses on children's developing sophistication in the use of counting strategies to solve counting, additive and subtractive tasks. The focus is on a progression through the stages of the SEAL model, from Stage 0 Emergent, to Stage 1 Perceptual, and Stage 2 Figurative, and on to Stage 3 Initial Number Sequence, which involves the development of the advanced counting-by-ones strategies: counting-up-from, counting-up-to and counting-down-from. Counting-down-to (Stage 4) is not necessarily an important instructional goal at this point because when the student attains Stage 3, the focus of instruction switches to structuring, that is, Domains 2B and 3B become increasingly important. Important settings for teaching Domain 2C include collections of counters and rows of dots (both unscreened and screened).

Middle Number

3A. Number Words and Numerals

The teaching chart has two sections: (I) number word sequences and numeral sequences by 1s and 10s, in the range to 1000 and beyond; and (II) reading and writing numerals, up to 5 digits and beyond. Instruction in sequences begins in the range to 100, extends to 1000, and later across and beyond 1000. Within each range, instruction progresses from using the numeral roll, to verbal and written tasks. Instruction in reading and writing numerals involves digit card and **arrow card** settings.

3B. Structuring Numbers 1 to 20

The instruction laid out for 3B is extensive, and we find it helpful to separate it into two charts: Chart $3B_{10}$ for the sub-domain of Structuring Numbers 1 to 10, and Chart $3B_{20}$ for Structuring Numbers 1 to 20. For Chart $3B_{10}$, instruction is based in the five-frame and ten-frame settings, progressing to verbal and written tasks. Standard five-wise and pair-wise patterns are established and progress to an organized and facile knowledge of all number combinations and partitions in the range 1 to 10. For Chart $3B_{20}$, instruction is based in the arithmetic rack setting. Again, standard five-wise, ten-wise and pair-wise patterns are established. Then instruction develops toward facility with mental strategies for addition and subtraction in the range 1 to 20, that do not involve counting by ones.

3C. Conceptual Place Value (CPV)

This domain involves flexibly incrementing and decrementing numbers by 1s, 10s and 100s. This informal knowledge of 1s, 10s and 100s is foundational in mental strategies for multi-digit computation, and can be distinguished from conventional place value knowledge. Instruction begins in the range to 100, then extends to 1000, and beyond. Instruction makes a progression in increasingly demanding increments and decrements, including multiple units, switching units and mixing units, and also a progression in distancing the setting, from visible through screened settings, to bare number tasks. Important settings include: bundling sticks, **base-ten dot materials** (ten-strips and 100-squares) and arrow cards.

3D. Addition and Subtraction to 100

This domain involves facility with mental computation for addition and subtraction in the range to 100, and beyond. Phases I and II of instruction address the sub-domain of Higher Decade Addition and Subtraction, using a setting of full ten-frame cards and ten-frame cards for 1 to 9, to work on adding and subtracting with a 2-digit number and a 1-digit number. Phases III and IV extend to general 2-digit addition and subtraction, using ten-frame cards again, and progressing to bare number tasks. Notating mental strategies becomes important in instruction, using notations such as the **empty number line**, **drop-down notation**, arrow notation and number sentences.

3E. Early Multiplication and Division

This domain focuses on children's developing sophistication with computation strategies to solve multiplicative tasks. Tasks are posed mostly in the range to 30, in settings of equal groups and arrays. Focus is on the progression through the levels of the Early Multiplication and Division model, learning to count in multiples and progressing from perceptual through figurative to abstract counting. Facility with number word sequences in multiples is developed – that is, skip-counting by 2s, 3s, 4s and 5s – along with familiarity with the first two ranges of multiplication basic facts – the smaller products. The aim is to build on these foundations, to progress from counting in multiples to truly multiplicative strategies, using multiplicative reasoning. Important settings include: counters, *n*-groups, *n*-tiles and small arrays.

3F. Multiplicative Basic Facts

This domain systematically works through the five multiplication ranges, to develop efficient multiplicative strategies for each range, and work toward habituation of all basic facts. Instruction emphasizes the structuring of multiplicative relationships in each family of products, such as how multiples of 4 relate to multiples of 2. Within each family of products, the multiplicative structuring leads to multiplicative strategies, then fluency with strategies leads to habituation. Early instruction in the first two ranges overlaps with the instruction of 3E, cultivating early multiplicative strategies, but with new focus on clarifying strategies, and habituating. Later instruction in the later ranges involves richer development of structuring and strategies, supported by informal notations and discussion. Settings include *n*-tiles, arrays, and multiplication and division fact cards.

LFIN Teaching Kit

The approach to instruction that we advocate includes an elaborated approach to the use of instructional settings. Instruction in each domain uses a few distinct key settings. The materials that constitute these settings are listed in the LFIN Teaching Kit, organized by domain (see below). As well, sketches and descriptions of these instructional settings appear in Appendix 1. Masters for materials in the LFIN Teaching Kit are included on the book's website.

Format of the teaching charts

The teaching charts list topics down the left-hand side. Each topic has a set of teaching procedures, which are listed across each row.

Topics

A topic is a small, important aspect of a domain of knowledge. The topics have evolved to be small enough that a teacher and student can focus their attention on a whole topic in a single episode of teaching, and make progress in a topic over just a few lessons. At the same time, each topic is sufficiently significant, that achieving facility in a topic entails real progress in number knowledge. Each domain has 10 to 20 topics.

Teaching procedures

A teaching procedure describes what a teacher does in any short episode of a lesson. Each cell across a row of a teaching chart represents a teaching procedure, with most topics addressed by three or four procedures. The teaching chart gives the briefest of descriptions of the procedures. The main idea of a procedure is written in italics, often just giving the instructional setting, and further pointers are added in non-italics. We recommend that further information on each procedure is sought through the Green Book, Red Book, video exemplars, or coaching conversations with a knowledgeable instructional leader.

Sections

Charts 2A, 3A and 3E are organized into two separate sections. For example, Chart 2A has Section I on number word sequences by 1s, and Section II on numerals and numeral sequences. These are simply distinct topic areas

LFIN Teaching Kit

2A / 3A	Number Words & Numerals
Numeral cards	A card for each numeral 1, 2, 3 … 100 and beyond.
Digit cards	Five sets of 0–9.
Arrow cards	1–9, 10–90, 100–900, 1000–9000.
Numeral track	Three large 10-flap tracks.
Numeral rolls	Seven different numeral sequences: by ones: 1–120 121–240 971–1030 1071–1130 by tens: 10–1200 4–334 876–1266

2B / 3B	Early Structuring / Structuring Numbers 1 to 20
Dot cards	Dice and pairs patterns for 1–6.
Five frame sets:	
Regular 0–5	6 cards. Black dots.
Partitions of 5	6 cards. Black & orange dots.
Ten-frame sets:	
Regular 0–10	22 cards: 11 five-wise, 11 pair-wise. Black dots.
Partitions of 10	16 cards: 11 five-wise, 5 evens pair-wise. Black & orange dots.
Combinations	36 cards: All combinations of 0–5 with 0–5. Red & blue dots.
Arithmetic rack	
Addition facts	120 cards: 25 (Range 1), 20 (Range 2), 55 (Range 3), 20 (totals).
Subtraction facts	120 cards: 25 (Range 1), 20 (Range 2), 55 (Range 3), 20 (totals).

2C	Early Arithmetical Strategies
Counters	20 of each of two colours (e.g. 20 red and 20 blue).
Counting row	A strip with a single row of 25 dots.

3C / 3D	CPV / Addition & Subtraction to 100
Bundling sticks	About 20 bundles of 10.
Base-ten dot materials	Single strips of 1 to 9 dots, 30 of ten-strips, 14 of 100-squares.
Full ten-frames	12 ten-dot ten-frame cards.

3E / 3F	Early Mult'n & Div'n / Multiplicative Basic Facts
Counters	About 30 (for posing division with equal groups).
N-groups	6 of each of 2-dot, 3-dot, 4-dot, 5-dot and 6-dot cards.
N-tiles	10 of each of 2-tiles, 3-tiles, … 9-tiles.
Small arrays	15 array cards: each of 2–6 × 2–6.
10×10 array	Used in conjunction with an L-cover.
50×35 array	
Multiplication facts	81 cards: 32 (Range 1), 9 (Range 2), 24 (Range 3), 16 (Range 4).
Division facts	81 cards: 32 Range 1, 9 Range 2, 24 Range 3, 16 Range 4.

that are addressed within the one domain, and so they are given separate sections in the one chart. Teaching does not progress from one section to the next; rather, these sections are likely to be addressed side-by-side in the same lessons, depending on the student's needs for work in each topic area.

Phases and ranges

Charts $3B_{20}$ and 3D are organized into a sequence of phases. For example, Chart $3B_{20}$ has Phase I on making and reading numbers 1 to 20, Phase II on adding numbers 1 to 10, and Phase III on adding and subtracting in the range 1 to 20. These phases are addressed broadly in sequence. It has been found that organizing these demanding domains into phases helps to give focus and direction to the instruction. Charts 3C and 3F are organized into a sequence of ranges. These are similar to phases.

Codes

The code for each chart matches the code for the domain: 2A, 2B, 2C, 3A and so on. Domain 3B has two charts, labelled $3B_{10}$ (Structuring 1 to 10) and $3B_{20}$ (Structuring 1 to 20). The code for each topic is written beside the topic, at the left end of the row. The code for any teaching procedure is determined by the grid of chart cells. For example, across row 3A4, the procedure codes are 3A4.1, 3A4.2, 3A4.3 and 3A4.4. This system of codes provides a simple and quick method to reference any cell in the charts.

Green Book references

The Green Book column on the far right of a teaching chart lists Green Book references for the topic and procedures in each row. Sometimes specific Green Book teaching procedures are listed; sometimes a whole Green Book Key Topic is listed. Some of the procedures now used are adaptations or extensions of the way they are described in the Green Book. In general, teaching procedures in the Early Number domains are closely aligned with the Green Book, whereas teaching procedures in the Middle Number domains are closely aligned with the Red Book.

Using the teaching charts

Linking the teaching charts with the models

Each teaching chart describes a broad progression in teaching through a domain. Each model in the LFIN (as described in Chapter 4) describes a broad progression in learning through a domain. While not identical, these progressions are closely aligned. In any domain, the relationship between a sequence of levels on a model and a sequence of teaching topics on a teaching chart is identifiable. For example, consider Domain 3D, Addition and Subtraction to 100. If a student is assessed at Level ④ on the A&S model – add/subtract across a decuple – then the student has probably consolidated knowledge of the topics up through Topic 3D7 on the 3D Teaching Chart – subtracting across a decuple. Similarly, Level ⑤ on the A&S model – addition with regrouping – indicates knowledge of the topics up to Topic 3D12 – addition with regrouping.

Important to realize is that instruction should be closely attuned to the student's current levels of knowledge. Instruction does not simply begin at the top of the teaching chart. Rather, a teacher plans the topics and procedures on the teaching chart corresponding to the student's level on the model. Since the correspondence from model levels to chart topics is not precise, teachers need to use professional judgement when developing a teaching plan, and continue to adjust the plan as teaching proceeds.

Three dimensions of mathematization in the teaching charts

In Chapter 1 we introduced the notion of dimensions of mathematization, and presented a framework of 10 dimensions. Typically, instruction in a domain progresses along at least the following three common dimensions of mathematization:

- extending the range,
- increasing the complexity, and
- distancing the setting.

For example, consider instruction with Teaching Chart 3A, beginning at the first topic: Sequences by 1s in the range to 130. Once a student has had success in the setting of the numeral roll (procedure 3A1.1), instruction can progressively distance the setting by first screening with the ten-lid frame (3A1.2) and later posing verbal tasks with no numeral roll (3A1.3). At the same time, instruction could increase the arithmetic complexity, by posing sequences by 10s with the numeral roll (3A2.1), rather than by 1s. Instruction could also extend the range of numbers, by posing sequences by 1s to 1000 with the numeral roll (3A3.1).

For a second example, consider progressions in Teaching Chart 3B$_{10}$, beginning from partitions of 10 with ten-frames (3B6.1). Distance the setting by posing verbal (3B6.2) and written (3B6.4) partitions of 10. Increase the complexity by posing additions up to 10 (3B8.1 and 3B9.1). Extend the range by posing partitions of other numbers up to 10 (3B7.1) and patterns beyond 10 (3B11.1). A fourth dimension of progression here is organizing and generalizing, by organizing a layout of all partitions of 10 (3A6.3 and 3A6.4).

Instructional progressions through the teaching charts

These three dimensions characterize much of the progression of instruction in the teaching charts. The two examples above are typical of how the three dimensions are laid out in each chart. Distancing the setting is shown in the horizontal progression across a row of procedures. The dimensions of making tasks more complex and extending the range are both shown in vertical progressions down to later topics.

Importantly, it is not imagined that you pursue a topic right through all the procedures in its row before moving down to the next topic – that is, completely distancing the setting before increasing the complexity or extending the range. Rather, instruction can progress along all three dimensions, alternating steps across to later procedures in the same row, and steps down to early procedures in the next few rows. This reveals the main purpose of the teaching charts: by laying out progressions in several dimensions, the charts create a space for flexible, responsive instruction. We might imagine the progression of instruction as a kind of dance across the chart.

Teaching charts and commentaries

The teaching charts are presented in order. Each teaching chart is presented in landscape format and comprises one or two full pages. Following each chart is a commentary which provides extensive details about the teaching procedures outlined in the chart.

EARLY NUMBER   Teaching Chart 2A: Early Number Words and Numerals

SECTION I: NUMBER WORD SEQUENCES BY 1s

	Topic	.1	.2	.3	.4	Green Book
		Copy and say short sequences	Say alternate number words	Say the next number word forwards	Say the number word after	
2A1	FNWS in the range 1 to 10	Copy and say short sequences	Say alternate number words	Say the next number word forwards	Say the number word after	5.1
2A2	BNWS " " "	"		" " " backwards	" " " before	5.1
2A3	FNWS in the range 1 to 20	"		Say the next number word forwards	Say the number word after	5.1
2A4	BNWS " " "	"		" " " backwards	" " " before	5.1
2A5	FNWS in the range 1 to 30	"		Say the next number word forwards	Say the number word after	6.1
2A6	BNWS " " "	"		" " " backwards	" " " before	6.1
2A7	FNWS in the range 1 to 100	"		Say the next number word forwards	Say the number word after	7.1
2A8	BNWS " " "	"		" " " backwards	" " " before	7.1

SECTION II: NUMERALS and NUMERAL SEQUENCES

	Topic	.1	.2	.3	.4	.5	.6	.7	.8	Green Book
		Numeral sequences Fwd only	Numeral sequences Fwd and bwd	Sequencing numerals		Numeral recognition	Numeral identification	Numeral tracks		
2A9	Numerals from 1 to 10	—	Numeral sequences Fwd and bwd	Sequencing numerals	—	Numeral recognition	Numeral identification	Numeral tracks 1 to 5, 1 to 10	—	5.2
2A10	Numerals from 1 to 20	—	"	"	—	"	"	Numeral tracks 11 to 15, 16 to 20 11 to 20	Numeral rolls 1 to 20, 1 to 50	6.2
2A11	Numerals from 1 to 100	—	"	"	Sequencing decuples and off-decuples	"	"	Numeral tracks range 20 to 100	Numeral roll 1 to 100	7.2

NOTE 1: In section II the rows of procedures are not in a clear progression. Instruction in this section involves selecting from the set of procedures, depending on what seems to be useful for the student.

NOTE 2: Transition from Chart 2A to Chart 3A (*Number Words and Numerals*). Section I and section II in this Chart 2A *both* develop toward section I (Number word and numeral sequences by 1s and 10s) in Chart 3A. The numeral identification procedures from section II of Chart 2A continue into section II (Reading and writing numerals) in Chart 3A, which otherwise begins somewhat new work on building, reading and writing 3- and 4-digit numerals.

Learning Framework in Number © Wright & Ellemor-Collins, 2018 (Sage)

Commentary on Teaching Chart 2A

Models: FNWSs (Levels ⓪–⑤), BNWSs (Levels ⓪–⑤) and Numeral Identification (Levels ⓪–④).

Section I: Number Word Sequences by 1s

References: Green Book, Key Topics 5.1 (pp. 74–8), 6.1 (pp. 99–104) and 7.1 (pp. 126–31).

Materials: None.

Chart 2A, Section I refers to saying a number word sequence forwards or backwards by 1s, that is, as compared with, for example, saying sequences by 2s (2, 4, 6, etc.) or by 5s (5, 10, 15, etc.). The broad focus of Section I is to develop facility with FNWSs and BNWSs first in the range to 10, then to 20, to 30 and to 100. All of the teaching procedures are verbally based, that is, they do not involve using settings or materials of any kind. Information from Assessment Schedule 2A including the student's levels on the FNWS and BNWS models is used to determine a starting point for instruction. Instructional activities focus on:

a. copying short sequences – for example, the teacher says a short sequence and then the student says the same sequence;

b. saying alternate number words – for example, the teacher says 'one', the student says 'two', the teacher says 'three' and so on;

c. saying the next number word forwards – the teacher says a short sequence and then the student says the next number word in the sequence; and

d. saying the number word after – the teacher says a number word, for example, 'six' and the student says 'seven'. The key goal of instruction is to extend the range over which these activities are undertaken and to strengthen knowledge within each range (to 10, to 30, etc.). An initial focus on the FNWS can extend to the BNWS, typically in a lower range than for the FNWS.

Section II: Numerals and Numeral Sequences

References: Green Book, Key Topics 5.2 (pp. 78–81), 6.2 (pp. 104–9) and 7.2 (pp. 130–7).

Materials: Numeral track, numeral roll.

Chart 2A, Section II refers mainly to learning to identify numerals and also includes learning to recognize numerals, that is, to select a stated numeral from a pseudorandomly arranged set of numerals (e.g. the numerals from 1 to 10 and the student's task is to point at, say, '7'). Simple activities use numeral cards (columns 1 to 6 on Chart 2A Section II).

- Student reads numeral cards in sequence, forwards and backwards;
- Student puts numeral cards in sequence when cards are presented mixed up;
- Student recognizes a requested numeral among a mixed set of numeral cards; and
- Student identifies numeral cards presented out of order.

We also use two settings that consist of numeral sequences: the *numeral track* and the *numeral roll* (columns 7 and 8). Both these settings allow for any numeral in the sequence to be displayed or screened. We have found simple instructional activities using these settings to be very effective. For all of the work with numeral tracks and numerals rolls, our view is that there is an interplay among three distinct facets of knowledge: FNWSs, BNWSs and numeral identification. Typically, knowledge of FNWSs is more advanced and students' relative facility with FNWS serves to enhance development of the other two facets.

When instruction is focused in the earlier ranges of 1 to 10 and 1 to 30 we strongly advocate the use of the numeral track setting. The numeral track can be used with the sequence from 1 to 10, and then extended to the sequence from 1 to 30. In order to build facility with the FNWS beyond 30, we find it advantageous to commence the numeral track sequence of 30 numerals at say 26 (i.e. 26, 27, … 55), rather than commence with a number at or near a decuple. The numeral track seems to work very well in that initial range up to 50 or 60 and with a sequence of 30 numerals. In that range, the numeral track has the advantage of not overwhelming the student with the extent of the setting, and has an ease of manipulation when screening and unscreening numerals. The numeral roll has a sequence of up to 100 or more numerals and provides for learning over a broader range than the numeral track. The numeral roll is used especially in Teaching Chart 3A, on Number Words and Numerals.

We describe key instructional activities for use with the numeral track or the numeral roll. The basic approach is to start with all of the numerals screened. The teacher unscreens one numeral, then the student names the numeral. The next numeral is unscreened and then the student names that numeral, and so on. We call this activity *See Then Say*. The more challenging alternative is for the student to name the next numeral *before* it is unscreened. We call this activity *Say Then See*. In *See Then Say*, the student can read the numeral that needs to be said next. In *Say Then See*, unscreening the numeral lets the student check the number they just said. These activities can involve going forwards or going backwards. Another activity is to unscreen one numeral and to simply point at a numeral several places away, asking the child to name the numeral and then check by unscreening.

EARLY NUMBER Teaching Chart 2B: Early Structuring

2B

	Topic	Teaching Procedures				Green Book
		.1	.2	.3	.4	
2B1	**Spatial configurations**	*Regular & irregular configurations* Ascribe numerosity	*Regular configurations* Make spatio-motor patterns to match	*Regular configurations* Make auditory patterns to match	—	5.4
2B2	**Finger patterns 1 to 5**	*Fingers seen* Raise fingers sequentially	*Fingers unseen* Raise fingers sequentially	*Fingers seen* Raise fingers simultaneously	*Fingers unseen* Raise fingers simultaneously	5.5.1, 5.5.2 5.5.3, 5.5.4
2B3	**Finger patterns Double 1 to double 5**	—	—	*Fingers seen* Raise fingers simultaneously	*Fingers unseen* Raise fingers simultaneously	5.5.5
2B4	**Finger patterns Fingers keeping track**	*Temporal sequences of sounds* Use fingers to keep track	*Temporal sequences of movements* Use fingers to keep track	—	—	5.5.6, 5.5.7
2B5	**Finger patterns Five-plus patterns for 6 to 10**	*Fingers seen* Make finger patterns	*Fingers unseen* Make finger patterns	—	—	6.5.1
2B6	**Finger patterns Doubles-plus-one patterns**	*Fingers seen* Make doubles-plus-one in two movements	*Fingers unseen* Make doubles-plus-one in two movements	*Fingers seen* Make doubles-plus-one in one movement	*Fingers unseen* Make doubles-plus-one in one movement	6.5.3
2B7	**Finger patterns Partitions of 10 fingers**	*Make partitions of 10*	*Make partitions systematically* In sequence	*Make partitions systematically* In commuted pairs	*Record partitions systematically*	6.5.4

Commentary on Teaching Chart 2B

Model: Structuring Numbers 1 to 20 (Levels ②–⑦).

References: Green Book, Key Topics 5.4 (pp. 83–5), 5.5 (pp. 85–9) and 6.5 (pp. 113–16).

Materials: None.

Chart 2B refers to the role of spatial configurations in the learning of early number. Regular spatial configurations can take the form of dots arranged in patterns that match those occurring on dice or dominoes. **Irregular spatial configurations** can be described as pseudorandom arrangements of dots. While both regular and irregular spatial configurations can be used, we recommend mainly using regular configurations.

A typical instructional activity using either regular or irregular configurations involves flashing the configuration for about a half a second with the student having the task of stating the number of dots on the configuration. We refer to this activity as ascribing number to a flashed configuration. A likely consequence of this activity is that students learn to visualize configurations and this can form a basis for additive reasoning. Thus if a simple additive task such as 4 + 3 is posed verbally, the student might visualize a four-pattern and a three-pattern and reason mentally in terms of the patterns to obtain the answer 7. These activities can be contrasted with early counting activities because the latter typically involve counting-by-ones and regarding numbers as composites whereas activities with regular configurations can involve regarding numbers as units. For this reason we regard these activities as involving early structuring of numbers. Assuming students do learn to reason by imaging these patterns as described above, then learning to visualize configurations is likely to be easier if the student is working with stylized regular configurations. Hence our preference for regular configurations in the form of dice patterns and so on.

A spatio-motor pattern involves the student pointing at, say, four imaginary points in sequence, and with those points making a four-pattern in space, more or less. Matching auditory patterns can involve the student clapping four times in response to seeing a flashed four-pattern.

Chart 2B also includes progressions of instructional activities involving building finger patterns. Virtually all children learn to build finger patterns to symbolize quantities. Becoming facile with finger patterns provides an important basis for early structuring of numbers – in this case seeing how quantities can be regarded in terms of their relationship to five, ten and doubles. Important progressions are from needing to see fingers to not needing to see them, and from raising fingers sequentially to raising fingers simultaneously. Just as numbers on a ten-frame can be in a five-wise or pair-wise arrangement so can finger patterns be built five-wise or pair-wise. Finger patterns for the numbers 6 to 9 are typically much more difficult than patterns for 1 to 5. After learning finger patterns for numbers in the range 1 to 10, students can learn to associate each finger pattern with a partition of 10, for example, the pattern for 8 is associated with the partition 8 & 2. The partitions of 10 can be recorded systematically in the form of a list of expressions (1 + 9, 2 + 8, etc.).

EARLY NUMBER   Teaching Chart 2C: Early Arithmetical Strategies

	Topic	Teaching Procedures				Green Book
		.1	.2	.3	.4	
2C1	**Counting visible items – collections**	*Count items in one collection*	*Establish a collection of given numerosity*	*Count items in two collections*	—	5.3.1, 5.3.2, 5.3.4
2C2	**Counting visible items – rows**	*Count items in a row Forwards and backwards*	*Establish a row of given numerosity*	*Count items of two rows*	—	5.3.3, 5.3.5
2C3	**Temporal sequences**	*Copy and count rhythmic sequences of sounds*	*Copy and count monotonic sequences of sounds*	*Copy and count arrhythmic sequences of sounds*	*Copy and count sequences of movements*	5.6.1, 5.6.2, 5.6.3, 5.6.4
2C4	**Figurative counting – collections**	*Count items in two collections First collection screened*	*Count items in two collections Second collection screened*	*Count items in two collections Both collections screened (Figurative counting)*	—	6.3.1, 6.3.2, 6.3.3
2C5	**Figurative counting – rows**	*Count items in a row First segment screened*	*Count items in a row Second segment screened*	—	—	6.3.4
2C6	**Additive tasks**	*Addition with two screened collections*	*Missing addend with two screened collections*	*Addition with two screened segments of a row*	*Removed items with a collection*	7.3.1, 7.3.2, 7.3.3, 7.3.4

Commentary on Teaching Chart 2C

Model: Stages of Early Arithmetical Learning (Levels ⓪–⑤).

References: Green Book, Key Topics 5.3 (pp. 81–3), 5.6 (pp. 89–91), 6.3 (pp. 109–10) and 7.3 (pp. 137–41).

Materials: Collections of counters in two colours, row of 25 dots, screen.

Chart 2C refers to developing sophistication in the use of counting to solve simple additive and subtractive tasks presented in settings such as collections of counters and rows of dots. Chart 2C is closely linked to the Stages of Early Arithmetical Learning (SEAL) model and Assessment Schedule 2C is used to determine the student's stage on SEAL as well as providing insight into the relative sophistication of the student's counting strategies.

Topics 2C1 to 2C3

The instructional activities in Topics 2C1 to 2C3 are aimed at progressing students who are at the Emergent Stage (Stage ⓪) and include:

a. carefully counting items in one or two collections to establish and consolidate one-to-one coordination of number words and items;

b. establishing a collection of given **numerosity**, for example, counting out 13 counters from a large collection of counters and carefully coordinating number words with items;

c. counting items in a row forwards and backwards, for example, counting along a row of dots from one to six (to eight, to fifteen, etc.) and back from six to one; and

d. activities involving **temporal sequences**.

The last mentioned are regarded as very useful in progressing students to Stage ①, Perceptual counting, and beyond on SEAL. These can take several forms – copying or counting rhythmic, arrhythmic and monotonic sequences of sounds (e.g. hand claps).

Topics 2C4 to 2C6

As students progress to robust perceptual counting, activities can extend to presenting simple additive tasks involving two collections, with first one collection screened (Topics 2C4 and 2C5), and then with both collections screened (Topic 2C6). Observe closely to determine whether students are counting from one or counting on. Additive tasks using a setting of one or two screened collections can be presented in four main orientations. Consider the case of the relation $8 + 5 = 13$:

a. *Addition* task:	'I have 8 under this screen, and 5 under this screen. How many altogether?'
b. *Missing addend* task:	'I have 8 under here. Now I have added some more and there are 13 under here altogether. How many did I add?'
c. *Removed items* task:	'I have 13 under here. Now I take 5 away. How many do I have left?'
d. *Missing subtrahend* task:	'I have 13 under here and now I take away some and there are 8 left. How many did I take away?'

We pose instructional tasks of the kinds described above so that if the student solves the task by counting on or back, the solution involves a count in the range 2 to 5 only. This conforms with our general rule of not posing tasks that are likely to involve students in long counts from one to keep track of their count (see Purple Book, p. 95).

MIDDLE NUMBER　Teaching Chart 3A: Number Words and Numerals

Topic	Teaching Procedures .1	.2	.3	.4	Green Book
SECTION I: NUMBER WORD AND NUMERAL SEQUENCES, BY 1s & 10s					
3A1 Range 1 to 130: by 1s (Forwards and backwards)	*Numeral roll* See then say. Say then see.	*Numeral roll with ten-lid frame* Naming numerals under lids.	*Verbal only* Say NWS starting from X.	*Written* Writing numeral sequences (e.g. ladders).	6.2.5, 6.2.6 7.1
3A2 Range 1 to 130: by 10s ON and OFF the decuple	"	"	"	"	"
3A3 Range 1 to 1000: by 1s	"	"	"	"	"
3A4 Range 1 to 1000: by 10s ON and OFF the decuple	"	"	"	"	"
3A5 Range across 1000: by 1s	"	"	"	"	"
3A6 Range across 1000: by 10s ON and OFF the decuple	"	"	"	"	"
3A7 Range beyond 1000: by 1s	"	"	"	"	"
3A8 Range beyond 1000: by 10s ON and OFF the decuple	"	"	"	"	"
SECTION II: READING AND WRITING NUMERALS					
3A9 Building, reading, writing 3-digit numerals	*Digit cards* No teens or 0s.	*Digit cards* With teens and 0s.	*Digit cards and arrow cards* Linking from digit cards to arrow cards.	*Written* Reading and writing numerals.	8.2
3A10 Building, reading, writing 4-digit numerals & beyond	"	"	"	"	8.2

Commentary on Teaching Chart 3A

Models: FNWSs (Levels ④–⑦), BNWSs (Levels ④–⑦) and Numeral Identification (Levels ③–⑥).

Section I: Number Word and Numeral Sequences, by 1s and 10s

Reference: Red Book, Chapter 3 (pp. 25–49).

Materials: Numeral roll.

Teaching Chart 2A focuses on students' beginning knowledge of the domain of number words and numerals and much of the instruction described there concerns the range 1 to 10 and extending this range to 30 and to 100. The focus of Teaching Chart 3A, Section I is to extend students' facility with FNWSs and BNWSs to at least the 10,000s (i.e. 5-digit numbers).

In Teaching Chart 2A, the numeral track is an important setting. In Teaching Chart 3A, working in the range beyond 100, we advocate using the numeral roll setting. The teaching procedures of *See Then Say, Say Then See* and naming numerals under lids are used with numeral rolls just as they are with numeral tracks – see the descriptions in the Commentary on Teaching Chart 2A, Section II. Numeral rolls typically have a sequence of more than 100 numerals. Thus the numeral roll enables the student to become aware of a large scope of numerals, to see the decades in turn, and to see the consistent pattern of numerals within each decade. We find it beneficial to distinguish by colour, alternate decades (1 to 10 white, 11 to 20 pink, 21 to 30 white, etc.). Initially we use the roll from 1 to say 120. Important modifications include rolls that hurdle higher centuples (200, 300, etc.) and this can be extended to bridging 1000. We also use rolls that progress by 10s rather than 1s. This enables a focus on a much larger range of the numeral sequence (10 times longer). These sequences by 10s are both on the decuple (10, 20, 30, ... 1200) and off the decuple (4, 14, 24, ... 1194), and also have each set of 10 numerals colour-coded.

Written sequences (column 4 in Teaching Chart 3A), can be organized in columns or 'ladders'. The teacher gives the student a starting numeral at the bottom of a column, and the student writes the sequence forwards up the column. Alternatively, the starting numeral is at the top, and the sequence is continued backwards down the column. Sequences can be by 1s, or by 10s. The particular numeral sequence is chosen according to the student's current knowledge.

A similar activity can be useful when students make a common error with BNWSs, for example: 'fifty-three, fifty-two, fifty-one, forty, forty-nine, forty-eight, ...'. The student is asked to write each numeral in turn, in a column, going down. The student is then asked to read the numerals *forwards*, commencing at the bottom of the column. This can bring the student into a sharp awareness of their error with the BNWS.

Section II: Reading and Writing Numerals

Reference: Red Book, Chapter 3.

Materials: Digit cards, arrow cards.

Teaching Chart 3A, Section II focuses on developing strong facility in learning to read and write numerals of up to 5 digits. We find the setting of digit cards to be useful. The teacher places out, say, 3 digits and builds a numeral, for example, 275. The student's task is to name the numeral. The teacher then rearranges the digits to build a new numeral (e.g. 527). The teacher poses tasks such as building a bigger numeral (725) or building a numeral in the 500s bigger than 527. The student's task can be either to build a numeral or to read a numeral built by the teacher.

As the student develops facility with building and reading, the teacher introduces numerals with a '1' in the tens place (e.g. 417) or with a zero (803, 740). We have found that learning to read 3-digit numerals can help students resolve difficulties in reading 2-digit numerals because reading a 3-digit numeral highlights the need to read the digits from left to right when naming a numeral. As students develop facility with reading 3-digit numerals it is relatively easy for them to extend this to reading 4- and 5-digit numerals.

The setting of arrow cards can be used in conjunction with digit cards. This can involve the teacher asking the student to use arrow cards to build a numeral that has been built already with digit cards. Used in this way, the arrow cards can support understanding of place value associated with the individual digits of a numeral built with digit cards. An interesting task is to build, say, 276 and 726 with digit cards, and to then build each numeral with arrow cards.

MIDDLE NUMBER   Teaching Chart 3B₁₀: Structuring Numbers 1 to 10

	Topic	Teaching Procedures .1	.2	.3	.4	Green Book
3B1	**Patterns for 1 to 5** Regular five-frames	*Five-frames shown/flashed* Say the number.	*Five-frames shown/flashed* Say the number, and the complement to 5.	*Set of five-frames* Organize a layout of all five-frames.		-
3B2	**Partitions of 5** Partition five-frames	*Partition five-frames shown/flashed* Say both parts and sum (5).	*Verbal* Given a number, say the complement to 5.	*Set of partition five-frames* Organize a layout of all partition five-frames.	*Written* Write out all partitions of 5.	7.4.1, 7.4.2
3B3	**Patterns for 1 to 10 Five-wise and pair-wise** Regular ten-frames	*Ten-frames shown/flashed* Say the number. 5-w & p-w sets separately. (Later, mixed.)	*Ten-frames shown/flashed* Say the number, and the complement to 10.	*Set of ten-frames* Organize a layout of all ten-frames.		-
3B4	**Small doubles** Ten-frames: doubles	*Ten-frame doubles shown/flashed* Say as a double: '3 and 3 is 6'.	*Verbal* Given a double, say the sum. '3 and 3 is ___.' ...	*Set of ten-frame doubles* Organize a layout of all ten-frame doubles.	*Written* Write out all small doubles.	-
3B5	**Five-plus** Five-wise ten-frames	*Ten-frames shown/flashed* Say top row, bottom row, altogether. '5 and 3 is 8'	*Verbal* Given a five-plus, say the sum. '5 and 3 is ___.' ...		*Written* Write out all five-plus sums.	7.4.3, 7.4.4
3B6	**Partitions of 10** Partition ten-frames	*Partition ten-frames shown/flashed* Say both parts and sum (10). 5-w & p-w sets separately.	*Verbal* Given a number, say the complement to 10.	*Set of partition ten-frames* Organize a layout of all partition ten-frames (& corresponding addition cards).	*Written* Write out all partitions of 10.	7.4.5, 7.4.6
3B7	**Partitions of 6, 7, 8, 9** Blank ten-frames or regular ten-frames	*Ten-frames and counters made/ shown/flashed* Say both parts (and record).	*Verbal* For partitioning 6 (or 7, 8, 9): Given a number, say the complement to 6.		*Written* Write out all partitions of 6 (or 7, 8, 9).	7.5.1, 7.5.2, 7.5.3
3B8	**Range 1 (Parts ≤ 5)** Combination ten-frames Range 1 addition cards	*Combination ten-frames shown/ flashed* Say top, bottom, altogether. (Also, say complement to 10).	*Verbal* Given a Range 1 task, say the sum.	*Set of combination ten-frames* Organize a layout of all combination ten-frames (& corresponding addition cards).	*Written: Range 1 addition cards* Read the card and say the sum.	-
3B9	**Range 2 (Whole ≤ 10)** Range 1 and 2 addition cards		*Verbal* Given a Range 1 or 2 task, say the sum.	*Written: addition cards* Read the card and say the sum. Range 2 addition cards alone. (Later: Ranges 1 and 2 mixed.)	*Written: set of addition cards* Organize a layout of Range 1 and 2 addition cards. Organize by sum, by addend, or both.	-

Commentary on Teaching Chart 3B$_{10}$

Model: Structuring Numbers 1 to 20 (Levels ②–⑦).

References: Red Book, Chapter 4 (pp. 50–76). Green Book, Key Topics 7.4 (pp. 141–5) and 7.5 (pp. 145–8).

Materials: Five-frames, ten-frames.

Structuring numbers 1 to 20 refers to learning to add and subtract in the range 1 to 20 with little or no reliance on counting-by-ones. Rather, students learn to reason from standard arithmetical structures of numbers in the range 1 to 20. This typically involves reasoning using doubles (3 + 3, 7 + 7), 5s and 10s.

Students who have learned to count on and back to solve addition and subtraction problems in the range 1 to 20 and who are relatively facile on early structuring (see Teaching Chart 2B) are ready to learn structuring numbers 1 to 20. This instructional topic begins with a focus on the range 1 to 10 and this is outlined in Teaching Chart 3B$_{10}$.

We can contrast two 2nd-grade students – Grace and Charlie. When their teacher verbally poses an addition or subtraction task in the range 1 to 20 (e.g. 8 + 7, 17 – 9), Grace answers quickly and confidently. Further, Grace warrants her answers with relatively sophisticated reasoning that does not involve long counts by ones:

8 + 7	'I know 8 is made up of 5 and 3, and 7 is made up of 5 and 2. I put the two 5s together, that's 10 and there is one more 5 from the 3 and the 2 so that is 15.'
17 – 9	'I know 8 and 8 are 16 so 9 and 8 are 17, so 17 take away 9 makes 8.'

By contrast, observe Charlie's responses:

8 + 7	He puts his hands under the table and starts counting sub-vocally. He makes 7 counts and stops at 15. He uses his fingers to keep track of his count and so he stops at 15 because he knows he has raised 7 fingers.
17 – 9	He attempts to count back 9 from 17, using his fingers under the table. But he makes an error with backward counting and so answers 7 rather than 8.

So the question is: What instructional programme would advance Charlie from his world of counting on or back by ones, to Grace's world of profound knowledge of the additive structure (i.e. addition and subtraction) of numbers in the range 1 to 20.

Charlie's instruction has to progress along four dimensions of mathematizing:

a.   a progression in *complexity*, from key combinations and partitions to all combinations and partitions;
b.   a progression in *range*, from Range 1 through to Range 4;
c.   a progression in *orientation*, from addition to subtraction;
d.   a progression in *setting*, from structured settings to bare numbers.

We explain each of these progressions below.

The progression in complexity involves first learning key combinations and partitions, and then progressing to learn all other combinations and partitions. Key combinations involve doubles, 5s or 10s only, whereas other combinations also involve other calculations. There are seven key combinations and partitions in structuring numbers to 20:

- Partitions of 5:   5 + 0, 4 + 1, 3 + 2, 2 + 3, 1 + 4, 0 + 5
- Five-pluses: 5 + 1, 5 + 2, 5 + 3, 5 + 4, 5 + 5
- Partitions of 10:   10 + 0, 9 + 1, 8 + 2, … 1 + 9, 0 + 10
- Ten-pluses: 10 + 1, 10 + 2, … 10 + 10
- Small doubles: 1 + 1, 2 + 2, 3 + 3, 4 + 4, 5 + 5
- Big doubles: 6 + 6, 7 + 7, 8 + 8, 9 + 9, 10 + 10
- Partitions of 20:   20 + 0, 19 + 1, 18 + 2, … 2 + 18, 1 + 19, 0 + 20

Key combinations and partitions are important because they become building blocks for the other additions and subtractions in the range 1 to 20. For example, if a student has sound knowledge of the big doubles they can work out 8 + 9 by using 8 + 8. As a second example, if a student knows 6 + 4 is a partition of 10, they can use that to work out 7 + 4.

The progression in range works through the four addition ranges (see Addition Ranges Grid in Chapter 1).

	Range	Examples			
Range 1	Parts ≤ 5	2 + 2	8 – 3	1 + □ = 5	10 – □ = 5
Range 2	Whole ≤ 10	3 + 6	9 – 7	2 + □ = 8	10 – □ = 4
Range 3	Parts ≤ 10	7 + 8	16 – 8	10 + □ = 16	11 – □ = 4
Range 4	Whole ≤ 20	13 + 3	19 – 11	15 + □ = 17	19 – □ = 13

The progression in orientation involves focusing on a set of addition combinations first, then progressing to subtractive orientations of the same combinations.

The progression in setting involves beginning work in visible settings, such as ten-frames and arithmetic racks, then progressively distancing the setting by screening and flashing, toward working with only spoken and written bare numbers. Importantly, this progression is recursive. For each new range, and each new set of combinations, instruction returns to visible settings, then progressively distances to bare numbers.

The progressions along these four dimensions are not pursued one at a time, or once and for all. Rather, they are interwoven. In Teaching Chart $3B_{10}$ these progressions are interwoven in the progressions down the rows, and across the columns. The topics down the left-hand column progress in range from Range 1 to Range 2, and also in complexity from key combinations (partitions of 5, small doubles, five-plus, partitions of 10) to all combinations (partitions of 6, 7, 8, 9; Range 1 and 2 additions and subtractions). (Ranges 3 and 4 are addressed in Teaching Chart $3B_{20}$.) The cells across each row progress in distancing the setting toward written forms. Written tasks can involve writing partitions, small doubles, large doubles and so on, systematically, which we refer to as organizing and generalizing.

We use the grid in Figure 6.1 to set out an example of this interwoven instructional path. The figure shows the progression from key combinations to all addition combinations and then to all subtraction combinations, and how this is staggered across the progression through Ranges 1 to 4. The fourth progression – distancing the setting – is applied within each cell in turn.

Step	Key combinations and partitions	All combinations – Addition	All combinations – Subtraction
A	Range 1: Partitions of 5 Small doubles Five-plus		
B	Range 2: Partitions of 10	Range 1: Additions	
C	Range 3: Ten-plus Big doubles	Range 2: Additions	Range 1: Subtractions
D	Range 4: Partitions of 20	Range 3: Additions	Range 2: Subtractions
E		Range 4: Additions	Range 3: Subtractions
F			Range 4: Subtractions

Figure 6.1 Structuring numbers 1 to 20: Steps in the teaching progression

Note: A progression from visible settings to bare numbers can apply in every cell.

Teaching Chart 3B₂₀: Structuring Numbers 1 to 20

3B₂₀

Topic		Teaching Procedures			Green Book
	.1	.2	.3	.4	
PHASE I: MAKING AND READING NUMBERS 1 to 20					
3B11 **Patterns for numbers 1–10** Ten-wise (top row only) Five-wise (6–10) Pair-wise	*Building patterns on rack* Build pattern in quick movements. Ten-wise, five-wise, pair-wise.	*Patterns on rack shown/flashed* Say the number.	*Imagining rack* Describe then build pattern.	—	8.5.1, 8.5.2
3B12 **Patterns for numbers 11–20** Ten-wise Five-wise (11–15) Pair-wise	"	"	"	—	8.5.3, 8.5.4, 8.5.5
PHASE II: ADDING NUMBERS 1 TO 10					
3B13 **Range 1 (parts ≤ 5)** (Review) Small doubles 5 + 1-to-5 1-to-5 + 1-to-5	*Both addends on rack* Say top, bottom, and sum. May transform beads.	*One addend shown/flashed on rack,* *task posed verbally/written* Solve task without touching.	*Verbal* Solve tasks posed verbally.	*Written* Range 1 addition cards: read the card and say the answer. Also do tasks in workbook.	–
3B14 **Range 2 (whole ≤ 10)** (Review) Partitions of 10 All sums ≤ 10	"	"	"	*Written* Range 2 addition cards: read the card and say the answer. Also do tasks in workbook.	–
3B15 **Range 3: Key combinations** Big doubles Ten-plus	"	"	"	*Written* Range 3 key combination cards: read the card and say the answer. Also do tasks in workbook.	–
3B16 **Range 3 (parts ≤ 10)** 5 + 6-to-10 1-to-5 + 6-to-10 6-to-10 + 6-to-10 all of 1-to-10 + 1-to-10	*Both addends on rack* Say top, bottom, and sum. Transform beads.	*One addend on rack,* *task posed verbally/written* Solve task by moving beads.	*One addend on rack,* *task posed verbally/written* Solve task without touching.	*Verbal and written* Ranges 1, 2, 3 addition cards: read the card and say the answer. Also do tasks in workbook, and tasks posed verbally.	8.5.6, 8.5.8

Chart continued overleaf....

Teaching Chart 3B₂₀: Structuring Numbers 1 to 20 continued

Topic	Teaching Procedures .1	.2	.3	.4	Green Book
PHASE III: ADDING AND SUBTRACTING IN THE RANGE 1 to 20					
3B17 **Range 4: Key combinations** Partitions of 20	*Building partition on rack* Teacher builds partition. Student builds partition.	*Partition on rack shown/flashed/ screened* Say (and record) the complement to 20.	*Verbal* Given a number, say the complement to 20.	*Written* Write out all partitions of 20.	-
3B18 **Range 4: Addition (one addend > 10)**	*One number on rack, task posed verbally/written* Solve task by moving beads.	*One number shown/flashed on rack, task posed verbally/written* Solve task without touching.	*Verbal and written* Solve tasks posed verbally. Do tasks in workbook.	—	-
3B19 **Range 3: Subtraction (both parts ≤ 10)** Various forms of subtraction	"	"	"	*Verbal and written* Ranges 1, 2, 3 subtraction cards. Read the card and say the answer or write the answer.	8.5.9
3B20 **Range 4: Subtraction (one part > 10)** Various forms of subtraction	"	"	"	—	-
3B21 **Addition and subtraction in the range 1 to 20** Consolidating topic	*Verbal and written* Solve mixed tasks posed verbally. Do tasks in workbook.	*Written* Write out various fact families.	*Written* Write out addition & subtraction tables. Annotate the tables.	*Written* Progress to algebraic tasks.	-

Commentary on Teaching Chart 3B$_{20}$

Model: Structuring Numbers 1 to 20 (Levels ②–⑦).

References: Red Book, Chapter 4 (pp. 50–76). Green Book, Key Topic 8.5 (pp. 141–5).

Materials: Arithmetic rack.

Teaching Chart 3B$_{20}$ continues the progressions described for Teaching Chart 3B$_{10}$. The phases in the chart progress from addition to subtraction, the topics within each phase progress through to Ranges 3 and 4, and each range progresses from key combinations to all combinations. Each row indicates the progression of distancing the setting. For structuring numbers in the range 1 to 20, our preferred setting is the arithmetic rack, referred to as the 'rack' in Chart 3B$_{20}$. Alternatively, double ten-frames can be used.

Teaching Chart 3B$_{20}$, Phase I – Making and Reading Numbers 1 to 20 – involves learning the *standard configurations* for the numbers 1 to 20 in the arithmetic rack setting, including the pair-wise, five-wise and ten-wise patterns. The student learns to *make* the patterns with facility – that is, without moving beads by ones – and to *read* the patterns – that is, to say the number when shown a pattern. This phase is an important preliminary to using the arithmetic rack setting effectively in Phases II and III. (See Red Book, pp. 57–8.)

Teaching Chart 3B$_{20}$, Phase II – Adding Numbers 1 to 10 – includes Range 1 and 2 combinations (Topics 3B13 and 3B14), which revisit topics from Teaching Chart 3B$_{10}$. The revision can be valuable in the context of the new arithmetic rack setting. The main work of Phase II is the progression to Range 3, with tasks which cross over 10. Instruction in Range 3 begins with the key combinations (Topic 3B15), which should be familiar as standard configurations from Phase I, then progresses to all Range 3 additions (Topic 3B16). Students need to develop non-counting strategies for these combinations, such as near-doubles, adding-through-ten and **compensation strategies**. Across the rows of the chart, the progression in distancing the setting is a distinctive progression in the handling of the arithmetic rack, designed to support the development of these strategies. The progression from reasoning in the context of manipulating beads on the rack, through to reasoning with bare written numbers, involves significant learning. (See Red Book, pp. 58–62.)

Teaching Chart 3B$_{20}$, Phase III – Adding and Subtracting in the Range 1 to 20 – commences with the last set of key combinations – the partitions of 20. The Range 4 Additions tasks (Topic 3B18) have one difference on the rack from Range 3: now that there is one addend greater than 10, we cannot build both addends separately on the rack, so 3B18.1 poses only *one* addend on the rack. The main work of Phase III is the progression to subtraction. For Topics 3B18 and 3B19, instruction can focus on various forms of subtraction tasks, such as take away ($13 - 5 = \square$), missing addend ($8 + \square = 13$), missing subtrahend ($13 - \square = 8$), difference (What is the difference between 13 and 8?) and partition (Tell me two numbers that make 13). Our view is that it is not necessary to focus on all of these comprehensively prior to progressing to Domain 3D. Again, the arithmetic rack can be a valuable setting for developing students' reasoning for the subtraction tasks. Particular care should be taken in progressing to written forms of subtraction. The notation for tasks can be developed alongside the use of the setting. Topic 3B21 involves working with verbal and written forms across all four addition ranges to consolidate the whole domain of Structuring Numbers 1 to 20. The progression to algebraic thinking involves focusing on patterns and generalizations, for example, in a list of the partitions of a number, noticing the sequences in the two addends: $1 + 11$, $2 + 10$, $3 + 9$, and so on.

MIDDLE NUMBER   Teaching Chart 3C: Conceptual Place Value

Topic	Teaching Procedures .1	.2	.3	.4
RANGE I: 0 to 130				
3C1 Inc- & decrementing by 10s ON and OFF the decuple	*Bundling sticks shown* After each inc-/decrement, say the number.	*Bundling sticks screened* After each inc-/decrement, say the number.	—	—
3C2 Inc- & decrementing by 1s & 10s Flexibly switching units	*Bundling sticks shown* After each inc-/decrement, say the number. (Extend to multiple unit jumps and mixed unit jumps.)	*Bundling sticks screened* After each inc-/decrement, say the number. (Extend to multiple unit jumps and mixed unit jumps.)	*Bundling sticks shown/screened, with arrow cards* Say the numbers, and also build arrow cards for some numbers.	*Verbal and written tasks* Given a number, say/write 10 more or 10 less.
RANGE II: 0 to 1000				
3C3 Inc- & decrementing by 10s ON and OFF the decuple	*Dot materials shown* After each inc-/decrement, say the number.	*Dot materials screened* After each inc-/decrement, say the number.	—	—
3C4 Inc- & decrementing by 100s ON and OFF the hundred	"	"	—	—
3C5 Inc- & decrementing by 1s, 10s & 100s Flexibly switching units	*Dot materials shown* After each inc-/decrement, say the number. (Extend to multiple unit jumps and mixed unit jumps.)	*Dot materials screened* After each inc-/decrement, say the number. (Extend to multiple unit jumps and mixed unit jumps.)	*Dot materials shown/screened, with arrow cards* Say the numbers, and also build arrow cards for some numbers.	*Verbal and written tasks* Given a number, say/write 10 more, 10 less, 100 more or 100 less.
RANGE III: 0 to 1000 and BEYOND				
3C6 Inc- & decrementing by 1s, 10s & 100s across 1000 switched, multiple & mixed units	"	"	"	"
3C7 Inc- & decrementing by 1s, 10s, 100s & 1000s beyond 1000 switched, multiple & mixed units	"	"	"	"

Notes: *Switch units:* e.g. increment by 10, then increment by 1, then increment by 10 again, then increment by 100, etc.

Multiple units: e.g. increment by two 10s, or by three 100s, not just by 10 or 100.

Mixed units: e.g. increment by one 10 and one stick; or by two 100s, one 10 and three 1s.

Missing units: e.g. there were 79 sticks, I added some, and now there are 100 sticks: how many did I add?

Commentary on Teaching Chart 3C

Model: Conceptual Place Value.

Reference: Red Book, Chapter 5 (pp. 77–98).

Materials: Bundling sticks, arrow cards, base-ten dot materials (plastic): ten-strips (a strip of 10 dots) and 100-squares (10×10-squares).

Conceptual place value refers to learning to increment and decrement flexibly by 1s, 10s and 100s in the range 0 to 130 (Range I) and 0 to 1000 and beyond (Ranges II and III). Developing facile conceptual place value supports students' development of strategies for adding and subtracting involving 2- and 3-digit numbers. Students who are not facile with conceptual place value frequently count by ones in order to increment or decrement a 2- or 3-digit number by 10. For example, when asked to say the number that is 10 less than 306, students will attempt to count down by ones from 306 and keep track of 10 counts.

The learning path from counting-by-ones to facile conceptual place value involves five dimensions of mathematizing. These are progressing:

a.   from *incrementing* by 10 to *decrementing* by 10;

b.   from working *on* the decuple to *off* the decuple;

c.   from incrementing and decrementing by 10s only, to incrementing and decrementing with increasing complexity involving switching, multiple, mixed and missing units;

d.   from base-ten materials to bare numbers, that is, formal arithmetic;

e.   from the range 0 to 130, to the range 0 to 1000 and beyond.

It is important that instruction takes full account of the student's current level of conceptual place value knowledge, so need not necessarily begin at the start of the teaching chart.

Instruction in Range I commences with a setting of bundling sticks to increment in the range 1 to 130, then makes each of the above progressions. At or before progressing to Range II, the setting changes from bundling sticks to plastic base-ten dot materials. Instruction typically develops a focus on tasks with screened setting and increased complexity, with sequences flexibly switching between 100s, 10s and 1s, incrementing by multiple 100s, 10s and 1s, and incrementing by a mixture of 100s, 10s and 1s. For example,

256 and 10 more (266); 1 more (267); two 10s more (287);

three 10s more (317); less 10 and 1 (306); less 10 (296);

less two 100s and a 10 (86). How many more to get up to 100? (14)

Missing units tasks are posed incidentally after a progression of increments and decrements, and typically (though not necessarily) involve a jump up to a centuple (100, 200, etc.) or a jump back from a centuple.

The progression of distancing the setting is important. An early aspect of this progression introduces arrow cards alongside the setting, to pose the task of symbolizing some of the numbers reached during the sequence of increments and decrements. Distancing progresses to increments and decrements expressed entirely as verbal or written tasks. A later written task type involves drawing up a table with base numerals in a central column, and the student to complete the columns on the left headed One Less, Ten Less; and the columns on the right headed One More, Ten More, possibly extending to One Hundred Less and One Hundred More. We have found the instructional settings and tasks described above to be very effective in advancing students' facility with conceptual place value.

Teaching Chart 3D: Addition and Subtraction to 100

	Topic	Teaching Procedures .1	.2	.3	Green Book
	PHASE I: DECUPLE AND 1-DIGIT				
3D1	**Locating nearest decuple**	*Ten-frames shown/screened* Given 2-digit number, say next decuple going forward/backward.	*Verbal* Given 2-digit number, say next decuple going forward/backward.		-
3D2	**Adding on from a decuple** e.g. $40 + 3$	*Ten-frames shown/screened* Given decuple and addend, solve task.	*Verbal/written* Solve tasks posed verbally. Do tasks in workbook.		8.4.1
3D3	**Subtracting down to a decuple** e.g. $43 − X = 40$	*Ten-frames shown/screened* Given 2-digit number, say next decuple going backwards, and say how far.	"		8.4.2
3D4	**Adding up to a decuple** 1–5 e.g. $37 + X = 40$ 6–9 e.g. $32 + X = 40$	*Ten-frames shown/screened* Given 2-digit number, say next decuple going forward, and say how far.	"		8.4.3, 8.4.5
3D5	**Subtracting down from a decuple** 1–5 e.g. $40 − 3$ 6–9 e.g. $40 − 8$	*Ten-frames shown/screened* Given decuple and subtrahend, solve task.	"		8.4.4, 8.4.6
	PHASE II: 2-DIGIT AND 1-DIGIT				
3D6	**Adding across a decuple** e.g. $37 + 6$	*Ten-frames shown/screened* Given 2-digit number and 1-digit number, solve task (and record).	*Verbal/written* Solve tasks posed verbally. Do tasks in workbook.	*Written* Write out linked number sentences systematically (algebraic thinking). e.g. $7 + 6 = 13$, $17 + 6 = 23$, $27 + 6 = \ldots$	9.5.3
3D7	**Subtracting across a decuple** e.g. $43 − 6$	"	"	"	9.5.4
3D8	**Adding within a decade** e.g. $43 + 5$	"	"	"	9.5.1
3D9	**Subtracting within a decade** e.g. $48 − 5$	"	"	"	9.5.2

Chart continued overleaf…

Teaching Chart 3D: Addition and Subtraction to 100 continued

	Topic	Teaching Procedures .1	.2	.3	.4	Green Book
PHASE III: BASIC 2-DIGIT AND 2-DIGIT						
3D10	**Adding/subtracting a decuple** e.g. 43 + 20, 63 − 20	*Ten-frames shown* Solve the written task. (Notate solution).	*Ten-frames for one number screened, one number shown* Solve the written task. (Notate solution).	*Ten-frames all screened* Solve the written task. Notate solution.	*Written* Solve the written task. Notate solution.	9.2.1, 9.2.4
3D11	**Addition with NO regrouping** e.g. 43 + 25	"	"	"	"	9.2.2, 9.4.1, 9.4.2
3D12	**Addition with regrouping** e.g. 43 + 29	"	"	"	"	9.2.3, 9.4.1, 9.4.2
3D13	**Subtraction with NO regrouping** e.g. 68 − 25	"	"	"	"	9.2.5, 9.4.5, 9.4.6
3D14	**Subtraction with regrouping** e.g. 68 − 29	"	"	"	"	9.2.6, 9.4.5, 9.4.6
PHASE IV: EXTENDING 2-DIGIT AND 2-DIGIT						
3D15	**Missing addend (and subtrahend)** e.g. 43 + X = 61, 61 − X = 43	*Ten-frames shown* Written task posed, and first number shown with ten-frames. Manipulate cards, and solve task. (Notate solution).	*Ten-frames screened* Solve the written task. Notate solution.	*Written* Solve the written task. Notate solution.		9.2.7, 9.4.3, 9.4.4
3D16	**Toward more flexible strategies and more formal notations** e.g. jump, split, over-jump, jump to the decuple, split-jump, compensation, transformation, complementary addition.	*Ten-frames screened* Given written task, solve task and notate solution. Discuss strategies and notations.	*Written* Given written task, solve task and notate solution. Discuss strategies and notations.	*Written* Progress to more formal notations. - Arrow notation - Number sentences.	*Written* Progress to algebraic tasks. e.g. - List fact families - List all partitions of X - Make a sequence of linked number sentences.	-
3D17	**3-digit addition and subtraction** e.g. 356 + 208, 134 − 21	*Ten-frames for one number screened, one number shown* Solve the written task. (Notate solution).	*Ten-frames screened* Solve the written task. Notate solution.	*Written* Solve the written task. Notate solution.	*Written* Progress to algebraic tasks.	-

Commentary on Teaching Chart 3D

Model: Addition and Subtraction to 100.

References: Green Book, Key Topics 8.4 (pp. 181–4) and 9.5 (pp. 220–2). Red Book, Chapter 6 (pp. 99–134).

Materials: Ten-frames, screen.

Phases I and II: Higher Decade Addition and Subtraction

Teaching Chart 3D, Addition and Subtraction to 100, refers to developing facile strategies for addition and subtraction involving two 2-digit numbers. We regard Addition and Subtraction to 100 as building on three critically important foundations: Structuring Numbers 1 to 20 (3B), Conceptual Place Value (3C) and Higher Decade Addition and Subtraction. Students can benefit significantly from direct instruction in these foundations. The first two foundations are addressed by the two previous teaching charts. The sub-domain of Higher Decade Addition and Subtraction is addressed as Phases I and II of Teaching Chart 3D.

Higher Decade Addition and Subtraction refers to tasks involving a 2-digit number plus or minus a 1-digit number. We distinguish nine different types of strategy within this sub-domain. The five topics of Phase I address the first five strategies. To illustrate these strategies, consider the following example of a computation strategy for a 2-digit addition task:

$$37 + 45 \text{ solved by jump strategy: } 37 + 40 \rightarrow 77 + 3 \rightarrow 80 + 2 \rightarrow \mathbf{82}$$

This strategy involves three steps. The second step is called *adding to a decuple* and the third step is called *adding from a decuple*. There are corresponding strategies for subtraction: *subtracting to a decuple* and *subtracting from a decuple*. Collectively these four strategies are referred to as *adding and subtracting to and from a decuple*. They are very important and we teach them explicitly in Phase I. Students without facile strategies for adding and subtracting involving 2-digit numbers typically do not have these strategies. These students will use counting-by-ones to work out the second and third steps above. Further, in the second step, they might not be able to determine that 80 is the next decuple after 77. We also teach this explicitly, in Topic 3D1, *locating the nearest decuple* above and below a given non-decuple number.

Phase II includes two further strategies that *cross* the decuple. *Adding across a decuple* refers to an addition such as 77 + 5. Subtracting across a decuple refers to corresponding subtraction tasks. Such tasks can be solved in two steps, as 77 + 5 was in the jump strategy example above, using adding to a decuple (77 + 3 → 80) then adding from a decuple (80 + 2 → 82). An alternative is to solve it in one step (77 + 7 → 82).

The last two topics in Phase II are referred to as adding and subtracting *within* a decade. These address the case where the sum of a 2-digit number and a 1-digit number does not cross the decuple. For example, 43 + 5, is less than 50 so this addition does not involve adding to or across the decuple 50. Similarly for subtraction: 48 – 5 is greater than 40 so this subtraction does not involve subtracting to or across the decuple 40.

All the strategies discussed in Phases I and II include steps that involve adding and subtracting in the range 1 to 10. This highlights the importance of students' knowledge of Structuring Numbers 1 to 10 as a basis for 3D – Addition and Subtraction to 100.

Instruction in Phases I and II involves using full ten-frames in conjunction with five-wise and pair-wise ten-frame cards to pose the specific task types for each topic. Progression across the chart involves distancing the setting, from ten-frames shown, to ten-frames screened, to verbal and written tasks.

Phase III: Basic 2-digit and 2-digit

Phase III addresses the main work of Domain 3D: adding and subtracting involving two 2-digit numbers. Instruction focuses on supporting students' development of efficient mental computation strategies. Students typically develop two main strategies: *jump* and *split*. Other strategies that arise include **over-jump**, split-jump, compensation and transformation. For an extensive description of students' strategies and how to support their development, see Red Book, pp. 99–107.

Topic 3D10 concerns the relatively simple case where one of the numbers involved is a decuple. As well as being important basic combinations in their own right, these cases arise as the first step in a jump strategy: 37 + 40 in the jump example described above. Although some students will solve this kind of task in one step, '37 + 40 makes 77', other students will increment 37 by 10 four times:

$$37 + 10 \text{ makes } 47, 47 + 10 \text{ makes } 57, 57 + 10 \text{ makes } 67, 67 + 10 \text{ makes } \mathbf{77}$$

This strategy is what we have called incrementing by 10 off the decuple and of course, students who do not have facile knowledge of conceptual place value might not be able to do this. This illustrates why conceptual place value is one of the three foundations for 3D Addition and Subtraction to 100.

Non-regrouping tasks (Topics 3D11 and 3D13) are typically much easier than regrouping tasks (Topics 3D12 and 3D14). Non-regrouping tasks can be solved by jump or split strategies:

$$53 - 12 \text{ solved by jump: } 53 - 10 \rightarrow 43 - 2 \rightarrow \mathbf{41}$$
$$53 - 12 \text{ solved by split: } 50 - 10 \text{ is } 40, 3 - 2 \text{ is } 1, \text{ and } 40 + 1 \text{ is } \mathbf{41}$$

For regrouping subtraction tasks, a split strategy presents particular difficulties. For example,

$$53 - 19, \text{ attempted by split: } 50 - 10 \text{ is } 40, 3 - 9 \text{ is } 6 \text{ (incorrect), answer } \mathbf{'46'}$$

One means by which students avoid this problem is to reason that 3 – 9 means 'go back six more from 40' and then correctly answer **34**.

Instruction begins in the setting of full ten-frames. Students can learn significantly from the opportunity to manipulate the ten-frames, visualize the ten-frames, and check answers against the ten-frames. Instruction progresses from left to right across the chart, distancing the setting toward bare number written tasks.

An important aspect of the instruction is notating students' strategies, which supports their awareness and facility. We advocate the use of four different systems for notating strategies: *empty number line (ENL)*, *drop-down*, *arrow* and *number sentences*. Typically, particular systems are suited to some strategies more than others, as illustrated in Figure 6.2. (For further examples of these notations, see Red Book, pp. 100–1.)

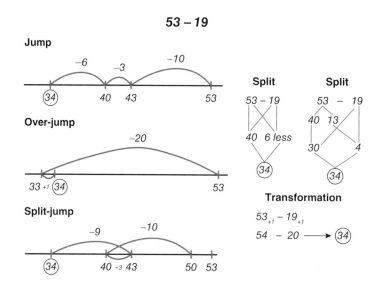

Figure 6.2 Informal notations for mental strategies for 53–19.

- *Empty number line* notation (ENL) is well suited to various kinds of jump strategies, as shown in the jump, over-jump and split-jump strategies notated in Figure 6.2.
- *Drop-down* is well suited to notating split strategies, as shown in Figure 6.2.
- *Arrow notation* can be adapted to a range of strategies.

$$\text{e.g. Jump for } 53 - 19: 53 - 10 \rightarrow 43 - 3 \rightarrow 40 - 6 \rightarrow 34$$

- *Number sentence notation*, using equations, can be regarded as the most formal, and also the most universal, in the sense that it can be used to notate any strategy by writing a number sentence for each step in the strategy.

$$\text{e.g. Jump for } 53 - 19:$$
$$53 - 10 = 43$$
$$43 - 3 = 40$$
$$40 - 6 = 34$$

Phase IV: Extending 2-digit and 2-digit

Phase IV refers to extending beyond basic cases and strategies, including posing tasks in a missing addend or missing subtrahend format, refining students' flexibility with strategies, and extending to simpler cases involving 3-digit addition and subtraction.

Examples of progressing to algebraic thinking (3D16.4) are:

- Listing a fact family for a given number sentence:

$$
\begin{array}{ll}
8 + 9 = 17 & 17 = 8 + 9 \\
9 + 8 = 17 & 17 = 9 + 8 \\
17 - 8 = 9 & 9 = 17 - 8 \\
17 - 9 = 8 & 8 = 17 - 9
\end{array}
$$

- Listing partitions of a number:

$$50 + 0 = 50, 49 + 1 = 50, 48 + 2 = 50, \ldots 2 + 48 = 50, 1 + 49 = 50, 0 + 50 = 50$$

- Making a sequence of linked number sentences:

$$
\begin{array}{ll}
7 + 2 = 9 & 14 - 8 = 6 \\
17 + 2 = 19 & 24 - 8 = 16 \\
27 + 2 = 29 & 34 - 8 = 26 \\
\ldots & \ldots\ldots\ldots \\
97 + 2 = 99 & 104 - 8 = 96
\end{array}
$$

3E

MIDDLE NUMBER   Teaching Chart 3E: Early Multiplication and Division

	Topic	Teaching Procedures .1	.2	.3	.4	Green Book
		SECTION I: EARLY MULTIPLICATIVE TASKS IN SETTINGS (Red Book, Chapter 7, instruction phase 1)				
3E1	**Equal groups: Multiplication** Determine total number	*N-groups out to manipulate/ to see only* Given number in each group and number of groups, determine total.	*N-groups face down* ------------------->	*N-groups screened* ------------------->	*(N-groups, with written task beside)* ------------------->	7.6.1, 8.6.1/.2
3E2	**Equal groups: Quotitive division** Determine number of groups	*Counters out to manipulate/ to see only* Given total and number in each group, determine number of groups.	*N-groups partially screened* ------------------->	*N-groups screened* ------------------->	*(N-groups, with written task beside)* ------------------->	7.6.2, 8.6.3
3E3	**Equal groups: Partitive division** Determine number in each group	*Counters out to manipulate/ to see only* Given total and number of groups, determine number in each group.	*N-groups face down* ------------------->	*N-groups screened* ------------------->	*(N-groups, with written task beside)* ------------------->	7.6.3, 8.6.4
3E4	**Arrays: Introduction**	*Array shown* Describe array in terms of rows, columns.	*N-tiles out to manipulate* Build arrays, then describe them.	—	—	7.6.4, 7.6.5
3E5	**Arrays: Multiplication**	*Array shown* Given number in each row and number of rows, determine total number.	*Array partially screened* ------------------->	*Array screened* ------------------->	*(Array, with written task alongside)* ------------------->	7.6.6, 8.6.5
3E6	**Arrays: Division**	‾‾‾ (Division not applicable with visible arrays)	*Array partially screened* Given total and number in a row, determine number of rows.	*Array screened* Given total and number of rows, determine number in each row.	*(Array, with written task alongside)* ------------------->	8.6.6, 8.6.7
		SECTION II: HABITUATING SEQUENCES OF MULTIPLES (Red Book, Chapter 7, instruction phase 2)				
3E7	**Sequences by 2s, up to 20** (Forwards and backwards)	*N-tiles* visible → face-down → screened Say cumulative number of dots.	*Verbal only* Say NWS.	*Numeral track* See then say. Say then see. Naming numerals under lids.	*Written* Writing numeral sequences. Extending range beyond 10th multiple, noticing patterns.	7.1, 8.1
3E8	**Sequences by 5s, up to 50**	"	"	"	"	"
3E9	**Sequences by 3s, up to 30**	"	"	"	"	"
3E10	**Sequences by 4s, up to 40**	"	"	"	"	"

Commentary Teaching Chart 3E

Model: Early Multiplication and Division.

References: Green Book, Key Topics 6.6 (pp. 116–18), 7.6 (pp. 148–53) and 8.6 (pp. 188–90). Red Book, Chapter 7 (pp. 135–72).

Materials: Counters of two colours; n-groups – dot cards showing equal groups of 2s, 3s, 4s, 5s; n-tiles – narrow dot cards showing equal rows of 2s, 3s, 4s, 5s; small objects for sharing; small arrays (3×3, 4×5, etc.).

Section I: Early multiplicative tasks in settings

Teaching Chart 3E Section I addresses the development from additive and counting-based strategies to multiplicative strategies and multiplicative reasoning. Instruction poses tasks in standard multiplicative settings of equal groups and small arrays, as contexts for developing students' awareness of multiplicative structure. The n-groups setting is used for three different orientations of multiplicative tasks:

- *Multiplication:* student determines the total in a collection, given the number of groups and the number in each group;
- *Quotitive division:* student determines the number of groups, given the number in each group (quota) and the total;
- *Partitive division:* student determines the number in each group, given the number of groups (parts) and the total.

In the arrays setting, **quotitive** and **partitive division** are not clearly distinguished from each other, so there are just the two orientations of multiplication and division.

Instruction with these settings can progress:
- from n-groups turned face up to face down;
- from seeing the n-group cards to the n-group cards being screened;
- from using n-group settings to using arrays;
- from seeing the rows of an array to the rows (or columns) being screened;
- from working entirely with settings to linking settings with written expressions.

Throughout instruction, draw attention to student's nascent efforts to coordinate counting composite units, and to recognize and use multiplicative relationships.

Section II: Habituating sequences of multiples

This section involves habituating sequences of multiples of 2, 5, 3 and 4, commonly referred to as *skip-counting*. Initially, students might not be able to skip count to the 10th multiple of a sequence, for example, they might skip count by 3s up to 12 or 15, without going all the way to 30. We use the setting of n-tiles as a context for students' skip-counting. Instruction can progress in the following ways:
- from skip-counting forwards to skip-counting backwards;
- from n-tiles face up, to n-tiles face down, to n-tiles screened;
- from n-tiles to numeral track activities such as *See Then Say*, and *Say Then See* (see Teaching Chart 2A);
- to writing sequences of numerals – 3, 6, 9, 12, and so on;
- to extending beyond the 10th multiple, for example 2, 4, 6, … 18, 20, 22, 24, …

Students can describe patterns in sequences of multiples. For examples:
- in the 5s sequence, every second multiple is a decuple;
- in the 4s sequence, there is a repeating pattern in the 1s digit involving all five even numbers: 4, 8, 2, 6, 0; 4, 8, 2, 6, 0 …

	Topic	.1	.2	.3	.4
	RANGE 1: 2S AND 10S				
3F1	**Structuring and strategies: Multiples of 2**	*2-tiles shown/screened* Inc- and decrement by 2s, and by multiple 2s. Track number of dots and number of tiles.	*N-tiles or arrays flashed/screened* Pose multiplication, partition, and quotition tasks. → Notate and refine strategies.	*Verbal or written tasks* Pose multiplication, partition, and quotition tasks. → Notate and refine strategies.	*Written* Systematically discuss set of multiples of 2, and preferred strategies.
3F2	**Structuring and strategies: Multiples of 10**	AS ABOVE for 10s.	AS ABOVE for 10s.	AS ABOVE for 10s.	AS ABOVE for 10s.
3F3	**Rehearsal: Range 1**	*N-tiles flashed/screened* Multiplication, partition, quotition.	*Given set of products, bare tasks* Multiplication, partition, quotition.	*Multiplication cards* Both mixed and organized.	*Division cards* Both mixed and organized.
	RANGE 2: LOW × LOW (Low 3s, 4s and 5s)				
3F4	**Structuring and strategies: Range 2**	*N-tiles shown/screened* Inc- and decrement by 3s, 4s, or 5s. Track number of dots and number of tiles.	*N-tiles or arrays flashed/screened* Pose multiplication, partition and quotition tasks. → Notate and refine strategies.	*Verbal or written tasks* Pose multiplication, partition and quotition tasks. → Notate and refine strategies.	*Written* Systematically discuss set of Range 2 facts, and preferred strategies.
3F5	**Rehearsal: Ranges 1 & 2**	*N-tiles flashed/screened* Multiplication, partition, quotition.	*Given set of products, bare tasks* Multiplication, partition, quotition.	*Multiplication cards* Both mixed and organized.	*Division cards* Both mixed and organized.
	RANGE 3: LOW × HIGH (High 3s, 4s and 5s)				
3F6	**Structuring and strategies: High multiples of 3**	*3-tiles shown/screened* Inc- and decrement by 3s, and by multiple 3s. Track number of dots and number of tiles.	*N-tiles or arrays flashed/screened* Pose multiplication, partition and quotition tasks. → Notate and refine strategies.	*Verbal or written tasks* Pose multiplication, partition and quotition tasks. → Notate and refine strategies.	*Written* Systematically discuss set of multiples of 3, and preferred strategies.
3F7	**Structuring and strategies: High multiples of 4**	AS ABOVE for 4s.	AS ABOVE for 4s.	AS ABOVE for 4s.	AS ABOVE for 4s.
3F8	**Structuring and strategies: High multiples of 5**	AS ABOVE for 5s.	AS ABOVE for 5s.	AS ABOVE for 5s.	AS ABOVE for 5s.
3F9	**Rehearsal: Range 3**	*N-tiles flashed/screened* Multiplication, partition, quotition.	*Given set of products, bare tasks* Multiplication, partition, quotition.	*Multiplication cards* Both mixed and organized.	*Division cards* Both mixed and organized.
3F10	**Rehearsal: Ranges 1–3**	AS ABOVE for all Ranges 1–3	AS ABOVE for all Ranges 1–3	AS ABOVE for all Ranges 1–3	AS ABOVE for all Ranges 1–3

Chart continued overleaf….

Teaching Chart 3F: Multiplicative Basic Facts continued

RANGE 4: HIGH × HIGH (High 6s, 7s, 8s and 9s)					
3F11	**Structuring and strategies: High multiples of 9**	*9-tiles shown/screened* Inc- and decrement by 9s, and by multiple 9s. Track number of dots and number of tiles.	*N-tiles or arrays flashed/screened* Pose multiplication, partition and quotition tasks. → Notate and refine strategies.	*Verbal or written tasks* Pose multiplication, partition and quotition tasks. → Notate and refine strategies.	*Written* Systematically discuss set of multiples of 9, and preferred strategies.
3F12	**Structuring and strategies: High multiples of 8**	AS ABOVE for 8s.	AS ABOVE for 8s.	AS ABOVE for 8s.	AS ABOVE for 8s.
3F13	**Structuring and strategies: High multiples of 7**	AS ABOVE for 7s.	AS ABOVE for 7s.	AS ABOVE for 7s.	AS ABOVE for 7s.
3F14	**Structuring and strategies: High multiples of 6**	AS ABOVE for 6s.	AS ABOVE for 6s.	AS ABOVE for 6s.	AS ABOVE for 6s.
3F15	**Rehearsal: Range 4**	*N-tiles flashed/screened* Multiplication, partition, quotition.	*Given set of products, bare tasks* Multiplication, partition, quotition.	*Multiplication cards* Both mixed and organized.	*Division cards* Both mixed and organized.
3F16	**Rehearsal: Ranges 1–4**	AS ABOVE for all Ranges 1–4.	*Multiplication and division cards* Both mixed and organized.	*Basic facts chart* Review of whole chart for families and strategies.	*Basic facts chart* Investigating patterns: doubling, evens and odds, squares and near-squares …
RANGE 5: FACTOR > 10 (Red Book, Chapter 7, instruction phase 6)					
3F17	**Multiplication with one factor > 10**	*Array shown/screened* Given number of rows and columns, determine total. Notate and refine strategies.	*Array screened, then notated* Solve tasks, then notate structuring on the array.	*Verbal/written* Solve verbal or bare number multiplication tasks. (Notate and refine strategies.)	*Written* Systematically discuss sets of products, and preferred strategies.
3F18	**Division with one factor > 10**	*Array shown/screened* Given total, and number of rows, determine number of columns. Notate and refine strategies.	*Array screened, then notated* Solve tasks, then notate structuring on the array.	*Verbal/written* Solve verbal or bare number division tasks. (Notate and refine strategies.)	*Written* Systematically discuss sets of products, and preferred strategies.
3F19	**Investigating primes, composites and factors**	*Square tiles* Given x tiles, make a rectangle. → Record factor pairs for each x.	*Verbal/numeral cards* Given any number 1–30, name the factors, or identify as prime.	*Factors grid* Generate factors grid for 1–24. Investigate patterns: primes, squares, related factors …	*100s chart* Annotate factors → Sieve of Eratosthenes. → Identify primes. → Identify factor families.

Commentary on Teaching Chart 3F

Model: Multiplicative Basic Facts.

References: Green Book, Key Topic 9.6 (pp. 223–5). Red Book, Chapter 7 (pp. 135–72).

Materials: *n*-tiles in 2s, 3s, … 9s; multiplication and division basic facts cards; large arrays.

Teaching Chart 3F – Multiplicative Basic Facts – aims to develop *grounded habituation* of the basic facts. Grounded habituation involves the ability to respond immediately and correctly when a basic fact task is posed, along with the ability to justify one's answer via a relatively sophisticated multiplicative strategy.

Instruction is organized by the five multiplication ranges (see the Multiplication Ranges Grid in Chapter 1):

	Range	Examples			
Range 1	2s and 10s	2×6	10×4	$10 \times \square = 70$	$18 \div 9$
Range 2	Low × low	3×4	5×5	$3 \times \square = 15$	$20 \div 4$
Range 3	Low × high	4×7	8×3	$5 \times \square = 45$	$24 \div 4$
Range 4	High × high	6×8	7×7	$9 \times \square = 54$	$42 \div 7$
Range 5	Factor > 10	12×4	5×36	$8 \times \square = 176$	$256 \div 4$

Within each range, the early topics address students' knowledge of multiplicative structuring and strategies for the range, then the later topics rehearse toward habituation of basic facts in that range. This follows the principle of having habituation build on the development of strong mental computation and reasoning, rather than being ungrounded memorization. Lessons can include segments on more than one range, pitching instruction to the different levels identified on the Multiplicative Basic Facts model. For example, a lesson might include rehearsing basic facts in Ranges 1 and 2 (at Levels ⓵d and ⓶d); refining strategies in Range 3 (at Level ⓷b); and beginning work in Range 4 (at Level ⓸a).

Instruction in multiplicative structuring and strategies works on subsets of multiples, seeking to raise students' awareness of the distinctive multiplicative relations specific to those multiples, and the associated multiplicative computation strategies. Examples of specific multiplicative relations are presented in Table 6.2. Note that, in Teaching Chart 3F, the subsets of multiples within each range are listed in a numerical order: for example, in Range 3 the high multiples of 3, of 4 and of 5. This order is simply for ease of reference on the chart. The order of instruction should respond to the student's developing knowledge: students may be ready to work on multiples of 5 before multiples of 3. In Range 4 in particular, while instruction on structuring and strategies may focus on the multiples of 9 first, instruction may work on structuring the multiples of 8, 7 and 6 mixed together.

Table 6.2 Multiplicative relations within sets of multiples

Multiples	Relations	Examples
2s	relating to doubles	7×2 can mean double 7
3s	even multiples of 3 are even, while odd multiples of 3 are odd	$2 \times 3 = 6, 4 \times 3 = 12, 6 \times 3 = 18 \dots$ $3 \times 3 = 9, 5 \times 3 = 15, 7 \times 3 = 21 \dots$
4s	relating to multiples of 2	7×4 as double 7×2
	high multiples of 4 can build from five 4s making 20	$6 \times 4 \to 20 + 4 \to 24$ $8 \times 4 \to 20 + 3 \times 4 \to 20 + 12 \to 32$
5s	even multiples of 5 are decuples, while odd multiples of 5 end in 5	$2 \times 5 = 10, 4 \times 5 = 20, 6 \times 5 = 30 \dots$ $3 \times 5 = 15, 5 \times 5 = 25, 7 \times 5 = 35 \dots$
6s	relating to multiples of 3	7×6 as double 7×3
	relating to multiples of 5	$7 \times 6 \to 5 \times 6 + 2 \times 6 \to 30 + 12$
9s	relating to multiples of 10	$7 \times 9 \to 10 \times 7 - 7 \to 70 - 7 \to 63$

For each subset of multiples, instruction in structuring and strategies can begin in the setting of *n*-tiles. Initial teaching procedures involve incrementing and decrementing by *n*-tiles (chart column 1). These tasks are similar to tasks for skip-counting in Teaching Chart 3E Section II, but with a new aspect – the student now keeps track of the *number of tiles*, as well as the total number of dots. For example, a sequence with screened 5-tiles:

5 and another 5 (10); another 5 (15); another 5 (20). How many 5s so far? (Four). Add two more 5s (30); another 5 (35). How many 5s now? (Seven).

Instruction can progress to procedures posing multiplication, quotition and partition tasks in the setting of screened *n*-tiles (chart column 2). These tasks are the same form as tasks with equal groups in Teaching Chart 3E Section I, but now the instruction focuses on a particular subset of multiples, to cultivate and refine the multiplicative structuring and strategies. Notating students' strategies can be important, to support students' awareness of their strategies, and lead to refinements in strategies. Instruction can progress to verbal and written tasks (chart column 3), and to the systematic recording of sets of tasks and answers (chart column 4), to support students' awareness of relationships among the multiples. Note that, in this progression, division can be developed alongside multiplication, and knowledge of each supports the other. Students can come to know, say, 5–6–30 as a multiplicative triple, with the fact $30 \div 6 = 5$ as familiar as the fact $5 \times 6 = 30$.

As students establish facile multiplicative strategies for all basic facts within a range, instruction can progress to rehearsing those basic facts toward habituation. Rehearsal can include tasks posed with various screened *n*-tiles (rehearsal column 1), with instructional attention now shifting from developing strategies to developing fluency. Some examples from rehearsing mixed Range 3 facts:

> *I have six 3s* (18). *I have 30 with six tiles?* (5s). *I have 4s making 28?* (Seven 4s).

Rehearsal can also involve listing a given set of multiplications for the student, such as listing the 12 Range 3 multiplications in a table, and then posing tasks drawn from that limited set (rehearsal column 2). Students' search to recall answers can be supported by referring to the limited set. Rehearsal within a range can also involve posing written tasks on cards (rehearsal columns 3 and 4).

Students can keep a times table chart, divided into the four ranges, and update their level of facility in each range with colour-coded shading. There can be benefits in students developing awareness of the progress in their knowledge, and of their next learning goal. As students establish habituation of Range 4, the final range of basic facts, instruction can consolidate students' knowledge across all four ranges (Topic 3F16). Achieving grounded habituation across all the multiplicative basic facts is a significant accomplishment.

Instruction can progress beyond the basic facts, to Range 5, with one factor greater than 10. Once students have habituated Ranges 1 and 2, and are working on Ranges 3 and 4, they can begin tasks in Range 5. Instruction can focus on developing students' structuring and strategies – there is no expectation of habituation in this range. For a setting, the *n*-tiles can become unwieldy with tasks in this range, so larger dot arrays are used. Notations can be drawn directly onto the dot arrays. Notating tasks and strategies becomes particularly important for developing students' awareness of the multiplicative relations involved. The final topic, 3F19, focuses on the further enrichment of students' knowledge of multiplicative relations, through investigations of factors, primes and squares, in the range to 100.

Glossary

Addend. A number to be added. In $7 + 4 = 11$, 7 and 4 are addends, and 11 is the sum.

Additive task. A generic label for tasks involving what adults would regard as addition. The label 'additive task' is used to emphasize that children will construe such tasks idiosyncratically, that is, differently from each other and from the way adults will construe them.

Algorithm. A step-wise procedure for carrying out a task. In arithmetic, a procedure for adding, subtracting, and so on. Also used to refer to the standard, written procedures for calculating with multi-digit numbers, for example, the division algorithm.

Arithmetic knowledge. A collective term for all the student knows about arithmetic (i.e. number and operations). The term 'knowledge' is sometimes juxtaposed with 'strategies' and in that case refers to knowledge not easily characterized as a strategy (for example, knowing the names of numerals).

Arithmetic rack. See Appendix 1.

Array. See Appendix 1.

Arrow cards. See Appendix 1.

Backward number word sequence (BNWS). A regular sequence of number words backward, typically but not necessarily by ones, for example, the BNWS from ten to one, the BNWS from eighty-two to seventy-five, the BNWS by tens from eighty-three.

Bare number tasks. Arithmetic tasks presented in the absence of a setting or context, for example $47 + 35$, 86×3. Referred to as formal arithmetic.

Base-ten. A characteristic of numeration systems and number naming systems whereby numbers are expressed in a form that involves grouping by tens, tens of tens and larger powers of ten (1000, 10,000, etc.).

Base-ten dot materials. See Appendix 1.

Base-ten materials. A generic name for instructional settings consisting of materials organized into ones, tens, hundreds, and so on, such as bundling sticks and base-ten dot materials.

Basic facts. Combinations or number bonds of the form $a + b = c$ (basic facts for addition) or $a \times b = c$ (basic facts for multiplication) where a and b are numbers in the range 0 to 10. Also, corresponding combinations involving subtraction or division.

Bundling sticks. See Appendix 1.

Centuple. A multiple of 100 (e.g. 100, 200, 300, 1300, 2500). Distinguished from century which means a sequence of 100 numbers, for example from 267 to 366 or a period of 100 years.

Colour-coding. Using colour to differentiate different parts of an instructional setting (a collection of 6 red counters and a collection of 3 green counters).

Compensation strategy. An arithmetical strategy that involves first changing one number to make an easier calculation and then compensating for the change, for example $17 + 38$: calculate $17 + 40$ and subtract 2.

Complementary addition. A strategy for subtracting based on adding up, for example $82 - 77$ is solved as $77 + ? = 80$, $80 + ? = 82$, answer 5.

Conceptual place value (CPV). An instructional topic focusing on developing students' facility to increment and decrement flexibly by ones, tens, hundreds, and so on. CPV is distinguished from conventional place value, that is the conventional instructional topic that is intended to provide a basis for learning formal written algorithms.

Counting-back-from. A strategy used by children to solve Removed Items tasks, for example 11 remove 3 – 'eleven, ten, nine – eight'. Also referred to as counting-off-from or counting-down-from.

Counting-back-to. Regarded as the most advanced of the counting-by-ones strategies. Typically used to solve missing subtrahend tasks, for example, have 11, remove some, and there are 8 left – 'eleven, ten, nine – three'. Also referred to as counting-down-to.

Counting-by-ones. Initial or advanced arithmetical strategies which involve counting-by-ones only. Examples of initial counting-by-ones strategies are perceptual and figurative counting, which involve counting-from-one. Examples of advanced counting-by-ones strategies are counting-up-from, counting-up-to, counting-back-from and counting-back-to.

Counting-on. An advanced counting-by-ones strategy used to solve additive tasks or missing addend tasks involving two hidden collections. Counting-on can be differentiated into counting-up-from for additive tasks and counting-up-to for missing addend tasks. Counting-on is also referred to as counting-up.

Counting-up-from. An advanced counting-by-ones strategy used to solve additive tasks involving two hidden collections, for example, 7 and 5, is solved by counting up five from 7.

Counting-up-to. An advanced counting-by-ones strategy used to solve missing addend tasks, for example, 7 and how many make 12, is solved by counting from 7 up to 12, and keeping track of five counts.

Decade. See Decuple.

Decimalizing. Developing base-ten thinking, that is approaches to arithmetic that exploit the decimal (base-ten) numeration system such as using 10 as a unit, and organizing calculations into ones, tens and hundreds.

Decrementing by tens. See Incrementing and decrementing by tens.

Decuple. A multiple of (e.g. 10, 20, 30, 180, 240). Distinguished from decade which means a sequence of ten numbers, for example from 27 to 36 or a period of ten years.

Difference. See Minuend.

Digit. The digits are the ten basic symbols in the modern numeration system, that is '0', '1', … '9'.

Digit cards. See Appendix 1.

Distancing materials. An instructional technique involving progressively reducing the role of materials, for example, materials are unscreened, then flashed and screened, then screened without flashing and used only to check, and so on.

Dividend. In a division equation such as $29 \div 4 = 7 \text{ r } 1$, 29 is the dividend, 4 is the divisor, 7 is the quotient and 1 is the remainder.

Divisor. See Dividend.

Domain. Used to refer to a broad area of arithmetical learning such as Number Words and Numerals, Conceptual Place Value.

Doubles. The addition basic facts that involve adding a number to itself: $1 + 1$, $2 + 2$, … $10 + 10$.

Drop-down notation. An informal notation for recording a split strategy for multi-digit addition and subtraction.

Early number. A generic label for the number work in the first three years of school and learned by children around 4 to 8 years of age. Also known as 'early arithmetic'.

Empty number line (ENL). See Appendix 1.

Enquiry-based teaching. An approach to teaching that emphasizes the enquiry mode. Thus tasks are designed to be at the cutting edge of students' current levels of knowledge.

Enquiry mode. A mode of working where students typically are investigating mathematical topics that are new to them and trying to solve tasks that are genuine problems for them. Contrasted with rehearsal mode, which is a mode of working that involves repeating something with which the student is acquainted, with the intention of increasing familiarity and ease, and perhaps working toward automatization.

Facile. Used in the sense of having good facility, that is, fluent or dexterous, for example, facile with a compensation strategy, or facile with the backward number word sequence.

Factor. If a number F, when multiplied by a whole number gives a number M, we call F a factor of M and M a multiple of F. For example, 3 is a factor of 27 and 27 is a multiple of 3, because $3 \times 9 = 27$.

Figurative. Figurative thought involves re-presentation of a sensory-motor experience, that is a mental replay of a prior experience involving seeing, hearing, touching, and so on. Figurative counting may be figural, in which visualized items constitute the material which is counted, motor, in which movements constitute the material which is counted, or verbal, in which number words constitute the material which is counted.

Finger patterns. Arrangements of fingers used by students when calculating.

Five-wise pattern. A spatial pattern on a ten-frame for a number in the range 1 to 10. Five-wise patterns are made by filling first one row, then the second. For example, a five-wise pattern for 4 has a row of 4 and a row of 0, a five-wise pattern for 7 has a row of 5 and a row of 2. Contrasted with pair-wise patterns, which are made by progressively filling the columns. For example, a pair-wise pattern for 4 has two pairs, a pair-wise pattern for 7 has three pairs and one single dot. On an arithmetic rack, these patterns can be made for numbers in the range 1 to 20. As well, ten-wise patterns can be made by first filling one row of the rack.

Flashing. A technique which involves briefly displaying (typically for half a second) some part of an instructional setting. For example, a ten-frame with 8 red and 2 black dots is flashed.

Formal arithmetic. Arithmetic at the adult level involving formal notation rather than involving informal notation such as an empty number line or a setting such as base-ten materials.

Forward number word sequence (FNWS). A regular sequence of number words forward, typically but not necessarily by ones, for example the FNWS from one to twenty, the FNWS from eighty-one to ninety-three, the FNWS by tens from twenty-four.

Generalizing. The process of proceeding from a few cases to many cases.

Groupable base-ten materials. Base-ten materials such as bundling sticks that can be aggregated into tens and disaggregated. Contrasted with base-ten materials already grouped into tens (or hundreds and tens, etc.) which are referred to as pre-grouped base-ten materials.

Habituated knowledge. Arithmetical knowledge that is recalled easily and quickly such as $10 - 2$ or 7×6.

Higher decade addition. Typically used to refer to addition involving a 2-digit number and a 1-digit number, for example $72 + 5$, $47 + 6$.

Higher decade subtraction. Typically used to refer to subtraction involving a 2-digit number and a 1-digit number, for example $37 - 4$, $52 - 7$.

Hurdle number. A number where students commonly have difficulty continuing a number word sequence. For example, students may say '106, 107, 108, 109, 200': there is a hurdle at 110.

Incrementing and decrementing by tens. Refers to the ability to say immediately, the number that is 10 more (incrementing) or 10 less (decrementing) than a given number.

Instructional setting. See Setting.

Inverse relationship. Commencing with a number N, if another number, for example 6, is added to N and then subtracted from the sum obtained, then the result will be N. Thus addition and subtraction have an inverse relationship – each is the inverse of the other. Similarly, multiplication and division have an inverse relationship.

Irregular spatial configuration. A configuration of dots that does not take the form of a pattern such as the patterns on dice or dominos.

Jump strategy. A category of mental strategies for 2-digit addition and subtraction. Strategies in this category involve starting from one number and incrementing or decrementing that number by first tens and then ones (or first ones then tens). Jump strategies are also used with 3-digit numbers.

Knowledge. A collective term for all of what the child knows about early number. The term 'knowledge' is sometimes juxtaposed with 'strategies' and in that case refers to knowledge not easily characterized as a strategy (for example, knowing the names of numerals).

Mathematics Recovery (MR). A programme originally developed in schools in New South Wales (Australia) which has been implemented widely in schools in a range of countries. The programme focuses on intensive teaching for low-attaining students and an extensive programme of specialist teacher development.

Mathematization. See Progressive mathematization.

Mental computation. Typically refers to doing whole number arithmetic with multi-digit numbers, and without any writing. Contrasted with written computation that is, computation that involves writing.

Micro-adjusting. Making small moment-by-moment adjustments in interactive teaching which are informed by one's observation of student responses.

Minuend. The number from which another number is subtracted, for example in 12 – 3 = 9, 12 is the minuend, 3 is the subtrahend, that is the number subtracted, and 9 is the difference, that is the number obtained.

Missing addend task. An arithmetical task where one addend and the sum are given, for example 9 + □ = 13.

Missing subtrahend task. A subtractive task where the minuend and the difference are given, for example, 11 – □ = 8.

Multi-digit. Involving numbers with two or more digits.

Multi-lid screen. See Appendix 1 – numeral roll and multi-lid screen.

Multiple. See Factor.

Multiplicand. The number multiplied, for example in 12 × 8 = 96 (interpreted as 12 multiplied by 8), 12 is the multiplicand, 8 is the multiplier and 96 is the product.

Multiplier. See Multiplicand.

Non-canonical. The number 64 can be expressed in the form of 50 + 14. This form is referred to as a non-canonical (non-standard) form of 64. Knowledge of non-canonical forms is useful in addition, subtraction, and so on.

Non-count-by-ones. A class of strategies which involve aspects other than counting-by-ones and which are used to solve additive and subtractive tasks. Part of the strategy may involve counting-by-ones but the solution also involves a more advanced procedure. For example, 6 + 8 is solved by saying 'six and six are twelve – thirteen, fourteen'. Also referred to as grouping strategies.

Non-counting strategy. See Counting-by-ones.

Non-regrouping task. See Regrouping task.

Notating. Purposeful writing in an arithmetical situation, for example, notating a jump strategy on an empty number line.

Number. A number is the idea or concept associated with, for example, how many items in a collection. We distinguish among the number 24 – that is, the concept – the spoken or heard number word 'twenty-four', the numeral '24' and also the read or written word 'twenty-four'. These distinctions are important in understanding students' numerical strategies.

Number word. Number words are names or words for numbers. In most cases in early number, the term 'number word' refers to the spoken and heard names for numbers rather than the written and read names.

Number word sequence (NWS). A regular sequence of number words, typically but not necessarily by ones, for example the NWS from 97 to 112, the NWS from 82 back to 75, the NWS by tens from 24, the NWS by threes to 30.

Numeral. Numerals are symbols for numbers, for example '5', '27', '307'.

Numeral cards. See Appendix 1.

Numeral identification. Stating the name of a displayed numeral. The term is used similarly to the term 'letter identification' in early literacy. When assessing numeral identification, numerals are not displayed in numerical sequence.

Numeral recognition. Selecting a nominated numeral from a randomly arranged group of numerals.

Numeral roll. See Appendix 1.

Numeral roll and multi-lid screen. See Appendix 1.

Numeral roll and window. See Appendix 1.

Numeral sequence. A regularly ordered sequence of numerals, typically but not necessarily a forward sequence by ones, for example the numerals as they appear on a numeral track.

Numeral track. See Appendix 1.

Numerosity. The numerosity of a collection is the number of items in the collection.

Ordering numerals. See sequencing numerals.

Over-jump strategy. A variation of a jump strategy that involves going beyond a given number and then adjusting, for example 53 – 19 as 53 – 20 and then 33 + 1.

Pair-wise pattern. A spatial pattern for a number in the range 1 to 10 made on a ten-frame (2 rows and 5 columns). The pair-wise patterns are made by progressively filling the columns. For example, a pair-wise pattern for 8 has four pairs, a pair-wise pattern for 5 has two pairs and one single dot.

Part-whole construction of number. The ability to conceive simultaneously of a whole and two parts. For example conceiving of 10 and also of the parts 6 and 4. Characteristic of students who have progressed beyond a reliance on counting-by-ones to add and subtract.

Partitioning. An arithmetical strategy involving partitioning a number into two parts without counting, for example, when solving 8 + 5, 5 is partitioned into 2 and 3.

Partitions of a number. The ways a number can be expressed as a sum of two numbers, for example, the partitions of 6 are 1 and 5, 2 and 4, 3 and 3, 4 and 2, and 5 and 1.

Partitive division. A division equation such as 15 ÷ 3 is interpreted as distributing 15 items into three groups, that is, three partitions. Contrasted with Quotitive division where 15 ÷ 3 is interpreted as distributing 15 items into groups of three, that is, groups with a quota of three.

Pedagogical engineering. The pedagogical process of designing, trialling and refining instructional procedures.

Perceptual. Involving direct sensory input – usually seeing but may also refer to hearing or feeling. Thus perceptual counting involves counting items seen, heard or felt.

Pre-grouped materials. See Groupable base-ten materials.

Procedure. See Strategy.

Product. See Multiplicand.

Progressive mathematization. The development over time, of the mathematical sophistication of students' knowledge and reasoning, with respect to a specific topic, for example, addition.

Quotient. See Dividend.

Quotitive division. See Partitive division.

Regrouping task. In the case of addition of two 2-digit numbers, a task where the sum of the numbers in the ones column exceeds 9, for example, in 37 + 48, 7 + 8 exceeds 9. In the case of subtraction involving two 2-digit numbers, a task where, in the ones column, the subtrahend exceeds the minuend, for example in 85 – 48, 8 exceeds 5. Similarly applied to addition and subtraction with numbers with three or more digits. The term Non-regrouping is used in the case of an addition task where the sum of the numbers in the ones column does not exceed 9 and in the case of a subtraction task where, in the ones column the minuend exceeds the subtrahend.

Regular spatial configuration. A configuration of dots that takes the form of a standard pattern such as the patterns on dice or dominos.

Rehearsal mode. See Enquiry mode.

Remainder. See Dividend.

Removed items task. A subtractive task where the minuend and the subtrahend are given, for example, 11 – 3 = □.

Scaffolding. Actions on the part of the teacher to provide support for students to reason about or solve a task beyond what they could manage on their own.

Screening. A technique used in the presentation of instructional tasks which involves placing a small screen over all or part of an instructional setting (for example, screening a collection of 6 counters).

Sequencing numerals. Putting in order, a set of numerals that constitute a standard sequence, for example, the numerals from 1 to 10 or from 46 to 55. When the set of numerals does not constitute a standard sequence the term ordering numerals is used, for example: 18, 9, 21, 12.

Setting. A setting is a situation used by the teacher when posing arithmetical tasks. Settings can be (a) materials (e.g. numeral track, ten-frame, counters), (b) informal written; (c) formal written; or (d) verbal. The term setting refers not only to the material, writing or verbal statements but also encompasses the ways in which these (materials, writing or verbal statements) are used in instruction and feature in students' reasoning. Thus the term setting encompasses the often implicit features of instruction that arise during the pedagogical use of the setting.

Split strategy. A category of mental strategies for 2-digit addition and subtraction. Strategies in this category involve splitting the numbers into tens and ones and working separately with the tens and ones before recombining them. Split strategies can also be used with 3-digit and larger numbers.

Split-jump strategy. A hybrid strategy for example, 47 + 25 as 40 + 20, 60 + 7, 67 + 5.

Strategy. A generic label for a method by which a child solves a task. A strategy consists of two or more constituent procedures. A procedure is the simplest form of a strategy, that is, a strategy that cannot be described in terms of two or more constituent procedures. For example, on an additive task involving two screened collections a child might use the procedure of counting the first collection from one and then use the procedure of continuing to count by ones, in order to count the second collection.

Structuring numbers. Coming to know numbers in the range 1 to 20 through organizing numbers in terms of five, ten and doubles, and applying that knowledge to addition and subtraction. For example, thinking of 16 is 10 + 5 + 1 or double 8.

Subitizing. The immediate, correct assignation of a number word to a small collection of perceptual items.

Subtractive task. A generic label for tasks involving what adults would regard as subtraction. The label 'subtractive task' is used to emphasize that children will construe such tasks idiosyncratically, that is, differently from each other and from the way adults will construe them.

Subtrahend. See Minuend.

Sum. See Addend.

Symbolization. A process of symbolizing in the sense of developing and using symbols in a context of arithmetical reasoning.

Symbolizing. See Symbolization.

Task. A generic label for problems or questions presented to a student.

Temporal sequence. A sequence of events that occur over time, for example, sequences of sounds or movements.

Ten-frame. See Appendix 1.

Ten-frames – combinations. See Appendix 1.

Ten-frames – five-wise. See Appendix 1.

Ten-Frames – Full. See Appendix 1.

Ten-frames – pair-wise. See Appendix 1.

Ten-frames – partitions. See Appendix 1.

Ten-wise pattern. See Five-wise pattern.

Transforming strategy. An arithmetical strategy that involves simultaneously changing two numbers to make an easier calculation, for example 17 + 38 is transformed to 15 + 40, 83 – 17 is transformed to 80 – 14.

Unit. A thing that is countable and therefore is regarded as a single item. For example, when one counts how many threes in 18: one 3, two 3s, three 3s, … six 3s; the threes are regarded as units.

Unitizing. A conceptual procedure that involves regarding a number larger than one, as a unit, for example 3 is regarded as a unit of three rather than three ones, and 10 is regarded as a unit of ten. Unitizing enables students to focus on the unitary rather than the composite aspect of the number.

Written computation. See Mental computation.

Appendix 1

Instructional Settings

Addition cards. A set of 100 expression cards showing all the tasks of the basic addition facts, that is, all additions with both addends in the range 1–10: 1 + 1, 1 + 2, 1 + 3... 1 + 10; 2 + 1, 2 + 2... 2 + 10;... 10 + 1, 10 + 2... 10 + 10. Typically colour-coded to be organised into Addition Ranges 1–3.

Arithmetic rack. An instructional device consisting of two rows of ten beads which can be moved like beads on an abacus. In each row the beads appear in two groups of five, demarcated by colour. The rack is used to support students' additive reasoning in the range 1 to 20.

Array. A rectangular grid of dots used as a setting for multiplication, for example a 6 × 4 array has six rows and four columns.

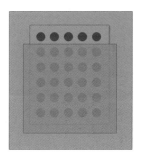

Arrow cards. A set of 36 cards with a card for each of the following numerals: 1, 2, ...9, 10; 11, ...90; 100, 200, ...900; 1000, 2000 ...9000. The cards are used to build multi-digit numerals, and each card has an arrow on the right hand side to support students' orienting and locating the cards.

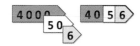

Base-ten dot materials. Materials consisting of strips with 1 to 9 dots, strips with 10 dots and squares with 100 dots. Dots are grey or black in order to demarcate a 5 in the 6- to 9-dot strips, two 5s in the 10-dot strip and two 50s in the 100-dot square.

Bundling sticks. Wooden sticks used to show 10s and 1s. Rubber bands are used to make bundles of 10 and groups of ten 10s.

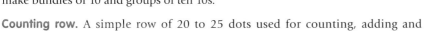

Counting row. A simple row of 20 to 25 dots used for counting, adding and subtracting.

Digit cards. A set of cards used to build numerals. Each card displays a digit (i.e. 0, 1, 2 ...9). A set includes several cards for each digit, in order to account for numerals with repeating digits (e.g. 464, 3333).

Division cards. A set of 100 expression cards showing all the tasks of the basic division facts, that is, all divisions with divisor and quotient in the range 2–10: 4 ÷ 2, 6 ÷ 2, 8 ÷ 2... 20 ÷ 2; 6 ÷ 3, 9 ÷ 3... 30 ÷ 3;... 20 ÷ 10, 30 ÷ 10... 100 ÷ 10. Typically colour-coded to be organised into Multiplication Ranges 1–4.

Empty number line (ENL). A setting consisting of a simple arc or line which is used by students and teachers to record and explain mental strategies for adding, subtracting, multiplying, and dividing.

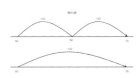

Expression card. A card containing a single arithmetic expression or task, presented in horizontal format, for example: 7 + 4, 17 – 13, 9 × 6, 24 ÷ 6.

Five-frame. An instructional setting consisting of a card with a 1 × 5 rectangular array used to support students' additive reasoning in the range 1 to 5.

Five-frames – Partitions. A set of six five-frames showing the partitions of 5 demarcated by colour (i.e. 5 & 0, 4 & 1, 3 & 2, … 0 & 5).

Five-frames – Regular. A set of six five-frames showing 0, 1, 2 …5 dots.

Multiplication cards. A set of 81 expression cards showing all the tasks of the basic multiplication facts, that is, all multiplications with both factors in the range 2–10: 2 × 2, 2 × 3, 2 × 4… 2 × 10; 3 × 2, 3 × 3… 3 × 10; … 10 × 2, 10 × 3… 10 × 10. Typically colour-coded to be organised into Multiplication Ranges 1–4.

N-groups. An instructional setting for multiplication consisting of cards with a group of a given number of dots. Hence 2-group, 3-group and so on.

N-tiles. An instructional setting for multiplication consisting of tiles with a single row of a given number of dots. Hence 2-tile, 3-tile and so on.

Numeral cards. A set of cards with each card displaying a numeral.

Numeral roll. An instructional setting consisting of a long strip of paper containing a relatively long sequence of numerals, increasing from left to right, for example, from 1 to 120 or 80 to 220.

Numeral roll and multi-lid screen. A numeral roll and a screen with 10 or more lids enabling screening and unscreening of individual numerals.

Numeral roll and window. A numeral roll threaded through a slotted card so that one numeral only is displayed.

Numeral track. An instructional setting consisting of a strip of cardboard containing a sequence of numerals and for each numeral, a hinged lid which can be used to screen or display the numeral.

Small arrays. An instructional setting for multiplication consisting of arrays of no more than five rows and no more than five columns.

Subtraction cards. A set of 100 expression cards showing all the tasks of the basic subtraction facts, that is, all subtractions with subtrahend and difference in the range 1–10: 2 – 1, 3 – 1, 4 – 1… 11 – 1; 3 – 2, 4 – 2… 12 – 2;… 11 – 10, 12 – 10… 20 – 10. Typically colour-coded to be organised into Addition Ranges 1–3.

Ten-frame. An instructional setting consisting of a card with a 2 × 5 rectangular array used to support students' additive reasoning in the range 1 to 10.

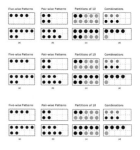

Ten-frames – Combinations. A set of ten-frames with the different combinations of (a) 0 to 5 dots in the upper row and (b) 0 to 5 dots in the lower row, typically with the rows in differing colours. A total of 36 cards.

Ten-frames – Five-wise. A set of 11 ten-frames showing the five-wise patterns for 0, 1, …10.

Ten-frames – Full. Ten-frames with 10 dots of one colour.

Ten-frames – Pair-wise. A set of 11 ten-frames showing the pair-wise patterns for 0, 1, …10.

Ten-frames – Partitions. A set of 11 ten-frames showing the partitions of 10 demarcated by colour (i.e. 10 & 0, 9 & 1, 8 & 2, … 0 & 10). Typically, a five-wise set and a pair-wise set.

Ten-frames – Regular. A set of 11 ten-frames showing 0, 1, 2 …10 dots. Typically, a five-wise set and a pair-wise set.

Appendix 2

LFIN Models Chart
Models of Learning Progressions

2A–3A **Number Word Sequences**

Forward (FNWS)   **Backward (BNWS)**

Forward (FNWS)	Backward (BNWS)
⓪ Emergent FNWS	⓪ Emergent BNWS
① Initial FNWS to 'ten'	① Initial BNWS to 'ten'
② Intermediate FNWS to 'ten'	② Intermed. BNWS to 'ten'
③ Facile FNWS to 'ten'	③ Facile BNWS to 'ten'
④ Facile FNWS to 'thirty'	④ Facile BNWS to 'thirty'
⑤ Facile FNWS to '100'	⑤ Facile BNWS to '100'
⑥ Facile FNWS to '1000'	⑥ Facile BNWS to '1000'
⑦ Facile FNWS to '10,000'	⑦ Facile BNWS to '10,000'

2A–3A **Numeral Identification**

(NID)

⓪ Emergent numeral ID
① Numerals to 10 – Identify
② Numerals to 20 – Identify
③ Numerals to 100 – Identify
④ Numerals to 1000 – ID & write
⑤ Numerals to 10,000 – ID & write
⑥ Numerals to 100,000 – ID & write

2–B **Structuring Numbers 1 to 20**

(SN20)

⓪ Emergent spatial patterns and finger patterns
① Finger patterns 1–5 and spatial patterns 1–6
② Small doubles and small partitions of 10
③ Five-plus and partitions of 5
④ Facile structuring numbers 1 to 10
⑤ Formal addition (parts ≤ 10)
⑥ Formal addition & subtraction (parts ≤ 10)
⑦ Formal addition & subtraction (whole ≤ 20)

2C **Stages of Early Arithmetical**

Learning (SEAL)

⓪ Emergent counting
① Perceptual counting
② Figurative counting
③ Initial number sequence – Counting-on and -back
④ Intermediate number sequence – Counting-down-to
⑤ Facile number sequence – Non-count-by-ones strategies

3C **Conceptual Place Value**

(CPV)

⓪ Emergent inc- & decrementing by 10
① Inc- & decrementing by 10, with materials, in range to 100
② Inc- & decrementing flexibly by 10s and 1s, with materials, in range to 100
③ Inc- & decrementing by 10, without materials, in range to 100
④ Inc- & decrementing by 10, without materials, in range to 1000

3D **Addition & Subtraction to 100**

(A&S)

⓪ Emergent addition & subtraction to 100
① Add-up-from/subtract-down-to decuple
② Add-up-to/subtract-down-from decuple – small
③ Add-up-to/subtract-down-from decuple – large
④ Add/subtract across a decuple
⑤ 2-digit addition with regrouping
⑥ 2-digit addition & subtraction with regrouping

3E **Early Multiplication & Division**

(EM&D)

⓪ Emergent grouping
① Perceptual items, counted by ones
② Perceptual items, counted in multiples
③ Figurative items, counted in multiples
④ Abstract groups, items counted in multiples
⑤ Abstract groups, facile repeated addition
⑥ Multiplicative strategies

3F **Multiplicative Basic Facts**

(MBF)

Range	ⓐ Count-based	ⓑ Mult've strategy	ⓒ Facile mult'n	ⓓ Facile div'n
1. 2s and 10s	⑴ₐ	⑴ᵦ	⑴ c	⑴ d
2. Low × low	⑵ₐ	⑵ᵦ	⑵ c	⑵ d
3. Low × high	⑶ₐ	⑶ᵦ	⑶ c	⑶ d
4. High × high	⑷ₐ	⑷ᵦ	⑷ c	⑷ d
5. Factor > 10	⑸ₐ	⑸ᵦ	⑸ c	⑸ d

Learning Framework in Number

Domains, Models, Assessment Schedules and Teaching Charts

Model names

FNWS:	Forward Number Word Sequences
BNWS:	Backward Number Word Sequences
NID:	Numeral Identification
SN20:	Structuring Numbers 1 to 20
SEAL:	Stages of Early Arithmetical Learning
CPV:	Conceptual Place Value
A&S:	Addition & Subtraction to 100
EM&D:	Early Multiplication & Division
MBF:	Multiplicative Basic Facts

BAND 2
Early Number (EN)

2A — Early Number Words & Numerals

▤ NID: ⓪①②③④…
▤ BNWS: ⓪①②③④⑤…
▤ FNWS: ⓪①②③④⑤…

2B — Early Structuring

▤ SN20: ⓪①②③…

2C — Early Arithmetical Strategies

▤ SEAL: ⓪①②③④⑤

BAND 3
Middle Number (MN)

3A — Number Words & Numerals

…③④⑤⑥
…④⑤⑥⑦
…④⑤⑥⑦

3B — Structuring Numbers 1 to 20

…②③④⑤⑥⑦

10
20

3C — Conceptual Place Value

▤ CPV: ⓪①②③④

3D — Addition & Subtraction to 100

▤ A&S: ⓪①②③④⑤⑥

3E — Early Multiplication & Division

▤ EM&D: ⓪①②③④⑤⑥

3F — Multiplicative Basic Facts

▤ MBF: ①abcd…⑤abcd

▢ Assessment schedule   ▯ Teaching chart   ▤ Model of a learning progression

⓪①②… level or stage numbers on model

Learning Framework in Number © Wright & Ellemor-Collins, 2018 (Sage)

Bibliography

Anghileri, J. (2000). *Teaching number sense*. London: Continuum.

Anghileri, J. (Ed.). (2001). *Principles and practices of arithmetic teaching*. Buckingham: Open University Press.

Aubrey, C. (1993). An investigation of the mathematical knowledge and competencies which young children bring into school. *British Educational Research Journal* 19: 27–41.

Baroody, A. (1985). Mastery of basic number combinations: Internalization of relationships or facts? *Journal for Research in Mathematics Education* 16: 83–98.

Baroody, A. (2006). Why children have difficulties mastering the basic number combinations and how to help them. *Teaching Children Mathematics* 13: 22–31.

Beishuizen, M. (1993). Mental strategies and materials or models for addition and subtraction up to 100 in Dutch second grades. *Journal for Research in Mathematics Education* 34: 394–433.

Beishuizen, M. (1999). The empty number line as a new model. In I. Thompson (Ed.), *Issues in teaching numeracy in primary schools* (pp. 157–68). Buckingham: Open University Press.

Beishuizen, M. (2001). Different approaches to mastering mental calculation strategies. In J. Anghileri (Ed.), *Principles and practices in arithmetic teaching* (pp. 119–30). Buckingham: Open University Press.

Beishuizen, M. & Anghileri, J. (1998). Which mental strategies in the early number curriculum? A comparison of British ideas and Dutch views. *British Education Research Journal* 34: 519–38.

Bobis, J. (1996). Visualisation and the development of number sense with kindergarten children. In J. Mulligan & M. Mitchelmore (Eds.), *Children's number learning: A research monograph of MERGA/AAMT* (pp. 17–34). Adelaide: Australian Association of Mathematics Teachers.

Bobis, J., Clarke, B., Clarke, D., Thomas, G., Wright, R., Young-Loveridge, J. & Gould, P. (2005). Supporting teachers in the development of young children's mathematical thinking: Three large-scale cases. *Mathematics Education Research Journal* 16(3): 27–57.

Cade, W.L., Copeland, J.L., Person, N.K. & D'Mello, S.K. (2008). Dialogue modes in expert tutoring. In B. Woolf, E. Aimeur, R. Nkambou & S. Lajoie (Eds.), *Proceedings of the Ninth International Conference on Intelligent Tutoring Systems* (pp. 470–9). Berlin: Springer-Verlag.

Carpenter, T.P., Fennema, E., Franke, M.L., Levi, L. & Empson, S.B. (1999). *Children's mathematics: Cognitively guided instruction*. Portsmouth, NH: Heinemann.

Carruthers, E. & Worthington, M. (2006). *Children's mathematics: Making marks, making meaning*. London: Sage.

Cayton, G.A. & Brizuela, B.M. (2007). First graders' strategies for numerical notation, number reading and the number concept. In J.H. Woo, H.C. Lew, K.S. Park & D.Y. Seo (Eds.), *Proceedings of the 31st Conference of the International Group for the Psychology of Mathematics Education* (Vol. 2, pp. 81–8). Seoul: PME.

Clarke, B., McDonough, A. & Sullivan, P. (2002). Measuring and describing learning: The early numeracy research project. In A. Cockburn & E. Nardi (Eds.), *Proceedings of the 26th Annual Conference of the International Group for the Psychology of Mathematics Education* (Vol. 1, pp. 181–5). Norwich: PME.

Clarke, D., Sullivan, P., Cheeseman, J. & Clarke, B. (2000). The early numeracy project: Developing a framework for describing early numeracy learning. In J. Bana & A. Chapman (Eds.), *Mathematics education beyond 2000: Proceedings of the 23rd annual conference of Mathematics Education Research Group of Australasia, Fremantle* (pp. 180–7). Sydney: MERGA.

Clements, D. & Sarama, J. (Eds.). (2004). *Engaging young children in mathematics*. Mahwah, NJ: Lawrence Erlbaum.

Clements, D. & Sarama, J. (2009). *Learning and teaching early math: The learning trajectories approach*. New York: Routledge.

Clements, D. & Sarama, J. (2011). Early childhood mathematics intervention. *Science* 333(6045): 968–70.

Cobb, P. (1991). Reconstructing elementary school mathematics. *Focus on Learning Problems in Mathematics* 13(3): 3–33.

Cobb, P. & Bauersfeld, H. (Eds.). (1995). *The emergence of mathematical meaning: Interaction in classroom cultures*. Hillsdale, NJ: Lawrence Erlbaum.

Cobb, P. & McLain, K. (2006). Guiding inquiry-based math learning. In R.K. Sawyer (Ed.), *The Cambridge handbook of the learning sciences* (pp. 171–86). Cambridge: Cambridge University Press.

Cobb, P. & Wheatley, G. (1988). Children's initial understandings of ten. *Focus on Learning Problems in Mathematics* 10(3): 1–36.

Cobb, P., Gravemeijer, K., Yackel, E., McClain, K. & Whitenack, J. (1997). Mathematizing and symbolizing: The emergence of chains of signification in one first-grade classroom. In D. Kirshner & J.A. Whitson (Eds.), *Situated cognition theory: Social, semiotic, and neurological perspectives* (pp. 151–233). Mahwah, NJ: Lawrence Erlbaum.

Cobb, P., McClain, K., Whitenack, J. & Estes, B. (1995). Supporting young children's development of mathematical power. In A. Richards (Ed.), *Proceedings of the Fifteenth Biennial Conference of the Australian Association of Mathematics Teachers* (pp. 1–11). Darwin: Australian Association of Mathematics Teachers.

Cobb, P., Wood, T. & Yackel, E. (1991). A constructivist approach to second grade mathematics. In E. von Glasersfeld (Ed.), *Radical constructivism in mathematics education* (pp. 157–76). Dordrecht: Kluwer.

Cobb, P., Yackel, E. & McClain, K. (Eds.). (2000). *Symbolizing and communicating in mathematics classrooms: Perspectives on discourse, tools, and instructional design.* Mahwah, NJ: Lawrence Erlbaum.

Copley, J. (Ed.). (1999). *Mathematics in the early years.* Reston, VA: National Council of Teachers of Mathematics.

Daro, P., Mosher, F. & Corcoran, T. (2011). *Learning trajectories in mathematics: A foundation for standards, curriculum, assessment and instruction.* Consortium for Policy Research in Education. CPRE Research Report #RR-68.

Davis, B., Sumara, D. & Luce-Kapler, R. (2008). *Engaging minds: Changing teaching in complex times.* New York: Routledge.

Denvir, B. & Brown, M. (1986). Understanding of number concepts in low attaining 7–9 year olds: Part 1. Development of descriptive framework and diagnostic instrument. *Educational Studies in Mathematics* 17: 15–36.

Dineen, A. (2014). *Use of grouping strategies to solve addition tasks in the range one to twenty by students in their first year of school: A teaching experiment.* Unpublished PhD thesis, Southern Cross University, Lismore, New South Wales.

D'Mello, S., Olney, A. & Person, N. (2010). Mining collaborative patterns in tutorial dialogues. *Journal of Educational Data Mining* 2(1): 1–37.

Dooren, W.V., Bock, D.D. & Verschaffel, L. (2010). From addition to multiplication ... and back: The development of students' additive and multiplicative reasoning skills. *Cognition and Instruction* 28(3): 360–81.

Dowker, A.D. (2004). *Children with difficulties in mathematics: What works?* London: DfES.

Dowker, A.D. (2005). *Individual differences in arithmetic: Implications for psychology, neuroscience and education.* Hove: Psychology Press.

Dowker, A. & Sigley, G. (2010). Targeted interventions for children with arithmetical difficulties. In R. Cowan, M. Saxton & A. Tolmie (Eds.), *Understanding number development and difficulties (British Journal of Educational Psychology Monograph Series II, 7)* (pp. 65–81). Leicester: British Psychological Society.

Downton, A. (2008). Links between children's understanding of multiplication and solution strategies for division. In M. Goos, R. Brown & K. Makar (Eds.), *Navigating currents and charting directions (Proceedings of the 31st Annual Conference of the Mathematics Education Research Group of Australasia)* (Vol. 1, pp. 171–8). Brisbane: MERGA.

Ellemor-Collins, D. & Wright, R.J. (2007). Assessing student knowledge of the sequential structure of numbers as a significant aspect of multi-digit addition and subtraction. *Educational and Child Psychology* 24: 54–63.

Ellemor-Collins, D. & Wright, R.J. (2008). How are your students thinking about arithmetic? Videotaped interview-based assessment. *Teaching Children Mathematics* September: 106–11.

Ellemor-Collins, D. & Wright, R.J. (2009). Structuring numbers 1 to 20: Developing facile addition and subtraction. *Mathematics Education Research Journal* 21(2): 50–75.

Ellemor-Collins, D. & Wright, R.J. (2011). Developing conceptual place value: Instructional design for intensive intervention. *Australian Journal of Learning Difficulties* 16(1): 41–63.

Ellemor-Collins, D. & Wright, R.J. (2011). Unpacking *mathematisation*: An experimental framework for arithmetic instruction. In B. Ubuz (Ed.), *Proceedings of the 35th Conference of the International Group for the Psychology of Mathematics Education* (Vol. 2, pp. 313–20). Ankara: PME.

Ellemor-Collins, D., Wright, R.J. & McEvoy, S. (2013). Instructional design for intervention in simple arithmetic. In M. Inprasitha (Ed.), *Proceedings of the 6th East Asia Regional Conference on Mathematics Education (EARCOME 6)* (Vol. 2, pp. 24–34). Phuket: International Commission on Mathematical Instruction.

Flexer, R. (1986). The power of five: The step before the power of ten. *Arithmetic Teacher* 31: 5–9.

Fosnot, C.T. & Dolk, M. (2001). *Young mathematics at work: Constructing multiplication and division.* Portsmouth, NH: Heinemann.

Fosnot, C. & Dolk, M. (2001). *Young mathematicians at work: Constructing number sense, addition and subtraction.* Portsmouth, NH: Heinemann.

Fountas, I.C. & Pinnell, G.S. (1996). *Guided reading: Good first teaching for all children.* Portsmouth, NH: Heinemann.

Fuson, K. (1988). *Children's counting and concepts of number.* New York: Springer-Verlag.

Fuson, K.C., Richards, J. & Briars, D. (1982). The acquisition and elaboration of the number word sequence. In C.J. Brainerd (Ed.), *Progress in cognitive development: Vol. 1: Children's logical and mathematical cognition* (pp. 33–92). New York: Springer-Verlag.

Fuson, K.C., Wearne, D., Hiebert, J., Human, P., Olivier, A., Carpenter, T. & Fenema, E. (1997). Children's conceptual structure for multidigit numbers and methods of multidigit addition and subtraction. *Journal for Research in Mathematics Education* 38: 130–63.

Geary, D.C., Hoard, M.K., Nugent, L. & Bailey, D.H. (2013). Adolescents' functional numeracy is predicted by their school entry number system knowledge. *PLoS ONE* 8(1): e54651.

Gelman, R. & Gallistel, C. (1978). *The child's understanding of number.* Cambridge, MA and London: Harvard University Press.

Ginsburg, H.P. (1997). *Entering the child's mind: The clinical interview in psychological research and practice.* New York: Cambridge University Press.

Ginsburg, H., Jacobs, S. & Lopez, L.S. (1998). *The teacher's guide to flexible interviewing in the classroom: Learning what children know about math.* Boston: Allyn and Bacon.

Gould, P. (2012). What number knowledge do children have when starting kindergarten in NSW? *Australian Journal of Early Childhood* 37(3): 105–10.

Graesser, A.C., Person, N.K. & Magliano, J.P. (1995). Collaborative dialogue patterns in naturalistic one-to-one tutoring sessions. *Applied Cognitive Psychology* 9(6): 1–28.

Gravemeijer, K.P.E. (1991). An instruction-theoretical reflection on the use of manipulatives. In L. Streefland (Ed.), *Realistic mathematics education in primary school* (pp. 57–76). Utrecht: Freudenthal Institute.

Gravemeijer, K.P.E. (1994). *Developing realistic mathematics education.* Utrecht: CD-β Press.

Gravemeijer, K.P.E. (1997). Mediating between concrete and abstract. In T. Nunes & P. Bryant (Eds.), *Learning and teaching mathematics: An international perspective* (pp. 315–43). Hove: Psychology Press.

Gravemeijer, K.P.E., Cobb, P., Bowers, J. & Whitenack, J. (2000). Symbolizing, modeling, and instructional design. In P. Cobb, E. Yackel & K. McClain (Eds.), *Symbolizing and communicating in mathematics classrooms: Perspectives on discourse, tools, and instructional design* (pp. 335–73). Mahwah, NJ: Lawrence Erlbaum.

Gray, E.M. (1991). An analysis of diverging approaches to simple arithmetic: Preference and its consequences. *Educational Studies in Mathematics* 33: 551–74.

Gray, E. & Tall, D. (1994). Duality, ambiguity, and flexibility: A 'proceptual' view of simple arithmetic. *Journal for Research in Mathematics Education* 25(2): 116–40.

Hackenberg, A.J. (2010). Students' reasoning with reversible multiplicative relationships. *Cognition and Instruction* 28(4): 383–432.

Hatano, G. (1982). Learning to add and subtract: A Japanese perspective. In T. Carpenter, J. Moser & T. Romberg (Eds.), *Addition and subtraction: A cognitive perspective* (pp. 211–22). Hillsdale, NJ: Lawrence Erlbaum.

Heirdsfield, A. (2001). Integration, compensation and memory in mental addition and subtraction. In M. Van den Heuvel-Panhuizen (Ed.), *Proceedings of the 25th Conference of the International Group for the Psychology of Mathematics Education* (Vol. 3, pp. 129–36). Utrecht: PME.

Hewitt, D. & Brown, E. (1998). On teaching early number through language. In A. Olivier & K. Newstead (Eds.), *Proceedings of the 22nd Conference of the International Group for the Psychology of Mathematics Education* (Vol. 3, pp. 41–8). Stellenbosh: PME.

Hiebert, J., Carpenter, T.P., Fenema, E., Fuson, K.C., Wearne, D., Murray, H., Oliver, A. & Human, P. (1997). *Making sense: Teaching and learning mathematics with understanding.* Portsmouth, NH: Heinemann.

Hughes, M. (1986). *Children and number: Difficulties in learning mathematics.* New York: Basil Blackwell.

Jacobs, V.R., Ambrose, R., Clement, L. & Brown, D. (2006). Using teacher-produced videotapes of student interviews as discussion catalysts. *Teaching Children Mathematics* 12(6): 276–81.

Jacobs, V.R., Lamb, L.L.C. & Philipp, R.A. (2010). Professional noticing of children's mathematical thinking. *Journal for Research in Mathematics Education* 41(2): 169–202.

Kamii, C. (1985). *Young children reinvent arithmetic.* New York: Teachers College Press.

Kamii, C. (1986). Place value: An explanation of its difficulty and educational implications for the primary grades. *Journal of Research in Early Childhood Education* 1: 75–86.

Kamii, C. & Dominick, A. (1998). The harmful effects of algorithms in grades 1–4. In L.J. Marrow (Ed.), *The teaching and learning of algorithms in school mathematics: 1998 Yearbook* (pp. 130–40). Reston, VA: National Council of Teachers of Mathematics.

Kaufman, E.I., Lord, M.W., Reese, T.W. & Volkmann, J. (1949). The discrimination of visual number. *The American Journal of Psychology* 62(4): 498–525.

Killion, K. & Steffe, L.P. (2002). Children's multiplication. *Putting research into practice in the elementary grades: Readings from journals of the NCTM.* Reston, VA: National Council of Teachers of Mathematics.

Klein, A.S., Beishuizen, M. & Treffers, A. (1998). The empty number line in Dutch second grades: Realistic versus gradual program design. *Journal for Research in Mathematics Education* 29(4): 443–64.

Lambdin, D.V. (2003). Benefits of teaching through problem-solving. In F.K. Lester & R. Charles (Eds.), *Teaching mathematics through problem-solving: Pre-kindegarten – Grade 6* (pp. 3–13). Reston, VA: National Council of Teachers of Mathematics.

Maclellan, E. (2010). Counting: What it is and why it matters. In I. Thompson (Ed.), *Teaching and learning early number* (2nd edn, pp. 72–81). Maidenhead: Open University Press.

McClain, K. & Cobb, P. (1999). Supporting children's ways of reasoning about patterns and partitions. In J.V. Copley (Ed.), *Mathematics in the early years* (pp. 113–18). Reston, VA: National Council of Teachers of Mathematics.

McClain, K. & Cobb, P. (2001). An analysis of development of sociomathematical norms in one first-grade classroom. *Journal for Research in Mathematics Education* 32: 236–66.

Menne, J. (2001). Jumping ahead: An innovative teaching programme. In J. Anghileri (Ed.), *Principles and practices in arithmetic teaching: Innovative approaches for the primary classroom* (pp. 95–106). Buckingham and Philadelphia: Open University Press.

Mix, K., Huttenlocher, J. & Levine, S. (2002). *Quantitative development in infancy and early childhood*. Oxford: Oxford University Press.

Mulligan, J.T. (1998). A research-based framework for assessing early multiplication and division. In C. Kanes, M. Goos & E. Warren (Eds.), *Proceedings of the 21st Annual Conference of the Mathematics Education Research Group of Australasia* (Vol. 2, pp. 404–11). Brisbane: Griffith University.

Mulligan, J.T. & Mitchelmore, M.C. (1997). Young children's intuitive models of multiplication and division. *Journal for Research in Mathematics Education* 28: 309–30.

Mulligan, J.T. & Mitchelmore, M.C. (2009). Awareness of pattern and structure in early mathematical development. *Mathematics Education Research Journal* 21(2): 33–49.

Munn, P. (1997). Writing and number. In I. Thompson (Ed.), *Teaching and learning early number* (pp. 19–23). Buckingham: Open University Press.

Munn, P. (2010). Children's beliefs about counting. In I. Thompson (Ed.), *Teaching and learning early number* (2nd edn, pp. 9–19). Maidenhead: Open University Press.

Olive, J. (2001). Children's number sequences: An explanation of Steffe's constructs and an extrapolation to rational numbers of arithmetic. *The Mathematics Educator* 11(1): 4–9.

Papic, M., Mulligan, J. & Mitchelmore, M.C. (2011). Assessing the development of preschoolers' mathematical patterning. *Journal for Research in Mathematics Education* 42(3): 237–68.

Pepper, K. & Hunting, R. (1998). Preschoolers' counting and sharing. *Journal for Research in Mathematics Education* 29: 164–83.

Piaget, J. (1941). *The child's conception of number*. New York: Norton.

Pirie, S.E.B. & Kieren, T.E. (1994). Growth in mathematical understanding: How can we characterise it and how can we represent it? *Educational Studies in Mathematics* 26: 165–90.

Rivkin, S.G., Hanushek, E.A. & Kain, J.F. (2005). Teachers, schools, and academic achievement. *Econometrica* 73(2): 417–58.

Rousham, L. (2003). The empty number line: A model in search of a learning trajectory? In I. Thompson (Ed.), *Enhancing primary mathematics teaching* (pp. 29–39). Maidenhead: Open University Press.

Sarama, J. & Clements, D.H. (2009). *Early childhood mathematics education research: Learning trajectories for young children*. New York: Routledge.

Sherin, M.G., Jacobs, V.R. & Philipp, R.A. (2011). *Mathematics teacher noticing: Seeing through teachers' eyes*. New York: Routledge.

Shulman, L.S. (1986). Those who understand: Knowledge growth in teaching. *Educational Researcher* 15(2): 4–14.

Siemon, D., Izard, J., Breed, M. & Virgona, J. (2006). The derivation of a learning assessment framework for multiplicative thinking. In J. Novotná, H. Moraová, M. Krátká & N. Stehlíková (Eds.), *Proceedings of the 30th Conference of the International Group for the Psychology of Mathematics Education* (Vol. 5, pp. 113–20). Prague: PME.

Simon, M. (1995). Reconstructing mathematics pedagogy from a constructivist perspective. *Journal for Research in Mathematics Education* 26(2): 114–45.

Steffe, L.P. (1988). Children's construction of number sequences and multiplying schemes. In J. Hiebert & M. Behr (Eds.), *Number concepts and operations in the middle grades* (pp. 191–41). Hillsdale, NJ: Lawrence Erlbaum.

Steffe, L.P. (1992a). Learning stages in the construction of the number sequence. In J. Bideaud, C. Meljac & J. Fischer (Eds.), *Pathways to number: Children's developing numerical abilities* (pp. 83–98). Hillsdale, NJ: Lawrence Erlbaum.

Steffe, L.P. (1992b). Schemes of action and operation involving composite units. *Learning and Individual Differences* 4(3): 259–309.

Steffe, L.P. (2004). On the construction of learning trajectories of children: The case of commensurate fractions. *Mathematical Thinking and Learning* 6(2): 129–62.

Steffe, L.P. & Cobb, P. (with E. von Glasersfeld) (1988). *Construction of arithmetic meanings and strategies*. New York: Springer-Verlag.

Steffe, L.P., von Glasersfeld, E., Richards, J. & Cobb, P. (1983). *Children's counting types: Philosophy, theory, and application*. New York: Praeger.

Stephan, M., Bowers, J., Cobb, P. & Gravemeijer, K. (2003). *Supporting students' development of measuring conceptions: Analyzing students' learning in social context, JRME Monograph #12* (Vol. 12). Reston, VA: National Council of Teachers of Mathematics.

Streefland, L. (Ed.). (1991). *Realistic mathematics education in primary school.* Utrecht: CD-B Press.

Sullivan, P., Clarke, D.M., Cheeseman, J. & Mulligan, J. (2001). Moving beyond physical models in learning multiplicative reasoning. In M. van den Heuvel-Panhuizen (Ed.), *Proceedings of the 25th Annual Conference of the International Group for the Psychology of Mathematics Education* (Vol. 4, pp. 233–40). Utrecht: PME.

Tabor, P. (2008). *An investigation of instruction in two-digit addition and subtraction using a classroom teaching experiment methodology, design research, and multilevel modeling.* Unpublished PhD thesis, Southern Cross University, Lismore, New South Wales.

Thomas, J. & Harkness, S. (2011). Implications for intervention: Categorising the quantitative mental imagery of children. *Mathematics Education Research Journal* 25(2): 231–56.

Thomas, J. & Tabor, P. (2011). Developing quantitative mental imagery. *Teaching Children Mathematics* 19: 175–83.

Thomas, J., Tabor, P. & Wright, R. (2011). First graders' number knowledge. *Teaching Children Mathematics* 17: 298–308.

Thompson, I. (1994). Young children's idiosyncratic written algorithms for addition. *Education Studies in Mathematics* 36: 333–45.

Thompson, I. (1997). Mental and written algorithms: Can the gap be bridged? In I. Thompson (Ed.), *Teaching and learning early number* (pp. 97–109). Buckingham: Open University Press.

Thompson, I. (Ed.). (1997). *Teaching and learning early number.* Buckingham: Open University Press.

Thompson, I. (Ed.). (1999). *Issues in teaching numeracy in primary schools.* Buckingham: Open University Press.

Thompson, I. (1999). Written methods of calculation. In I. Thompson (Ed.), *Issues in teaching numeracy in primary schools* (pp. 167–83). Buckingham: Open University Press.

Thompson, I. (Ed.). (2003). *Enhancing primary mathematics teaching.* Buckingham: Open University Press.

Thompson, I. (2003). Place value: The English disease? In I. Thompson (Ed.), *Enhancing primary mathematics teaching* (pp. 181–90). Maidenhead: Open University Press.

Thompson, I. & Bramald, R. (2002). *An investigation of the relationship between young children's understanding of the concept of place value and their competence at mental addition (Report for the Nuffield Foundation).* Newcastle upon Tyne: University of Newcastle upon Tyne.

Thompson, I. & Smith, F. (1999). *Mental calculation strategies for the addition and subtraction of 2-digit numbers (Report for the Nuffield Foundation).* Newcastle upon Tyne: University of Newcastle upon Tyne.

Threlfall, J. (2002). Flexible mental calculation. *Educational Studies in Mathematics* 50(1): 29–47.

Threlfall, J. (2010). Development in oral counting, enumeration and counting for cardinality. In I. Thompson (Ed.), *Teaching and learning early number* (2nd edn, pp. 61–71). Maidenhead: Open University Press.

Tolchinsky, L. (2003). *The cradle of culture and what children know about writing and numbers before being taught.* Mahwah, NJ: Lawrence Erlbaum.

Tran, L.T. (2016). *Targeted, one-to-one instruction in whole-number arithmetic: A framework of key elements,* PhD thesis, Southern Cross University, Lismore, NSW.

Tran, L.T. & Wright, R.J. (2014). Beliefs of teachers who teach intensive one-to-one intervention about links to classroom teaching. In J. Anderson, M. Cavanagh & A. Prescott (Eds.), *Proceedings of the 37th Annual Conference of Mathematics Education Research Group of Australasia, Sydney* (pp. 621–9). Sydney: MERGA.

Tran, L.T. & Wright, R.J. (2014). Using an experimental framework of key elements to parse one-to-one, targeted intervention teaching in whole-number arithmetic. In C. Nicol, S. Oesterle, P. Liljedahl & D. Allan (Eds.), *Proceedings of the 38th Conference of the International Group for the Psychology of Mathematics Education and the 36th Conference of the North American Chapter of the Psychology of Mathematics Education* (Vol. 5, pp. 265–72). Vancouver: PME.

Tran, L.T. & Wright, R.J. (2017). Teachers' professional noticing from a perspective of key elements of intensive, one-to-one intervention. In E.O. Schack, M.H. Fisher & J.A. Wilhelm (Eds.), *Teacher noticing: Bridging and broadening perspectives, contexts, and frameworks* (pp. 481–504). New York: Springer.

Treffers, A. (2001). Grade 1 (and 2) – Calculation up to 20. In M. van den Heuvel-Panhuizen (Ed.), *Children learn mathematics* (pp. 43–60). Utrecht: Freudenthal Institute, Utrecht University/SLO.

Treffers, A. & Beishuizen, M. (1999). Realistic mathematics education in the Netherlands. In I. Thompson (Ed.), *Issues in teaching numeracy in primary schools* (pp. 27–38). Philadelphia: Open University Press.

Treffers, A. & Buys, K. (2001). Grade 2 and 3 – Calculation up to 100. In M. van den Heuvel-Panhuizen (Ed.), *Children learn mathematics* (pp. 61–88). Utrecht: Freudenthal Institute, Utrecht University/SLO.

Van de Walle, J.A. (2004). *Elementary and middle school mathematics: Teaching developmentally* (5th edn). Boston: Pearson.

Van den Heuvel-Panhuizen, M. (1996). *Assessment and realistic mathematics education.* Utrecht: Freudenthal Institute, Utrecht University.

Van den Heuvel-Panhuizen, M. (Ed.). (2001). *Children learn mathematics: A Learning–teaching trajectory with intermediate attainment targets.* Utrecht: Freudenthal Institute, Utrecht University.

Von Glasersfeld, E. (1982). Subitizing: The role of figural patterns in the development of numerical concepts. *Archives de Psychologie* 50: 191–318.

Von Glasersfeld, E. (1987). Learning as a constructive activity. In C. Janvier (Ed.), *Problems of representation in the teaching and learning of mathematics* (pp. 3–17). Hillsdale, NJ: Lawrence Erlbaum.

Von Glasersfeld, E. (1995). *Radical constructivism: A way of knowing and learning.* London: Falmer.

Vygotsky, L.S. (1963). *Mind in society: The development of higher psychological processes.* Cambridge, MA: Harvard University Press. (Translator M. Lopez-Morillas, original work published 1934.)

Wheatley, G. & Reynolds, A. (1999). *Coming to know number.* Tallahassee, FL: Mathematics Learning.

Wigley, A. (1997). Approaching number through language. In I. Thompson (Ed.), *Teaching and learning early number* (pp. 113–22). Buckingham: Open University Press.

Willey, R., Holliday, A. & Martland, J.R. (2007). Achieving new heights in Cumbria: Raising standards in early numeracy through Mathematics Recovery. *Educational and Child Psychology* 24(2): 108–18.

Worthington, M. & Carruthers, E. (2003). *Children's mathematics: Making marks, making meaning.* London: Sage.

Wright, R.J. (1989). *Numerical development in the kindergarten year: A teaching experiment.* Doctoral dissertation, University of Georgia [DAI, 50A, 1588; DA8919319].

Wright, R.J. (1991). An application of the epistemology of radical constructivism to the study of learning. *Australian Educational Researcher* 18(1): 75–95.

Wright, R.J. (1991). The role of counting in children's numerical development. *Australian Journal of Early Childhood* 16(2): 43–8.

Wright, R.J. (1991). What number knowledge is possessed by children entering the kindergarten year of school? *Mathematics Education Research Journal* 3(1): 1–16.

Wright, R.J. (1992). Number topics in early childhood mathematics curricula: Historical background, dilemmas, and possible solutions. *Australian Journal of Education* 36: 125–42.

Wright, R.J. (1994). Mathematics in the lower primary years: A research-based perspective on curricula and teaching practice. *Mathematics Education Research Journal* 6(1): 23–36.

Wright, R.J. (1994). A study of the numerical development of 5-year-olds and 6-year-olds. *Educational Studies in Mathematics* 36: 35–44.

Wright, R.J. (1996). Problem-centred mathematics in the first year of school. In J. Mulligan & M. Mitchelmore (Eds.), *Research in early number learning: An Australian perspective* (pp. 35–54). Adelaide: AAMT.

Wright, R.J. (1998). Children's beginning knowledge of numerals and its relationship to their knowledge of number words: An exploratory, observational study. In A. Olivier & K. Newstead (Eds.), *Proceedings of the 22nd Conference of the International Group for the Psychology of Mathematics Education* (Vol. 4, pp. 201–8). Stellenbosch: PME.

Wright, R.J. (2000). Professional development in recovery education. In L.P. Steffe & P.W. Thompson (Eds.), *Radical constructivism in action: Building on the pioneering work of Ernst von Glasersfeld* (pp. 134–51). London: Falmer.

Wright, R.J. (2001). The arithmetical strategies of four 3rd-graders. In J. Bobis, B. Perry & M. Mitchelmore (Eds.), *Proceedings of the 25th Annual Conference of the Mathematics Education Research Group of Australasia* (Vol. 4, pp. 547–54). Sydney: MERGA.

Wright, R.J. (2003). Mathematics Recovery: A program of intervention in early number learning. *Australian Journal of Learning Disabilities* 8(4): 6–11.

Wright, R.J. (2008). Interview-based assessment of early number knowledge. In I. Thompson (Ed.), *Teaching and learning early number* (2nd edn, pp. 193–204). Maidenhead: Open University Press.

Wright, R.J. (2008). Mathematics Recovery: An early number program focusing on intensive intervention. In A. Dowker (Ed.), *Mathematics difficulties: Psychology and intervention* (pp. 203–23). San Diego, CA: Elsevier.

Wright, R.J. (2013). Assessing early numeracy: Significance, trends, nomenclature, context, key topics, learning framework and assessment tasks. *South African Journal of Childhood Education* 2: 21–40.

Wright, R.J., Ellemor-Collins, D. & Lewis, G. (2007). Developing pedagogical tools for intervention: Approach, methodology, and an experimental framework. In J. Watson & K. Beswick (Eds.), *Proceedings of the 30th Annual Conference of the Mathematics Education Research Group of Australasia* (Vol. 2, pp. 843–52). Sydney: MERGA.

Wright, R.J., Ellemor-Collins, D. & Tabor, P. (2012). *Developing number knowledge: Assessment, teaching and intervention with 7–11 year olds.* London: Sage.

Wright, R.J., Martland, J. & Stafford, A. (2006a). *Early numeracy: Assessment for teaching and intervention* (2nd edn). London: Sage.

Wright, R.J., Martland, J., Stafford, A. & Stanger, G. (2006b). *Teaching number: Advancing children's skills and strategies* (2nd edn). London: Sage.

Wright, R.J., Stanger, G., Stafford, A. & Martland, J. (2014). *Teaching number in the classroom with 4–8 year olds* (2nd edn). London: Sage.

Yackel, E. (2001). Perspectives on arithmetic from classroom-based research in the United States of America. In J. Anghileri (Ed.), *Principles and practices in arithmetic teaching: Innovative approaches for the primary classroom* (pp. 15–31). Buckingham: Open University Press.

Young-Loveridge, J. (1989). The development of children's number concepts: The first year of school. *New Zealand Journal of Educational Studies* 34(1): 47–64.

Young-Loveridge, J. (1991). *The development of children's number concepts from ages five to nine* (Vols 1 and 3). Hamilton, NZ: University of Waikato.

Young-Loveridge, J. (2002). Early childhood numeracy: Building an understanding of part-whole relationships. *Australian Journal of Early Childhood* 27(4): 36–42.

Index

Note: Page numbers in *italics* refer to charts and teaching charts.